Spirit, Soul, and City

Spirit, Soul, and City

Shakespeare's Coriolanus

Jan H. Blits

LEXINGTON BOOKS

A division of
ROWMAN & LITTLEFIELD PUBLISHERS, INC.
Lanham • Boulder • New York • Toronto • Oxford

LEXINGTON BOOKS

A division of Rowman & Littlefield Publishers, Inc.
A wholly owned subsidary of The Rowman & Littlefield Publishing Group, Inc.
4501 Forbes Boulevard, Suite 200
Lanham, MD 20706

PO Box 317
Oxford
OX2 9RU, UK

British Library Cataloguing in Publication Information Available

Library of Congress Cataloging-in-Publication Data

Blits, Jan H.
   Spirit, soul, and city : Shakespeare's Coriolanus / Jan H. Blits.
     p. cm.
   Includes index.
   ISBN-13: 978-0-7391-1541-1 (cloth : alk. paper)
   ISBN-10: 0-7391-1541-3 (cloth : alk. paper)
   ISBN-13: 978-0-7391-1542-8 (pbk. : alk. paper)
   ISBN-10: 0-7391-1542-1 (pbk. : alk. paper)
   1. Shakespeare, William, 1564-1616. Coriolanus. 2. Coriolanus, Cnaeus Marcius—
In literature. 3. Generals in literature. 4. Rome—In literature. I. Title. II. Title:
Shakespeare's Coriolanus.
PR2805.B65 2006
822.3'3—dc22   2006008145

Printed in the United States of America

⊗™ The paper used in this publication meets the minimum requirements of
American National Standard for Information Sciences—Permanence of Paper for
Printed Library Materials, ANSI/NISO Z39.48-1992.

To Harvey Flaumenhaft

Table of Contents

Acknowledgments

I wish to thank Harvey Flaumenhaft, Mera Flaumenhaft, and Linda Gottfredson for their thoughtful comments on the manuscript and their innumerable discussions of the play. I also wish to thank John Alvis for his generous review of the manuscript.

~

Introduction

It is hard to fight against spirit (*thumos*); for whatever it wants it buys at the cost of soul (*psychê*). —Heraclitus, frag. 85

Coriolanus portrays the founding of the Roman republic and the life and soul of Coriolanus, Rome's legendary warrior. Exemplifying the Roman view that virtue is valor, Coriolanus is unmatched in courage and war. Never beaten in battle, he fights when others flee, stands firm even when his sword bends, conquers a city single-handedly, is strengthened by his own bloody wounds, transforms his general's retreat into victory, beats his greatest rival in single combat and, leading his soldiers "like a thing / Made by some other deity than nature" (4.6.91–92),[1] by his "rare example" makes even "the coward / Turn terror into sport" (2.2.104–5). It is no wonder that friends and foes alike take him for Mars, the god of war (2.1.216–19; 4.5.119, 196–97; 4.6.91–93).

By single-handedly defeating the city of Corioles, Martius wins his new name "Coriolanus." Named by reason of his birth after the god of war (". . . he springs of / The noble house o'th'Martians" [2.3.235–36]), Martius becomes named, by reason of his deed, after the enemy he defeats. Like Rome itself, whose own name means "strength" or "force,"[2] Coriolanus is characterized chiefly by opposition and conflict. And, as with Rome, the opposition and conflict are both external and internal. Just as Rome is frequently at war against foreign enemies and always divided at home between its two major classes, Coriolanus is constantly divided both against others and within himself.[3] Moreover, much as Rome's internal division gives rise to its external

1

wars, Coriolanus's spirited opposition to everything in his nature except spiritedness itself gives rise to his spirited opposition to his enemies in battle. Seeking to be altogether spirited, he is always at war against others.

Spirit or spiritedness—*animus* in Latin, *thumos* in Greek—rules Coriolanus's soul. While seeming almost by nature identical to valor,[4] spirit, unlike the bodily appetites, has the peculiar character of having no specific content or natural object. Its content and end are determined not by itself, but, rather, by something outside itself. Essentially reactive, spirit is aroused by threats to our sense of worthiness or dignity. As we see in *Coriolanus*, its manifestations, comprising virtually every important aspect of man's inner life, include, among many other things, pride and shame, praise and blame, admiration and scorn, hope and fear, friendship and enmity, joy and grief, sympathy and antipathy, delight and disgust, self-sacrifice and self-assertion, competition and compassion, remorse and revenge, ambition and emulation, love of fame and fear of obscurity, constancy and resolve, integrity and austerity, absolutism and idealism, and, perhaps most commonly and most obviously, anger and the indignant desire to punish, particularly for injury to our dignity or pride.

While its phenomena constitute what classical writers consider the distinctly human in man—manifestations of our nature that cannot be traced simply to either our animal or our rational nature—spirit, at bottom, seems to stem from the combination of the soul's two powers or functions. According to the dominant classical tradition, the soul is the source both of thinking—human cognition in all its forms—and of life—animal motion of every sort. The twin powers of the soul thus make man a rational animal. The soul's double aspect, furthermore, makes man a natural unity or whole. Because thinking and life have a single cause, man's composite nature as a rational animal has a single source. Man is a whole because his nature, though composite, is one. The single source of his doubleness renders him whole or one.[5] Now, as a rational animal, man is the only animal aware of his own mortality. What essentially defines man as human naturally brings about phenomena that distinguish him as human. Man's recognition of his own mortality prompts him, in particular, to resist or oppose all the things that threaten to drag him down, violate his wholeness, and deny him his self-worth. It causes man to fight against or strive to overcome his own mortality, whether in the form of mastering or punishing the body's desires, seeking fame through a noble death, or aspiring to become more than human. If spirit often manifests itself as indignation, indignation—literally, "regarding as unworthy"—consists not only of anger at unworthy acts but, more generally, of contempt for what is unworthy. Indignity is the ground of indignation.

Spirit is therefore closely related to justice as well as being almost identical to courage.[6] Reacting to a sense of right and wrong, noble and base, it wishes to see the good and the noble rewarded and the bad and the base punished. Sharply distinguishing what is deserved from what is undeserved, spirit ultimately demands a world in which virtue alone rules and merit alone is rewarded. Coriolanus, accordingly, fiercely resists the nobles' compromises with the commoners, particularly the establishment of the tribunate and hence of Rome's mixed regime. In his view, the people have no virtue and therefore should have no political power. Cowardly in war and impudent in peace, they should not govern, but be governed. Only what is noble deserves a share in the city's rule. Similarly, since only virtue deserves reward, Coriolanus invokes the gods and Fortune not for victory in battle, as others do (e.g., 1.2.34–36; 1.3.45; 1.5.20–22; 1.6.6–9; 2.1.169–70; also 1.3.45; 2.1.169–70), but simply for the opportunity to fight and prove his virtue (e.g., 1.4.10–12, 44–45; 4.5.136). Wanting fully to deserve his victory, he wants virtue alone to determine the outcome and for nothing to interfere with or obscure the true order of merit. Victory should verify virtue.[7]

Coriolanus thus embraces Rome's aristocratic principle in its pure or absolute form. Virtue itself should reign in both the city and the soul. On the level of the city, only the nobles should rule; the people should simply obey. Virtue should not share power with or make concessions to non-virtue. Likewise, on the level of his own soul, Coriolanus wants his virtue to be "absolute" (3.2.39; 4.5.137). He wants it to be unconditional in two respects: his virtue must depend on nothing outside itself, and it must also be its own reward. It must come entirely from within himself and be practiced entirely for its own sake. It must be wholly self-sufficient, in both its origin and end. Like Coriolanus himself, his virtue must stand "alone" (1.4.51–52; 1.6.76; 1.8.8; 2.1.161–62; 2.2.110–12; 4.1.29–30; 5.6.116).

Coriolanus is therefore deeply ambivalent about public honor. Rome is an honor-loving city. The Romans, vying with one another for glory, "venture all [their] limbs for honour" (2.2.80). Seeking unrivaled renown, they strive to surpass one another in battle in order to win the city's highest honors. "[I]t is incredible to report," Sallust writes, "in how short a time, the city, having obtained . . . liberty in government, increased and prospered, so infinite a desire for glory had possessed the minds of all sorts."[8] Honor, for the Romans, is life's highest good. Coriolanus, however, both desires and rejects honor. He desires it because, like other Romans, he seeks to have his estimation of his own worth confirmed by others and wishes to have his proud rivals concede his claim to superiority. Loving excellence and victory, he loves honor. There is, consequently, a theatrical element in much that he does. To be looked up to, he must be looked at. Since noble deeds must be seen to win honor, whenever Coriolanus acts, he performs for others. Even as he indignantly claims indifference to honor ("[Y]ou shout me forth / In acclamations hyperbolical, / As if I lov'd my little should be dieted / In praises sauc'd with lies" [1.9.49–52]), he goes so far as to describe his fellow soldiers, not as having fought in the battle with him, but as having "beheld the doing" (1.9.40). They were simply spectators of his great deeds. But Coriolanus also repudiates honor, for its pursuit implicitly denies the self-sufficiency of virtue. Not only does honor depend upon others and is only as good as those who bestow it, but the desire for it implies that virtue is not an end in itself, but rather a means to a further end—"[a] bribe to pay [one's] sword" (1.9.38). The pursuit of honor thus appears to devalue the virtue and deed for which the honor is given. Paradoxically, it shows that a man does not truly deserve the honor that he seeks or claims.

Coriolanus's ambivalence toward honor seems to demonstrate the inherent logic of honor itself. No honor, however great, can do justice to what most deserves honor. The concern for honor thus ultimately leads away from caring about honor, turning the demand for honor into a disdain for honor. Forced by its own claim to merit, the wish to be honored rises above itself and comes to scorn what it seeks in order truly to deserve it. The ambition for honor thus perfectly illustrates the soul's characteristic, spirited tendency to surpass itself in order to affirm itself—to go beyond itself in order to be true to itself. This paradoxical tendency goes to the heart of Coriolanus.

Not only the concern for honor, but virtually everything important about Coriolanus turns back against itself. His pursuit of wounds turns into his refusal to show his wounds; his defense of Rome, into his treason to Rome; his insistence on constancy and integrity, into his betrayal of both the Romans and the Volscians; his crowded, jubilant entry into Rome, into his solitary, sad departure; his enmity to Aufidius, into his friendship with Aufidius; his desire to express gratitude toward a benefactor, into his forgetting the man's name and dropping the matter; his refusal to play a false part, into his playing the part; his unwillingness to humble himself before his countrymen, into his willingness to humble himself before his archenemy; his opposition to accepting anything from Rome, into his thinking that he is nothing but what he has received from Rome; his public boasting of having no private interest, into his public yielding to his private interest; his contempt for popular support in Rome, into his welcoming popular support in Antium; his being a manly warrior, into his being a "boy of tears" (5.6.101); and, in general, his victories, into his defeats. A man who does not allow for contradictions, Coriolanus becomes the embodiment of self-contradiction. He cannot seek to be true to himself ("Would you have me / False to my nature? Rather say I play / The man I am" [3.2.14–16]) without necessarily contradicting himself. If spirit leads us to rise above ourselves, it does so only by turning against itself. As it is defined by opposition and hence by overcoming, negation constitutes its core. Self-destruction is not so much the contrary as the consequence of spirit's self-affirmation.

A man of self-contradictions, Coriolanus is at once the exemplar and the antithesis of republican Rome. He repudiates what he exemplifies. Although Coriolanus wants his virtue to be unconditional, nothing in Rome is unconditioned. Everything high depends upon things that are low, even while much that is low smacks of things that are high. Rome publicly stands for honoring courage ("It is held / That valour is the chiefest virtue and / Most dignifies the haver" [2.2.83–85]), and the Senate presents itself as standing no less than the gods above the people: "[Y]ou may as well / Strike at the heaven with your staves, as lift them / Against the Roman state, whose course will on / The way it takes . . ." (1.1.66–69). Yet the Senate repeatedly makes concessions to the people's cowardice, particularly for the sake of maintaining at least a modicum of domestic peace amid the city's continual political strife. If "Not to be other than one thing" (4.7.42) could be Coriolanus's public motto, "[A]s partly 'tis" (2.3.260) could well be the republic's implicit maxim. Coriolanus, however, who has the most vehement contempt for the concessions, refuses to recognize that they are necessary for Rome's pursuit of war and hence for the exercise of his virtue. Without the concessions, Rome would have no domestic peace, and without domestic peace, it would have no army for war.[9] The performance of Coriolanus's own spirited virtue is thus conditioned on satisfying the people's ordinary desires for safety, wealth, and some degree of respect, and hence on the Senate's concessions. Moreover, Coriolanus would not only deny the people the Senate's concessions, but have them submissively obey the nobles' commands. Yet, just as his opportunity for war rests on satisfying their desires, the people's performance in war is conditioned on their spiritedness in the city. For if the people are unspirited in the city, they will be unspirited in battle. Coriolanus wishes, above all, to free virtue from its conditions, but, in doing so, he would deny the conditions that make his own virtue possible.

Machiavelli tries to understand human life not in terms of its ultimate end, as the classical writers do,[10] but in terms of its origins and conditions. The low replaces the high; expediency replaces nobility. Virtue, rather than being the end of human life, becomes merely a means that may or may not be used, depending on conditions.[11] With the shift from ends to means, Machiavelli also effaces the significance of the political regime. The regime, in the classical view, is a country's form of government and its specific way of life. At once the type of men who rule the city and what the city honors above all, it is the country's manner of life as activity directed toward the end for which it exists.[12] Hence, a regime is no longer the same when it is no longer guided to the same end.[13] Coriolanus, who embodies the type of man that Rome claims to honor, staunchly champions the classical view that Machiavelli rejects. Just as he believes that virtue alone should determine the city's order, be its sole end, and rest entirely on itself, so he believes that the central political issue in the city is the character of the rulers and hence the nature of the regime. According to Coriolanus, in a mixed regime, unlike in an aristocratic regime, not only are the virtuous controlled by the non-virtuous ("where gentry, title, wisdom, / Cannot conclude but by the yea and no / Of general ignorance" [3.1.143–45]), but the city consequently has no end or purpose: "Purpose so barr'd, it follows / Nothing is done to purpose" (3.1.147–48). A mixed regime is, in effect, no regime. Lacking an end, "the state" lacks "that integrity which should becom't" (3.1.157–58).[14] The tribune Sicinius understands perfectly the implication of Coriolanus's uncompromising emphasis on the regime. Believing that only the virtuous should have power, Coriolanus "would depopulate the city and / Be every man himself" (3.1.262–63). The one virtuous man alone would be citizen. The city would no longer be a city. It is no small irony that the more Coriolanus lives up to what Rome publicly honors, the more he would do away with Rome itself.

Seeing things as spirit would have them, Coriolanus simplifies the world by reducing wholes to parts and taking parts for wholes. The commoners, to him, are just "fragments" (1.1.221), mere "voices" (2.3.124); the tribunes are "tongues of the common mouth" (3.1.22); Coriolanus himself is his "sword" (1.6.76) and his "heart" (1.9.37); and his courage is his "wounds" (1.9.28) and "drops of blood" (4.5.70). Dividing wholes and exaggerating parts, spirit demands and creates well-defined distinctions. Thus, in addition to frequently using synecdoche and metonymy,[15] Coriolanus often speaks in stark antitheses,[16] strong comparisons,[17] hyperboles,[18] and negations. Time and again, he describes himself by declaring what he is not or would prefer not to be or to have,[19] what he will not or cannot do,[20] and what he cannot seem.[21] While he often speaks in negatives, the sense of many of them is not simply to negate, but to state something's opposite: "Suffer't, and live with such as cannot rule, / Nor ever will be rul'd" (3.1.39–40); "I will not do't, / Lest I surcease to honour my own truth" (3.2.120–21). More than thirty of his words begin with the privative prefix *dis-*, *im-*, *in-*, or *un-* or end with the privative suffix *less*.[22] Coriolanus is, of course, not the only one to speak in this way. Most of the characters in the play do. But Coriolanus does so more consistently and more forcefully than anyone else. As Menenius says, "His heart's his mouth: / What his breast forges, that his tongue must vent" (3.1.255–56).

A "most absolute sir" (4.5.137), Coriolanus demands that everything be "absolute" (3.2.39), that everything be single and certain. Just as he rails against the "double worship" of the mixed regime (3.1.141) and the "multitudinous tongue" of "the many-headed multitude" (2.3.16–17; 3.1.155), he fights "alone" against "all the city" (1.4.51–52; also 1.8.8; 2.1.161; 2.2.110; 5.6.116), wins singular honors for his deeds ("[He] cannot in the world / Be singly counter-pois'd" [2.2.86–87]), departs Rome "alone / Like to a lonely dragon" (4.1.29–30) and finally wishes to be "author of himself / And kn[o]w no other kin" (5.3.36–37). From the start, he seeks to be entirely single-sided—"[n]ot to be other than one thing." He oversimplifies himself, just as he oversimplifies the world. He accepts only one aspect of himself and, absolutizing it, denies everything that tends to contradict or degrade it. He wants to be nothing but spirited virtue.

As already noted, in the classical view, man's wholeness arises from the dual nature of his soul. Man is one because his dual nature as a rational animal has a single source. Yet, although spirit seems to stem from the combination of the soul's twin powers, it seems ultimately to deny man's composite nature. In seeking to go beyond man's mortal condition, it tends to deny its own dual source. The tension in Rome and in Coriolanus between spiritedness and appetitiveness, which some commentators emphasize,[23] is, at bottom, a tension within the soul between spirit and life, virtue and birth. Coriolanus was bred by his mother to be a warrior. As her praises made him a soldier, he fights largely to please her. But while Volumnia raised him for heroic valor, his aspiration for absolute virtue leads him to deny his maternal origins. Just as he tries to separate himself from the political conditions in Rome that make the practice of his virtue possible, so, more deeply, he tries to separate himself from his birth and to make himself stand alone and apart from his family. Seeking to show himself dependent on no one but himself, he finally wishes to be "author of himself / And kn[o]w no other kin." His spirited end repudiates his maternal origin. Determined to prove himself self-sufficient, Coriolanus acts—or attempts to act—as though he were self-generated. His attack on Rome is an attack not just on "[t]he country, our dear nurse," or even on "thy mother's womb / That brought thee to this world," as his mother warns (5.3.110, 124–25), but on natural generation itself. It surely is no accident that Coriolanus describes his victories as the destruction of families (1.4.41; 2.1.176–78; 4.4.2–6; see also 5.6.121–22). Nor is it accidental that, if he is sometimes spoken of as the god of war, he is also described—and describes himself—as a lifeless mechanism of death and even as death itself (e.g., 1.4.53–56; 1.6.76; 2.1.157–60; 2.2.105–14; 4.6.90–96; 5.4.18–23). The fulfillment of his virtue not only involves pursuing death in battle, but ultimately denies natural generation and hence life as such. Virtue's victory is thus also its defeat. The perfection of one power of the soul is the death of the other—and hence the death of the soul itself. Just as Coriolanus's unconditioned virtue would destroy the city, so, too, it would destroy the soul.

Notes

1. All references to *Coriolanus* are to the Arden edition, ed. Philip Broadbank (London: Methuen, 2001). I have occasionally revised quotations, based on the New Variorum Edition, ed. Horace Howard Furness, Jr. (Philadelphia: J.B. Lippincott, 1928). References are to act, scene, and line.

2. Plutarch, *Romulus*, 1.1.

3. The adversative preposition "against" (including "'gainst") appears a third more often in *Coriolanus* (forty-five times) than in any other Shakespeare play.

4. Aristotle, *Nicomachean Ethics*, 1116b23–17a4.

5. See Jan H. Blits, *Deadly Thought: "Hamlet" and the Human Soul* (Lanham: Lexington Books, 2001), 11, and n25.

6. Plato, *Republic*, 440c1–d6.

7. The word "deserve" (along with its cognates) appears two-dozen times in *Coriolanus*, more than twice as often as in any other of Shakespeare's tragedies and more often than in any of his other plays.

8. Sallust, *Catiline Conspiracy*, 7.3; *Heywood's Sallust* (1608; reprint: London: Constable and Co., 1924), 61–62. I have modernized the spelling and punctuation of Elizabethan translations throughout.

9. See 4.3.40–48; also Plutarch, *Coriolanus*, 5.3; Livy, *History of Rome*, 2.24–25, 32.

10. Plato, *Republic*, 544d6ff.; Aristotle, *Nicomachean Ethics*, 1094a1–b11.

11. Machiavelli, *The Prince*, 8, 18. For the reversal of the relation between an end and its conditions, cf., e.g., Aristotle, *Politics*, 1257b38–58a10, 1323b7–10, and Machiavelli, *Prince*, 3.

12. Plato, *Republic*, 544d6ff.

13. Cicero, *The Republic*, 1.39.

14. See also, e.g., 1.1.209–11, 218–20; 3.1.37–40, 67–73, 90–111, 134–38, 141–48, 157–59, 236–38.

15. Lawrence Danson, "Metonymy and *Coriolanus*," *Philological Quarterly*, 52 (1973), 30.

16. E.g., "The one affrights you, / The other makes you proud" (1.1.168–69); "Where he should find you lions, find you hares" (1.170–71); "[B]acks red, and faces pale" (1.4.37); "Wouldst thou have laugh'd had I come coffin'd home, / That weep'st to see me triumph?" (2.1.175–76); "You are plebeians / If they be Senators" (3.1.100–1); "I shall be lov'd when I am lack'd" (4.1.15); ". . . an eagle in a dovecote" (5.6.114).

17. E.g., "Now put your shields before your hearts, and fight / With hearts more proof than shields" (1.4.24–25); "Oh! Let me clip ye / In arms as sound as when I woo'd" (1.6.29–30); "The mouse ne'er shunn'd the cat as they did budge / From rascals worse than they" (1.6.44–45); "I do hate thee / Worse than a promise-breaker" (1.8.1–2); "I'll give my reasons / More worthier than their voices" (3.1.118–19); ". . . whose breath I hate / As reek o'th'rotten fens" (3.3.120–21); "Mine ears against your suits are stronger than / Your gates against my force" (5.2.86–87); "I melt, and am not / Of stronger earth than others" (5.3.28–29).

18. E.g., "I'd make a quarry / With thousands of these quarter'd slaves, as high / As I could pick my lance" (1.1.197–99); "All the contagion of the south light on you" (1.4.30); "In acclamations hyperbolical" (1.9.50); ". . . teach my mind / A most inherent baseness" (3.2.122–23); ". . . deliver you as most / Abated captives to some nation / That won you without blows!" (3.3.131–33); ". . . bitterest enmity, . . . fellest foes" (4.4.18); "Drawn tuns of blood out of thy country's breast" (4.5.100); ". . . chaste as the icicle / That's curdied by the frost from purest snow / And hangs on Dian's temple" (5.3.65–67).

Coriolanus, similarly, often adds emphasis to a point by speaking in asyndeton, dispensing with conjunctions between parallel words, phrases or clauses within a sentence. See, e.g., 1.1.182–83, 204–7; 1.6.30–31, 35–39, 56–58, 67–72; 2.3.123; 3.1.96–100, 142–43; 3.2.10–11; 3.3.70–72, 120–22; 4.1.5–9; 4.4.24–26; 5.2.80. On asyndeton, see Anonymous, *Ad herennium*, 4.41; Quintilian, *Institutio oratoria*, 9.3.50.

19. E.g., "I had rather be their servant in my way / Than sway with them in theirs" (2.1.201–2); "I had rather have my wounds to heal again / Than hear say how I got them" (2.2.69–70); "I had rather have one scratch my head i'th'sun / When the alarum were struck, than idly sit / To hear my nothings monster'd" (2.2.75–77); "'[T]was never my desire yet to trouble the poor with begging" (2.3.70–71); "I have shed my blood, / Not fearing outward force" (3.1.75–76).

20. E.g., "But cannot make my heart consent to take / A bribe to pay my sword" (1.9.37–38); "I cannot / Put on the gown, stand naked . . ." (2.2.136–37); "I cannot bring / My tongue to such a pace" (2.3.52–53), "I cannot do it to the gods, / Must I then do't to them? (3.2.38–39); "I will not do't, / Lest I surcease to honour mine own truth" (3.2.120–21); "I would not buy / Their mercy at the price of one fair word" (3.3.90–91); "I will not hear thee speak" (5.2.90); "I'll never / Be such a gosling to obey instinct, but stand / As if . . ." (5.3.34–36); "[W]e'll / Hear nought from Rome in private" (5.3.92–93).

21. E.g., "Would you have me / False to my nature? Rather say I play / The man I am" (3.2.14–16); "[T]his extremity / Hath brought me to thy hearth, not out of hope / (Mistake me not) to save my life" (4.5.79–81).

22. "Discharge" (3.2.106), "disclaim" (3.1.35), "disdain" (1.4.26; 3.1.79, 143), "disgrace" (5.3.42), "dishonor" (3.1.157; 3.2.60), "dismiss" (5.3.82), "disobedience" (3.1.117), "displeasure" (4.5.72), "dissension" (4.4.17), "dissentious" (1.1.164), "dissolved" (1.1.204), "impossibility" (5.3.61), "inevitable" (4.1.26), "ingrate" (5.2.86), "invincible" (4.1.10), "measureless" (5.6.102), "needless" (2.3.116), "reckless"

(3.1.91), "thankless" (4.5.70), "unaching" (2.2.148), "unbarb'd" (3.2.99), "unborn" (3.1.129), "unbruis'd" (4.1.47), "unburied" (3.3.122), "uncertainty" (3.3.124), "unmusical" (4.5.58), "unnatural" (5.3.84, 184), "unroof'd" (1.1.218), "unsaluted" (5.3.50), "unseparable" (4.4.16), "unstable" (3.1.148), "unswept" (2.3.119), "unvulnerable" (5.3.73), "unwise" (3.1.91).

23. E.g., Maurice Charney, *Shakespeare's Roman Plays* (Cambridge: Harvard University Press, 1961), 143–57; Paul Cantor, *Shakespeare's Rome: Republic and Empire* (Ithaca: Cornell University Press, 1976), 21–23, 31–39.

ACT ONE

~

Act One, Scene One

1.

Coriolanus begins with civil strife in the streets of Rome. The common people, armed and mutinous, have risen up against the patricians, demanding corn at their own price. The First Citizen, egging the crowd on, takes pains to explain that he is urging action against the nobles and, most especially, against Caius Martius, the "chief enemy to the people," "in hunger for bread, not in thirst for revenge" (1.1.6–7, 23–24). "Let us kill him, and we'll have corn at our own price" (1.1.9–10). The people's grievance, the Citizen seems to say, is economic, stemming from their stomachs rather than from their hearts. The Citizen, accordingly, emphasizes the people's starvation. They are "famish[ing]" (1.1.4), he says, afflicted with "leanness" (1.1.19), from which (he says twice) they need to be "relieved" (1.1.15, 17). But even as he denies that he speaks this "in . . . thirst for revenge," the Citizen, in the same breath, expressly calls for revenge: "Let us revenge this with our pikes, ere we become rakes" (1.1.21–22). The Citizen may think that only the pain of hunger—not the pleasure of revenge—can justify rebellion against the Senate: to be justifiable, the rebellion must be compelled by necessity and not be a matter of choice. But despite insisting that he speaks only in hunger for food, the Citizen wishes to defend the people's dignity no less than their lives: "You are all resolved rather to die than to famish?" (1.1.3–4). "[T]o die," here, means to die fighting, with self-respect. It means placing something higher than—and even in opposition to—one's life. The Citizen thus has two grievances, though he openly acknowledges just one. One grievance pertains to the injury: the patricians withhold food from the people, charge high prices for what there is, and even eat in excess what the people could live on. The other pertains to the insult: the patricians despise the people and maliciously starve them so that they can take satisfaction in the contrast between their own plenty and the people's want (1.1.14–21).[1] The two grievances not only differ, but also are potentially at odds. While the first, based on hunger, arises from a concern with preserving life, the second, based on anger, is compatible with accepting death. And just as their effects may be opposite, so too, at bottom, are their causes. While hunger rests on a person's sense of what he lacks or needs, anger rests on his sense of what he possesses and deserves. The former levels us; the latter shows our concern for being treated as worthy by others.

Coriolanus, like some commentators, will stress the opposition between spirit and appetite. But our first glimpse of Coriolanus's Rome shows not so much their opposition as their paradoxical combination. The people's desire is transformed by their spiritedness: they would rather die than famish, so that they could have corn at their own price. Spirit raises desire above the body even as it serves the body. But, on the other hand, even while raising desire above the body, the Citizen's spirit justifies itself as bodily necessity. The Citizen's thirst for revenge disguises itself as his hunger for bread. His spirited desire, which he describes with a metaphor of bodily appetite, dissembles itself as necessity: since necessity excuses, the people cannot be justly blamed for their rebellion. Thus, while spirit elevates appetite above the level of the body, it also, paradoxically, lowers itself, here, to the level of the body in order to justify itself. It raises desire above the body in order to serve the body and then descends to the body in order to claim something higher than the body.

The Citizen, voicing his indignation in pointed antitheses,[2] reflects spirit's tendency also to clarify the moral world by simplifying it. While anger characteristically claims to be in the right, its self-righteous claims typically rest on taking a part for the whole and exaggerating differences. The Citizen thus asks whether the people are "resolved" to act, and the people respond, "Resolved, resolved" (1.1.3, 5). By "resolved," the Citizen means "having a fixed determination," "being resolute in one's purpose." But the word also has another—indeed, a more fundamental—meaning: "to reduce something to its simpler parts." On the Citizen's lips, the two meanings go together, the latter making the former possible: the people's spirited determination rests largely on their moral simplification. And while the Citizen simplifies the moral world by exaggerating differences, the people accomplish the same result in the opposite fashion. Rather than exaggerate, they suppress key distinctions. The first time they speak for themselves and do not simply repeat the Citizen's words, they ignore the difference between a likeness and the thing it resembles. Martius, they say, does not merely resemble a dog, but is "a very dog to the commonality" (1.1.27–28). As the hyperbolic "very," modifying the substantive, implies,[3] Martius is in every respect a dog to the people. The metaphor is meant in its full and unrestricted sense, as though it were not a metaphor, but literally true.

In the play's opening line, the Citizen stops the crowd and calls to be heard: "Before we proceed any further, hear me speak." And the people shout in unison, "Speak, speak" (1.1.1–2). Public speech is central to Rome's political life. It is both a cause and an effect of the city's freedom and strife. While free men are governed by persuasion and hence by political oratory, political oratory itself flourishes on political strife and even seeks to perpetuate it, since its principal rewards come from igniting rather than extinguishing political fires. Public rhetoric is essentially republican.[4] Public speech is the major means by which a Roman takes part in the city's civil life. Not surprisingly, the verb "speak" occurs repeatedly—eighty-five times—in the play, thrice in the first two lines alone, "hear" eighty-one times, including once in the opening line, "say" a hundred and one times,[5] the noun "voice" forty-eight times (far more than in any other Shakespeare play) all but four times meaning the people's vote,[6] "words" thirty-one times, and the synecdochical "tongue" and "mouth" twenty-one and six times, respectively. While nearly every important event in the play is preceded or provoked by some form of speech—"by formal oration or informal argument, outright insult or sly innuendo, boldly asserted truth or whispered lie"[7]—almost every one is also accompanied by a public oration. Speech-making—both informal and formal—determines the action as well as the mode of speaking in the play. In addition, while preceding and accompanying action in Rome, speech is also a principal spur to action: "I, considering . . . that [comeliness] was no better than picture-like to hang by th'wall, if renown made it not stir, was pleased to let him seek danger where he was like to find fame" (1.3.9–14). As the Romans vie with one another for honor and fame, renown both inspires and rewards their valor. Renown itself leads to military success.[8] Even the commoners are aroused by what is said about them ("We are accounted poor citizens" [1.1.14]) and act to avoid or to refute a public reproach (e.g., 1.6.69–70; 2.3.14ff.).[9]

Another citizen speaks up for Martius. This citizen is actually grateful to his oppressor for the service he has done "for his country" (1.1.29–30). He seems to think that Martius's service to Rome outweighs his malice to the people. The First Citizen, however, disagrees. He would be grateful to Martius ("give him good report"), he says, "but that he pays himself with being proud" (1.1.31–33). Service to one's country deserves repayment, but Martius's payment to himself in pride prevents the First Citizen's payment to him in gratitude. Defending himself against the charge of speaking "maliciously" (1.1.34), the First Citizen denies that Martius acted for the sake of Rome. What Martius has done "famously" (1.1.35), he says, he did "to that end" (1.1.36), that is, for the sake of his fame, and not "for [the sake of] his country" (1.1.37). Acting in support of one's country ("for his country" [1.1.29–30]) is one thing; acting for the sake of one's country ("for his country" [1.1.37]) is something else. Gratitude requires more than benefiting another. A matter of wishing well rather than simply of doing well, it requires having the intention to benefit the other and doing so for the other's sake. Martius, however, did what he did partly "to please his mother," the First Citizen says, and partly "to be . . . proud, which he is, even to the altitude of his virtue" (1.1.38–39). Martius's private motives cancel his beneficiaries' debt.

The First Citizen's retort is the play's first mention of Volumnia. Significantly, it pairs Martius's pride and his mother as the twin motives of his action. The tension between the two motives will prove to lie at the core of his tragedy.

None of the commoners, not even Martius's supporter, looks favorably upon pride. To all the plebeians, "pride" is a "fault"—a dangerous fault (2.1.17, 18). Thus, instead of defending Martius's pride as something that he merits, the Second Citizen, trying again to blunt his fellow citizen's anger, says that the First Citizen blames as a vice what Martius "cannot help in his nature" (1.1.40). Anger presupposes responsibility. Only what is voluntary or depends on a person's choice deserves blame. What could not have been otherwise should not be blamed (see 1.1.40; 4.7.10–12). Like gratitude, anger and blame require intention. Perhaps feeling that his defense is lame, the Second Citizen abruptly shifts and assuredly states that the First Citizen can in no way accuse Martius of being "covetous" (1.1.42). Some patricians may oppress the people out of greed (1.1.18–21, 80–84), but Martius, the Second Citizen seems to mean, does so purely out of scorn and pride. We might wonder whether such a defense extenuates or intensifies the First Citizen's charge. Martius was so odious to the people in the disputes concerning their debts, Plutarch writes, because "they knew well enough that it was not for any gain or benefit he had gotten thereby, so much as it was for spite and displeasure he thought to do them."[10] His indifference to wealth, in the context of his opposition to easing the people's debt, indicates his insolence toward them. The Second Citizen's attempted vindication of Martius points to an incongruous but significant political alliance in the Senate. While the Senate as a whole, as we shall see, is split between those willing and those unwilling to accommodate the people's demands, the latter faction is itself split between the avaricious and the spirited. Greed and spirit, although opposed to each other in principle (as the Second Citizen implies), converge in a self-contradictory alliance of nobles resisting the commoners' demands.[11]

Suddenly, there are shouts elsewhere. "The other side o'th'city is risen" (1.1.46–47). The uprising is broader than this single group. The First Citizen, though the leader here, proves to be just a follower, not the rebellion's overall leader. Hearing the shouts, the Citizen, who began by asking to be heard before the group proceeded any further, now reverses himself and belittles their speaking: "[W]hy stay we prating here? To th'Capitol!" (1.1.47; cf. 1.1.11–12). But the Citizen no sooner reverses himself than he does so again and asks the crowd to wait: "Soft, who comes here?" (1.1.49). Demonstrating his own inconstancy, the Citizen frames the play's opening discussion of Martius by prefiguring Martius's central criticism of the people.

2.

Menenius enters. But before we hear from him, we hear both the First and Second Citizen praise him. "Worthy Menenius Agrippa, one that hath always loved the people"; "He's one honest enough, would all the rest were so!" (1.1.50–53). Menenius is the only patrician the plebeians largely trust. A man who describes himself as overly fond of bodily goods, particularly of the belly (2.1.46–52; see also 2.1.110; 4.2.49; 5.1.50–58; 5.2.33–34), and—no less important to the people—the only major patrician not described as a warrior,[12] Menenius appears to provide an amiable link between Rome's two classes.[13] Yet, notwithstanding what the two citizens suppose, it is by no means clear that he either loves the people or is honest with them. To him, as to Martius, the people are Rome's "rats" (1.1.161), "beastly plebeians" (2.1.94–95), "multiplying spawn" (2.2.78), and "musty chaff, . . . smelt / Above the moon" (5.1.31–32). Nor is Menenius averse to deceiving them, as we shall see in a moment. It is clear, though, why, in addition to his lack of patrician austerity and military manner, they think of him as they do. Flattering the people, which they take to be a sign of his good will, he calls them "my countrymen," "masters, my good friends, mine honest neighbors," and "friends" (1.1.54, 61, 64), gives them a hearing, asking where they are going with bats and clubs and what the matter is, implores them rather than commands ("Speak, I pray you" [1.1.55]), wheedles rather than threatens, and seems concerned that they will harm themselves ("Will you undo yourselves?" [1.1.62]). No other patrician normally speaks to the people in so obliging or solicitous a fashion.

When the First Citizen replies that the people cannot undo themselves since they are already undone, Menenius attempts to persuade them that the patricians have "most charitable care" of them (1.1.64). This is the nobles' first attempt to persuade the commoners, to rule them through speech. Menenius begins by invoking the Senate's authority and admonishing the people. "For your wants, / Your suffering in this dearth, you may as well / Strike at the heaven with your staves," he says,

> as lift them
> Against the Roman state, whose course will on
> The way it takes, cracking ten thousand curbs
> Of more strong link asunder than can ever
> Appear in your impediment.
>
> (1.1.65–71)

In contrast to the modern conception of the state, which understands the state as an artificial, abstract sovereign standing between the rulers and the ruled,[14] Menenius, like all the Roman nobles, identifies the state, according to the classical notion of the regime, with the ruling body and hence with the country itself. The Senate is "the Roman state" (see also 1.1.76; 2.1.107; 2.2.50; 3.1.117, 122, 150, 157; 3.2.34; 5.1.20; 5.3.18). Grounding its political authority in its moral authority and its moral authority in the people's reverence for the gods, Menenius sets the Senate as high as the gods, above the people. The Senate, just like the gods, he warns, will go its way no matter what the people think or want. Even as he invites comparison of the people to the Senate, Menenius implicitly denies the possibility of such a comparison.[15] As for the dearth, Menenius says that "[t]he gods, not the patricians, make it, and / Your knees to them, not arms, must help" (1.1.72–73). The gods, he strongly suggests, are punishing the people with the dearth for their disobedience to the patricians. Their insolence toward the one amounts to their impiety toward the other. And while the people have been carried away by their suffering and made more disobedient, further disobedience can bring them only further suffering:

> Alack,
> You are transported by calamity
> Thither where more attends you; and you slander
> The helms o'th'state, who care for you like fathers,
> When you curse them as enemies.
>
> (1.1.73–77)

Unlike the Athenians, who treat the gods as largely irrelevant,[16] the Romans think of the gods in everything they do, turn to them for everything they want, and thank them for everything they gain.[17] After Romulus founded Rome by force of arms, Numa, wishing to reduce the Romans to civil obedience, tamed them by fear of the gods. Persuaded by him that the gods take part in human affairs, the Romans esteem the power of the gods more than that of men.[18] Religion, which the patricians at once respect and manipulate, is particularly vital to Rome's unity. While freedom in Rome, as we shall see, requires the mutual antagonism and suspicion of the classes, religion serves to temper and contain the class hostility, by helping to make it appear to the people that Rome is a single community with a single common good and that the patricians (literally, "fathers"[19]) provide for them like fathers. If Rome is really not one but two cities within a single set of walls,[20] the Roman gods help make it seem to be one. "Superstitious fear of the gods holds the Roman commonwealth together" (Polybius, 6.56.7).

Despite invoking the sacred quality of the Senate, Menenius fails to awe the people into submission. The First Citizen immediately and indignantly challenges him. The nobles never cared for the commoners, he answers. They not only allow the people to famish while their storehouses are full. They also make laws that hurt the poor and favor the rich, including ones that enslave ("chain up and restrain" [1.1.83]) the poor to their usurious creditors.[21] "If the wars eat us not up, they will" (1.1.84). The Senate's laws or its wars will devour the people.

Having failed to subdue the commoners with awe, Menenius tries to assuage them with a "pretty tale" (1.1.89). Instead of invoking the Senate's magistracy and authority, he offers a homespun, well-known tale,[22] with which he seeks to charm and shame the people. Like much of Roman pedagogy, Menenius's tale has the character of an old, familiar fable: "[I]t may be you have heard it, / But since it serves my purpose, I will venture / To stale't a little more" (1.1.89–91). The First Citizen agrees to hear it. While most Romans take pleasure in hearing as well as in telling ("Speak, . . . / Leave nothing out for length . . ." [2.2.48–49]), fables are particularly attractive to, and effective with, the people. For while the novelty of fables gives pleasure, the people's rude and uneducated minds (as Quintilian explains, referring specifically to Menenius's tale) are largely unsuspicious in hearing fictions and, when pleased, readily agree with the arguments from which their pleasure comes. The source of pleasure appears to them as the source of wisdom.[23] The Citizen, however, seems to recognize that Menenius might try to use his tale to trick the people, and so he warns that they will not be gulled: "Well, I'll hear it, sir; yet you must not think to fob off our disgrace with a tale"

(1.1.92–93). Just as he seems to think it would be a disgrace to be fooled, the Citizen, now silent about the people's hunger, describes their plight as a "disgrace." The people may have two grievances, but they see their deprivation, above all, as a humiliation.

Menenius's tale, in the style of traditional fables, has an introductory commendation of the fable (1.1.88-91), a narration (1.1.95–104, 106–13, 126–45), and an interpretation or moral of the story (1.1.147–54).[24] The tale, blurring the difference between political prosecution and political rebellion, takes the form of a mock trial, in which the accusers are at the same time the jurors (cf. 1.1.10; 3.1.264–68). There was a time, Menenius tells, when all the parts of the body rebelled against the belly, thus accusing it:

> That only like a gulf it did remain
> I'th'midst o'th'body, idle and unactive,
> Still cupboarding the viand, never bearing
> Like labour with the rest, where th'other instruments
> Did see, and hear, devise, instruct, walk, feel,
> And, mutually participate, did minister
> Unto the appetite and affection common
> Of the whole body.

> (1.1.97–104)

As Menenius presents it, the body has an appetite and desire common to the whole and a division of labor among all its parts, which serve that appetite and desire, whose satisfaction should be shared by all. According to the accusation, however, the belly got all the food but did no work, while the rest of the body did all the work but got no food. The belly remained idle and yet was rich; the rest of the body labored and yet remained poor.

When the Citizen, intrigued, asks what the belly replied, Menenius alters the character of both the belly and its accusers. Where he initially ignored everything but the body, he now describes both parties as spirited rather than appetitive. The belly, knowing it could deceive the other parts, "[w]ith a kind of smile, / Which ne'er came from the lungs . . . / . . . tauntingly replied" (1.1.106–7, 109). Its smile was contemptuous, just as its answer was derisive. And the mutinous members, no longer complaining of hunger, are now said to have "envied [the belly's] receipt" (1.1.111). Whereas the belly looked down in contempt at the other parts' gullibility, the other parts looked up in envy at its wealth. The mutinous parts were "discontented" (1.1.110), not because they were famished, but because the belly was "not such as [they]" (1.1.113). Both the belly and the other parts compare themselves to each other—the one in satisfaction (as the Citizen had accused the nobles

[1.1.19–20]), the other in discontent. Neither is any longer simply a part of a whole, as in Menenius's original version. In fact, the belly, able to smile and to speak, has become a whole in its own right—an organ with organs of its own. The emergence of spiritedness is the emergence of individuation.

Impatient for the belly's answer, the First Citizen, breaking into verse and recasting the accusers, assigns military and political roles to the body's various parts: "The kingly crown'd head, the vigilant eye, / The counsellor heart, the arm our soldier, / Our steed the leg, the tongue our trumpeter" (1.1.114–16). Instead of a society of workers feeding the body, with a division of labor but not of rank, the Citizen describes an armed camp ready for battle, with a division of rank as well as of labor. Where Menenius's original depiction is limited to what the body needs for internal health, the Citizen describes a body set on expansion. If eating is the former's characteristic activity, war is the latter's. Accordingly, in Menenius's description, the belly rules the body, which the mind serves ("devise, instruct" [1.1.101]). In the Citizen's, the heart ("[t]he counsellor") rules the body, whose head wears a kingly crown. Despite the difference, however, in one respect the two accounts are alike. In Menenius's, the mind merely ministers to the belly; in the Citizen's, the head is nothing but a figurehead (see 1.1.135). Reason is either merely an instrument for the stomach or an ornament to the heart.

The Citizen, whose impatience to hear the belly's answer only delays his hearing it, cannot imagine what the belly could reply ("What could the belly answer?" [1.1.123]). To him, the charge of the oppressive greed of the "cormorant" belly, "the sink o'th'body" (1.1.120, 121), appears unanswerable. Menenius, who only paraphrased the "rash" members' accusation (1.1.128), expressly quotes ("quoth he"; "—this says the belly, mark me—" [1.1.129, 140]) the "most grave belly['s] . . . deliberate" answer (1.1.127). Like Menenius, the belly was much more careful than his accusers in speaking. Following rules of classical forensic rhetoric for rebutting a charge, the belly admitted the act but denied the injury or injustice. Instead of harming the accusers, his action, he said, benefits them.[25] It is true, he granted, that he at first receives "the general food" (1.1.130) which all the parts live upon. But that is only fitting, he went on to explain, since he is "the storehouse and the shop / Of the whole body" (1.1.132–33). Then, reminding the accusers of what they themselves should know ("if you do remember" [1.1.133]), the belly described how he distributes the food to all of the body's parts. All the other parts "receive [from him] that natural competency / Whereby they live" (1.1.138–39). Where the accusers charged that the belly selfishly remained idle while hoarding all the food, the belly answered that he stores and processes the food and distributes it to all the rest. Far from benefitting only himself, he benefits all the others. Indeed, he alone directly benefits them.

Although one might think that, with this, he had completed his case, the belly nevertheless continued, partly qualifying what he just explained. Whereas initially he appealed to what the various parts know firsthand (1.1.133), the belly now acknowledged that "all at once cannot / See what I do deliver out to each" (1.1.141–42). Each part can know only part of what the belly does—only what that part itself receives. The belly alone can know what is true of the whole. The belly therefore offered his assurance. Combining a proverbial phrase[26] with commercial metaphors, he declared, "Yet I can make my audit up, that all / From me do back receive the flour of all, / And leave me but the bran" (1.1.143–45). Everything good that the various parts have comes from what the belly returns to them, and the belly is left with just the worthless husks. The belly is the poor, selfless, public servant. We might note that the belly assured the other parts not that he would provide such an audit, but that he could. The accounting, like the selfless service, remains unseen.

The Citizen is eager for the moral ("How apply you this?" [1.1.146]). Even though Menenius made the analogy explicit by comparing the mutinous parts to the Roman people and the belly to the senators (1.1.111–13), the Citizen wants to hear the situation in the fable expressly applied to Rome. "The senators of Rome are this good belly, / And you the mutinous members," Menenius answers;

> for examine
> Their counsels and their cares, digest things rightly
> Touching the weal o'th'common, you shall find
> No public benefit which you receive
> But it proceeds or comes from them to you,
> And in no way from yourselves.
>
> (1.1.148–53)

The people are useless to themselves and cannot do without the Senate's rule. They under no circumstances benefit themselves. No longer speaking of what the people receive "back" (1.1.144), Menenius says that everything good that they have comes entirely from the Senate and in no way from themselves. It is the people, not the Senate, who have a selfish appetite, perform no labor, and yet receive plenty.

Menenius's fable presents the living body as the model of the city. The city is said to be an organic whole—a "body politic"—in which all the parts are naturally inclined to a single end, which is the union and well-being of the whole. The sole good—the body's good—is a common good. The fable, completely disregarding one of the people's two complaints, assumes that all the parts of the city are concerned only with being well fed and that no part is concerned with its dignity or self-respect. Moreover, by reducing the city to an organic body, the fable renders the accusers' charge of starvation not only false but self-refuting, for the health of each part of a body depends on the health of all. No part tries to starve another. The city's parts are, indeed, "incorporate friends" (1.1.129). None could have a private good which it might serve at the expense of the rest. Menenius's fable thus does not so much argue that the Senate is not selfish as it presupposes that no part of the city could possibly be. No part could be greedy or ambitious for itself at the expense of another or of the whole. As Menenius presents it, there could be no class animosity, contention, oppression, competition, fear, envy, rivalry, or resentment in the city. Menenius's fable, refuting itself, thus denies the most obvious truths about Rome. Ironically revealing what it is meant to conceal, it is contradicted by the very complaint it purports to answer.

Menenius asks the Citizen what he thinks, but rather than let the man reply, he cleverly deflects his response by the way he addresses him: "What do you think, / You, the great toe of this assembly?" (1.1.153–54). Menenius's mock insult distracts the Citizen: "I the great toe? Why the great toe?" (1.1.155). The Citizen's provoked question allows Menenius to replace the Citizen's reply with his own: "For that being one o'th'lowest, basest, poorest / Of this most wise rebellion, thou goest foremost" (1.1.156–57). The fact that being called "the great toe" is an insult belies Menenius's tale. In contrast to the tale's presumption, the city is not parallel to the body. Not only are there goods higher than those of the body, and not only might some part seek its own good at the expense of the rest. But some people may not like being treated as the lowest part of the body, no matter how well they eat.

Menenius's fable attempts what his appeal to the authority of the Senate and the gods tried to do. It presents Rome as a single community with a single common good, which the Senate selflessly provides for all the community's members. The fable tries to teach engagingly what Roman religion teaches gravely. But it, too, fails. Menenius momentarily silences the Citizen, but his fable does not get rid of the people's complaint. Menenius seems to recognize his failure. After insulting the Citizen again—this time, apparently less good-naturedly ("Thou rascal, that art worst in blood to run" [1.1.158])—he concedes that a destructive fight will not be avoided: "Rome and her rats are at the point of battle; / The one side must have bale" (1.1.161–62). Contrary to his fable's premise, Menenius identifies Rome with the patricians alone and describes them as contending against the plebeians, who, moreover, eat parasitically at their expense.

3.

Hailed by Menenius as "noble Martius," Martius, entering, offers his "[t]hanks," in return, with a single, monosyllabic word (1.1.162, 163). Wanting to depend only upon himself and be indebted to no one, Martius will prove incapable of giving thanks to others for recognizing his nobility.

Martius immediately affronts the people: "What's the matter, you dissentious rogues / That, rubbing the poor itch of your opinion, / Make yourselves scabs?" (1.1.164–66). Martius associates the people with the body. He associates them, however, not with a starving body, but with a sick or infected body. To him, the people are rebelling not because they are hungry, but because they think too highly of themselves. Their sore distress is the result entirely of their excessive self-estimation. By scratching their unreasonable opinion of themselves, the people (as Martius says with a pun) make sores for themselves ("scabs") and turn themselves into loathsome creatures ("scabs"). Their suffering is completely of their own making.

When the First Citizen, unintimidated, sarcastically responds, "We have ever your good word" (1.1.165), Martius launches into his first tirade. He begins, as he is given to do when indignant, by hurling back the speaker's words: "He that will give good words to thee, will flatter / Beneath abhorring" (1.1.166–67).[27] Martius, in effect criticizing Menenius, declares that any good words for the people amount to the basest flattery, for there is nothing good to be said about them. Then, using a question not to get an answer but to reproach or upbraid, as he is also inclined to do when angry and as he has already done in his first words to the people,[28] Martius asks, "What would you have, you curs, / That like nor peace nor war? The one affrights you, / The other makes you proud" (1.1.167–69). Neither war nor peace satisfies the people. War frightens them; peace makes them impudent. When at war, they are cowardly, not brave; when at peace, presumptuous, not orderly. Always showing qualities opposite to the ones they should, they are neither good soldiers nor good citizens. More particularly, the people are untrustworthy in battle:

> He that trusts to you,
> Where he should find you lions, finds you hares;
> Where foxes, geese; you are no surer, no,
> Than is the coal of fire upon the ice,
> Or hailstone in the sun.

> (1.1.169–73)

The people lack prudence as well as courage. Just as they are cowardly when they should be fierce, they are guileless when they should be cunning. Still worse, they are not only inconstant, but, like fire quenched by ice and hailstone melted by the sun, they are altered by external conditions. The people, in short, are never satisfied, never what they should be, never constant, and never their own masters.

The people do, however, have one "virtue": "Your virtue is, / To make him worthy whose offense subdues him, / And curse that justice did it" (1.1.173–75). The people's one good quality, Martius says, is to make a man "worthy" by giving him something to hate and, when he then offends the people, to bring him down ("whose offense subdues him"), allowing the worthy man to curse "justice" for his downfall.[29] Martius curses justice in the name of worthiness. He curses democratic justice in the name of aristocratic justice, equality in the name of excellence. While democratic justice presupposes equality or commonality, for Martius there is no equality or commonality between the classes, let alone between him and the people. He and the people are, he has already suggested, of different species (1.1.167).[30] The people, he says, are good only to provoke his deep contempt, give him an enemy to battle and allow him to curse plebeian justice for their defeating him. We are forced to wonder whether Martius courts popular defeat in pursuit of worthiness.

Martius stresses that the hatred between the people and the great is no mere misunderstanding. "Who deserves greatness, / deserves your hate" (1.1.175–76). He who deserves to be great is, indeed, "chief enemy to the people" (1.1.6–7). The people's hatred of him is not at all misplaced. By the same token, he who would seek the people's love ("affections") has "[a] sick man's appetite, who desires most that / Which would increase his evil" (1.1.176–77). Such a man desires what would make his malady ("evil") worse. As Martius presents it, the only choice is whether to seek the people's hatred or their love. Speaking nearly entirely in stark antitheses and sharp inversions,[31] Martius never considers the possibility that someone could be indifferent to both (cf. 2.2.16–23). He is constitutionally incapable of such indifference.

Inconstant in war and peace, the people are no less inconstant in their heroes and foes. "He that depends / Upon your favours," Martius continues,

> swims with fins of lead,
> And hews down oaks with rushes. Hang ye! Trust ye?
> With every minute you do change a mind,
> And call him noble that was now your hate,
> Him vile that was your garland.

> (1.1.178–83)

The people's favor is as worthless as their courage and cunning. Just as one cannot depend on their virtue in battle, one cannot depend on their favor in the city. From minute to minute, the people, always at one extreme or the other, reverse their judgments completely.

Concluding his denunciation, Martius, partly echoing his opening rhetorical question, turns to the people's protests against the Senate. "What's the matter," he asks or, rather, exclaims,

> That in these several places of the city,
> You cry against the noble Senate, who
> (Under the gods) keep you in awe, which else
> Would feed on one another?

(1.1.183–87)

Menenius said that the people are useless to themselves and can do nothing without the Senate's rule. Martius, going further, says that they would destroy themselves without it. Unable to rule themselves, the people must be ruled by the Senate. And, the Senate, in order to rule them, must keep them in awe, rooted in their reverence for the gods. There must be an unbridgeable gap between the Senate and the people. Far from devouring them, as the First Citizen claimed (1.1.84–85), the distance between the classes is indispensable to protecting the people from devouring one another.

Instead of giving the people a chance to answer, Martius asks Menenius what they want. And when told that they seek "corn at their own rates, whereof they say / The city is well stor'd" (1.1.188–89), he ignores the question of food and responds solely to the people's presumption: "Hang em! They say?" (1.1.189). Rather than show proper deference, the people "presume to know / What's done i'th'Capitol" (1.1.190–91). For Martius, who never takes seriously the people's complaint about food, there is only one issue—the people's growing presumption and their growing political power. To him, the issue of hunger is purely a pretext.

Martius is angry not only at the people, however, but also at at least some of the nobles, for they will not lay aside their compassion ("ruth") "[a]nd let me use my sword." If they would, "I'd make a quarry," he boasts, "With thousands of these quarter'd slaves, as high / As I could pick my lance" (1.1.196–99). Anger naturally seeks action. Joining the inner soul and the outer world, it seeks to strike at what arouses it. Martius's thwarted wish to use his sword contains his first (and repeated) references to himself ("... me ... my ... I'd ... I ... my ..."). Even as it links the internal to the external, anger, like spiritedness in general, sharply individuates. While connecting the soul and the world, it emphatically distinguishes between them. Martius refers to himself on six occasions in the scene. All six times, the immediate context is anger or action (1.1.196–99, 216–18, 224–25, 229–31, 232–35, 238–39). Similarly, throughout the play, nearly all of Martius's references to himself occur in the context of anger or action—action which, we shall see, is ultimately grounded in his anger.

Prevented from using his sword, Martius uses his words as a weapon against the people. Vituperation substitutes for slaughter. While Menenius uses speech to persuade the people, Martius uses it to defeat them. Menenius, accordingly, now urges persuasion: "Nay, these are almost thoroughly persuaded; / For though abundantly they lack discretion, / Yet are they passing cowardly" (1.1.200–2). Menenius is ironic and oblique. Lacking discretion, he says, the people might be expected to have valor; but despite having no discretion or good sense, they are exceedingly cowardly. Menenius, appealing directly to Martius's opinion of the people (cf. 1.1.169–71) while speaking over their heads, tries to persuade Martius to permit him to persuade them. This is not the last time that he will attempt to persuade Martius to be moderate and permit persuasion in place of bloodshed.

It now becomes clear why Martius is so angry. When Menenius asks about the group of commoners on the other side of Rome, Martius, repeating his curse ("Hang em!" [1.1.203]), reports that the people said they were hungry, recited proverbs about hunger and food, and then the Senate (contrary to Menenius's admonishment of the Citizen [1.1.66–71]) yielded to their demands. "With these shreds," he says, referring to the people's scraps of wisdom,

> They vented their complainings, which being answer'd
> And a petition granted them, a strange one,
> To break the heart of generosity
> And make bold power look pale, they threw their caps
> As they would hang them on the horns o'th'moon,
> Shouting their emulation.

> (1.1.207–13)

While scorning the people for their proverbial cast of speech,[32] Martius implicitly contrasts their feebleness in making their demands with the height of their ambitious aims. Just as their "[s]houting their emulation" showed both their rivalry with one another to shout the loudest and their malicious grudge against the nobles for being superior,[33] so their throwing their caps as high as they could expressed their rising aspirations as well as their immediate political triumph.[34] Indeed, punning on the word "generosity," Martius declares that the senators' generous giving will prove to destroy the nobility ("break the heart of generosity").[35] For the senators' leniency will give the people enough strength to make the Senate ("bold power") look weak and afraid ("pale"), and that will encourage the people to become ever more disobedient and ambitious. The Senate's concessions are the first step toward its ultimate destruction.

The measure granted was "a strange one," however, not so much because the strong gave power to the weak, but because the people asked for bread and got a political office, instead: "Five tribunes to defend their vulgar wisdoms, / Of their own choice" (1.1.214–15).[36] The rebellion was not an uprising for food, as the First Citizen insisted and the moderate senators seem to think, but a democratic political revolt. It results in the establishment of the tribunate, Rome's first plebeian office.[37] The tribunate, consisting of five officers chosen by the commoners from their own class, divides political power in Rome, creating a system of checks and balances between the classes. Serving as an intermediary between the people and the Senate, the office is intended to safeguard the people against the nobles' insolence. By possessing the power to veto anything the Senate proposes (3.1.143–45), the tribunes make it necessary for the nobles to moderate their treatment of the people.[38] Martius, who says that the rabble should have first "unroof'd the city" before they should have so prevailed with him (1.1.217), restates, with greater explicitness, the concession's danger: "[I]t will in time / Win upon power, and throw forth greater themes / For insurrection's arguing" (1.1.218–20). Martius is of course correct, though what he sees as a danger will help lead, instead, to Rome's greatness. The people will, over time, encroach upon the patricians' power, and each victory, rather than satisfying them, will produce greater demands, further contention, and fresh insurrections. Once the tribunate has politically awakened the people, their desires—and the tribunes' powers—will only continue to grow, as will Rome's conquests. But just as Martius fails to grasp the connection between Rome's mixed regime and its freedom and conquests, he also, more particularly, ignores his own and his political allies' role in arousing the people's demands. The people might well have been willing to remain quiet even without a share in Rome's power (as they had under the kings), provided the nobles, and Martius especially, had not insulted their dignity as well as denied them corn (1.1.78–85).[39] Men often rebel when their dignity has been offended. "[Even] slaves bitterly resent insult" (Gellius, *Attic Nights*, 10.3.17). Martius blames the moderate senators' concessions, but not the spirited or covetous senators' provocations that made them necessary.

Plutarch describes the greatest of all the many contests between Virtue and Fortune, to determine which of them produced the mighty power of

Rome. Even if Fortune and Virtue are engaged in a direct and continual strife with each other, he says, it is likely that they suspended hostility and joined forces in completing Rome (Plutarch, *On the Fortune of the Romans*, 1–2). Here, at the dawn of the republic, the Senate, faced with the need to quell a rebellion, establishes a key political institution that will fundamentally alter the regime, but treats it as a minor concession to a passing problem. While Lycurgus, to whom Menenius will unfavorably compare the tribunes (2.1.54), founded Sparta from the beginning and at a single stroke,[40] Rome's regime is the product of fortune or accident rather than of wisdom or planning. Menenius agrees that the concession was "strange" (1.1.220), but only Martius gives any thought to its lasting effects, and he is continually ignored. Hence, the head's subordinate role in Menenius's tale: the heart—"th'seat o'th'brain" (1.1.135)—is what thinks.

4.

A messenger arrives with news that the Volscians are in arms. The news pleases Martius. "I am glad on't; then we shall ha' means to vent / Our musty superfluity" (1.1.224–25). It is not clear whether Martius is glad at the prospect of getting rid of some plebeians only or of some moderate senators as well. Whatever the case, he is pleased that some Romans will be killed.

Martius has anticipated the attack. "Martius, 'tis true, that you have lately told us, / The Volsces are in arms" (1.1.226–27). Aufidius will soon complain that the Romans always anticipate his battle plans. Shakespeare leaves unclear whether Martius knows his plans because he has a spy among the Volscians, as Aufidius will think (1.2.1–6), or because he has the judgment to know that the Volscians will try to take advantage of Rome's internal turmoil, as they frequently do.[41]

Martius, hearing the messenger's news confirmed, praises Aufidius's nobility:

> They have a leader,
> Tullus Aufidius, that will put you to't.
> I sin in envying his nobility;
> And were I anything but what I am,
> I would wish me only he.
>
> (1.1.227–31)

Martius describes Aufidius by referring to himself. While declaring that Aufidius will put his opponent to the test, he says that he envies his nobility. The two parts of his description are of a piece. Martius needs someone to test him, someone against whom he can measure himself. He needs to overcome opposition in order to confirm his own excellence. And because he can know himself only on the basis of what he can subdue, he needs an opponent worthy of himself, an opponent whose defeat would measure his own virtue. Martius therefore needs someone who is, paradoxically, his equal and yet someone he can vanquish—his equal, so that he would be a worthy opponent; someone he can vanquish, so that Martius can prove himself superior. Martius's need to have a worthy opponent—to have "a lion / That [he is] proud to hunt" (1.1.234–35)—will force him continually to exaggerate Aufidius's nobility.

Martius describes how proud he is to fight Aufidius. "Were half to half the world by th'ears, and he / Upon my party, I'd revolt to make / Only my wars with him" (1.1.232–34). Proud to fight such a man, Martius is indifferent to the cause for which he fights. Even if half the world were fighting the other half, were he and Aufidius on the same side, he would switch sides just to be able to fight him. The private duel is all that matters to him. Right from the start, Martius's ties to his country appear tenuous.

Before departing to prepare for the battle for which he will be greatly honored, Martius and the other senators briefly allude to three senses or aspects of honor. When the First Senator, glad to hear his eagerness to fight, urges Martius to serve under Cominius's command and Cominius reminds Martius that "[i]t is [his] former promise," Martius replies, "Sir, it is, / And I am constant" (1.1.237–38). Martius considers keeping a promise a point of honor, for failure to do so, particularly in the face of danger, shows a failure of courage. Honor, in this sense, is identical to virtue. Turning, then, to Lartius, Martius vows that Lartius will see him once more "strike at Tullus' face" (1.1.239). Honor, in this sense, is connected with a person's physical body, and especially with the head and face, for while the head seems symbolic or synecdochical for the person himself, "the face is the image of the soul" (Cicero, *Orator*, 18.60).[42] Thus, just as the Citizen spoke of "[t]he kingly crowned head" (1.1.114) as displaying the city's highest honor and Coriolanus will describe the people's "bare heads" (3.2.10) and his own "unbarb'd sconce" (3.2.99) as signs of their shameful status,[43] so for Martius to defeat Aufidius by striking at his face would be for him to dishonor him doubly. Lartius, eager to follow Martius into battle although wounded and on crutches, next, explicitly offers him precedence. Already honoring him more highly than all but the present consul, he bids Martius, "Follow Cominius, we must follow you, / Right worthy you priority" (1.1.244–45). Precedence implies priority; precedence of place indicates estimation of worth.[44] Honor, in this sense, is the outward sign of the respect in which a man is held. The three senses, passing from the internal to the external, from what depends on oneself to what is given by others, consist of what is identical to virtue itself, what stands for the person himself and what depends on the recognition of others. For most Roman nobles, the three senses are hard to distinguish.

Before the messenger brought news of the impending war, Martius, disgusted with the establishment of the tribunate, scornfully ordered the people to go home: "Go get you home, you fragments!" (1.1.221). But, hearing the First Senator reiterate his order ("Hence to your homes, be gone!" [1.1.247]), Martius now reverses himself and says the people should follow him and the other nobles to the Capitol:

> Nay, let them follow.
> The Volsces have much corn: take these rats thither,
> To gnaw their garners. Worshipful mutiners,
> Your valour puts well forth: pray follow.

> (1.1.247–50)

Martius's words combine mock praise of the people's valor with open insult of their appetite for food. Earlier, Martius said that anyone who has a good word for the people flatters them beneath abhorring (1.1.166–67). But, now, he does it himself, even if he mixes his praise—and perhaps conceals it from himself—with insults and obvious sarcasm. If he is to battle Aufidius, Martius requires soldiers to fight the Volscians; and if the soldiers are to win, they must be spirited.[45] Martius therefore not only holds out to the commoners the prospect of their winning much corn in the battle, but praises their spiritedness in the rebellion as a prospect of their spiritedness in battle. Martius's words point to a political truth that Martius himself refuses to accept or to see. Although he would deny the people political power and have them stay at home and simply obey the nobles' commands, such docility would make them unfit for war. If the people are to be spirited in battle, they will also be spirited in the city. Martius may try, here, to pretend that he is not praising them. That he praises them in spite of himself, however, and now entreats them ("pray follow") instead of ordering them ("Go get you home, you fragments!"), shows his unacknowledged need to make compromises with the non-virtuous conditions that make his practice of his virtue possible. For him to have the battles that he seeks, the nobles must make the concessions that he deplores.

The awaited attack changes the people, too. "*Citizens steal away*" (s.d. 1.1.250). Threatened by war, the people recognize their need of Martius, whom they had resolved to kill just a short while ago, and of the nobles, in general, against whom they were rebelling. Foreign wars bring the two classes closer together, each recognizing its dependence on the other. Whereas in peace the patricians think they can safely oppress the people and the people think they can safely do without the patricians as their leaders, in war the patricians recognize their need of soldiers and the people recognize their need of leaders. Foreign wars thus moderate both parties, as they unite their interests. And because foreign wars temper the domestic strife, Rome's domestic strife, in turn, makes its foreign wars necessary. The people's spiritedness is thus not only needed to fight foreign wars, but is a direct cause of them. As wars abroad moderate conflict at home, conflict at home necessitates war abroad. Foreign wars and domestic strife, not peace either at home or abroad, serve Rome's common good.

The wars also directly serve the people's political interests. Because war frightens them and peace makes them proud (1.1.168–69), the people are more inclined to obey the nobles in times of war than in times of peace. But, even as they make the people more governable, foreign wars add to their political influence and wealth. For in order to raise the troops it requires, the Senate must listen to their complaints and grant them concessions. It must pay the people with power as well as with food. That war brings the people both power and corn helps to explain the First Citizen's earlier ambivalence. Although he cursed the wars along with the laws for eating up the people, the Citizen approvingly understood war as the city's principal activity (1.1.84, 113–18). War may devour soldiers, but it also feeds them and helps to protect them against the patricians' oppressive laws.

5.

The scene ends, much as it began, with Martius's enemies discussing him. Although claiming indifference to public opinion, Martius is constantly under public scrutiny, as he has been since a young boy (see 1.3.7–9; also 2.2.89–90, 93–94). Not even in *Hamlet* do the other characters analyze and judge the central figure as much as in *Coriolanus*.[46] This should not be surprising. Public scrutiny is characteristic of Rome. Men seeking honor seek public attention. Because public honor is the greatest good in Rome and a man's honor is a public verdict on him, Romans—particularly ambitious or outstanding Romans—live under the constant gaze of others. Acting for the public good, they live in the public eye. Honor, by its very nature, is public.[47]

Here, when everyone else leaves, Sicinius and Brutus, who entered with the senators (s.d. 1.1.225) but have said nothing, remain behind to discuss Martius's pride and its political import for them. After declaring that no one ever was "so proud as is this Martius" (1.1.251), they remark on his contemptuous "lip and eyes" as well as on his "taunts" when they were chosen tribunes (1.1.254). Throughout the play, characters pay close attention to and interpret gestures, for gestures—whether formal or informal, intended or otherwise—often bespeak honor or dishonor, respect or scorn. Some gestures are traditional rituals, such as precedence in serial order, as we have already seen (1.1.244–46), kneeling in reverence or submission (1.1.73; 2.1.170; 3.2.75; 4.6.22–23; 5.1.5–6, 65–66; 5.3.50, 57, 75, 169, 175), customary election garb and procedures (2.1.231–34; 2.2.134–50; 2.3), triumphal entries (s.d. 2.1.160) as well as canons and practices of hospitality (1.10.23–27; 4.5.132ff.; 5.3.2–3, 5), sworn vows (1.2.35; 3.1.140–41; 5.3.20–21), rules of single combat (1.8.14–15), rites of friendship (1.6.55–58) and rituals of departure and return (2.1.193–96; 4.1.44–58; 5.5). Other gestures are objects or tokens of status, office or position, for example, titles and surnames (1.9.61–66; 2.1.161–66; 4.5.66–72; 5.1.11–15; 5.6.88–90), garlands of war (1.9.58; 2.1.123–24, s.d. 160; 2.2.101), the consul's horse (1.9.60–61), the Lictors' *fasces* (s.d. 2.2.36), symbols and insignia of office (s.d. 2.2.1; 2.3.139–40; 3.1.100; 4.7.43; 5.4.21–22), the clothing of beggars and mourners (s.d. 4.4.1; 4.5.12–53; 5.3.94–96), and funeral rites and memorials (5.6.148–53). Still other gestures involve the use of space and time, including where people meet (e.g., 2.2.231; 2.3.143–47; s.d. 2.2.1; 5.2.92–93), how long they meet (2.3.137), how long a person speaks (2.2.48–51) and a person's position at the table (4.5.197–98), while yet another type includes one's characteristic manner such as one's posture, the tone and timbre of one's voice, and the look of one's face (1.4.56–61; 1.6.21–27; 2.1.217–19; 4.5.61–63; 5.3.38–40).

Most frequently, however, gestures in *Coriolanus* involve informal bodily signs—whether intentional, unintentional or half-intentional—of one's inward thoughts and passions. Besides what the tribunes have just noted, these gestures include blanching from fear (1.4.37–38; 4.6.102–3), blushing from shame or embarrassment (1.9.67–68; 2.2.144–45; 4.6.4–5; 5.6.98–100), crying from joy or sorrow (e.g., 2.1.158, 176, 182), smiling in scorn or wonderment (1.1.106–10; 1.9.3), biting one's lip in anger (5.1.48), laughing in glory or contempt (2.1.183; 3.3.51–52; 5.3.183–85), baring one's head in respect (s.d. 1.9.40; 2.1.68; 2.2.27; 2.3.98, 165; 3.2.10, 73, 99; 4.5.198–99), casting up one's cap in celebration (1.1.211; s.d. 1.6.76; s.d. 1.9.40; 2.1.104, 264–66; s.d. 3.3.137; 4.6.131–33), waving one's head in self-correction (3.2.77), raising one's sword in exhortation and exaltation or in defense and defiance (s.d. 1.6.75; 3.1.221–24), turning one's back in scorn or turning away in fear (3.3.133–35; 5.3.168), shouting approval or hooting abuse (4.6.124, 132; 3.3.137–39; 4.6.130–37; 5.5.4), shaking with fear and sorrow (5.3.100), stealing away (s.d. 1.1.250), forgetting a name (1.9.88), grasping hands (2.1.192;

4.1.57; 4.5.133, 148; s.d. 5.3.182), supplicating with raised hands (5.3.173–77), dismissing with a silent hand (5.1.66–67), sneering (2.1.114–15), frowning (3.1.106; 4.5.63), drooping (4.1.20), shrugging (1.9.4), quaking (1.9.6), embracing (1.9.29–32; 107–14), and seemingly countless other gestures. Because honor and dishonor are largely indicated indirectly by signs, virtually everything said or done in Rome carries a second significance often outweighing the first. The world of honor is a world of hermeneutics.

The tribunes, having mentioned his facial gestures, go on to describe how Martius, his pride limitless, takes neither failure nor success well. In failure "he will not spare to gird the gods" and "[b]emock the modest moon" (1.1.255–56). In success he "disdains the shadow / Which he treads on at noon" (1.1.259–60). Failure makes him furious at what lies above him; success makes him scorn what lies beneath his feet. In failure, he thinks the gods and the moon despise him. In success, he despises his earthly home. Martius's pride, the tribunes suggest, is incompatible with his being or remaining human.

When Sicinius then wonders how Martius can endure to serve under the command of a superior, Brutus answers, "Fame, at the which he aims, / . . . cannot / Better be held, nor more attain'd than by / A place below the first" (1.1.262–65). Martius can best satisfy his ambition for fame by serving second to another in authority. For if things go badly, Brutus explains, the general will get all the blame, even though he performed as well as any man could have, and "giddy censure" (1.1.267) will credit Martius for what he might have done, had he been in command. "Besides, if things go well," Sicinius adds, "Opinion, that sticks so on Martius, shall / Of his demerits rob Cominius" (1.1.269–71).[48] As he would escape all the blame in failure, Martius would get all the credit in success. Brutus, fully agreeing, goes so far as to say that half of Cominius's honors and all of his faults have already turned into Martius's honors, none of which Martius deserves. It is perhaps telling that, notwithstanding his reminding Martius of his promise to fight, Cominius, not normally taciturn, said remarkably little—just three half-lines, totaling eleven words (1.1.231, 237, 246)—when Martius expressed his eagerness to fight Aufidius and the First Senator proposed that he accompany Cominius in battle. Even the Senator said more. While the tribunes, no doubt, maliciously exaggerate, they nevertheless draw attention to an important circumstance in Rome. The Romans honor merit, but they tend to give the benefit of the doubt to the man out of office and place the burden of proof on the one in office.[49] The double standard stems, on the one hand, from the people's fickle judgment, ingratitude, forgetfulness, and, most of all, fear of Rome's military heroes, and, on the other hand, from the nobles' envious ambition.

For opposite reasons, both the people and the nobles want frequent turnover in office. Neither wants honor to rest long with any hero—the people, from fear of ambition; the nobles, from pursuit of ambition. And though rooted in the private interests and passions of the two classes, the double standard greatly benefits the city. It forces ambitious nobles to compete continually with one another in serving Rome. Even the consul must compete with his subordinates. And bringing new men into the city's political life while inspiring valor, it offers spirited young men the prospect of working their way up through public service and being rewarded for their brave deeds by the city's highest honors.[50] The people's fear and the nobles' envy combine to make the interest of the man and the interest of the city serve each other.

Although the tribunes are silent about their own ambitions and how their new office can serve Rome or satisfy themselves, two points might be stressed. The tribunate provides a lawful object for the ambitions of the most spirited plebeians, by providing them with an office to which they can aspire. It is surely no mere coincidence that "Junius Brutus and Sicinius Vellutus were the first Tribunes of the people that were chosen, who had only been the causers and the procurers of this sedition" (Plutarch, *Coriolanus*, 7.1; North, 2:149).[51] As we shall see, by giving them a stake in the status quo, the tribunate turns potentially dangerous enemies into defenders of the regime (see 3.1.173–74; 3.3.17, 64).[52] In addition, the office, while protecting the commoners, makes their opposition less chaotic or random and more easily controlled by the nobles. It institutionalizes and stabilizes the tumult, keeping Rome's political disorder from becoming a battle to the death for final victory by either party. Like foreign wars, the office that adds to the people's power also, paradoxically, adds to the Senate's ability to govern them.[53]

The tribunes, ending the scene, decide to follow after the nobles and go to the Capitol to hear how the present military matters are to be arranged and, specifically, what Martius's powers and appointment are to be. They have reason to be concerned. As they will later make explicit (2.1.203–21), and as Sicinius indicates with his pun on "singularity" (1.1.277), Martius's great success in war could eclipse their new powers in the city.

Act One, Scene Two

Aufidius is discussing with certain Volscian senators his intended attack on Rome. He believes the Romans have a spy in Corioles's councils. Before the Volscians can ever bring their "thought" to "bodily act" (1.2.4, 5), he says, the Romans have warning and circumvent their plans. In the present case, he is sure that the Romans have a spy in Corioles because he has one in

Rome who has informed him that the Romans have conscripted an army, Cominius, Martius, and Lartius are rumored to lead it, and although it is not known where in the Volscian territory they will go, their most likely destination is Corioles.

Aufidius is evidently trying to take advantage of Rome's political strife and famine. As the spy reports, "The dearth is great, / The people mutinous," and Martius "is of Rome worse hated than of you" (1.2.10–11, 13). When the First Senator doubts that Rome's swift response will change anything—the Volscian army is in the field, he says, and the Volscians never doubted that Rome was ready to meet their attack—Aufidius sharply corrects him. It is never folly, he says, to keep your designs "veil'd, till when / They needs must show themselves" (1.2.20–21). Surprise and hence secrecy are essential in war. Just as Aufidius relies on spies, he practices deception.[54] Intentions should be kept cloaked as long as possible. The discovery of their plans, however, has forced the Volscians to curtail their aim, which was to capture many towns almost before the Romans knew what they were doing. The discovery has cost them surprise and speed. The Romans' rapid response has already blunted the Volscians' strategy.

The Second Senator thus offers a revised strategy. Aufidius is to lead his troops out right away, while other Volscians stay behind to guard Corioles. Then, if the Romans attack the city, Aufidius can return to fight them from the rear. Besides reducing the Volscians' aims, the Roman response has split the Volscian forces and turned a purely offensive operation into a partly offensive and partly defensive one. The Senator, apparently thinking that the Romans are too distracted by their internal troubles to prepare for war, makes light of their preparations: "[B]ut I think you'll find / Th'have not prepar'd for us" (1.2.29–30). Aufidius is certain that he is wrong: "Oh, doubt not that, / I speak from certainties" (1.2.30–31). Contrary to his spy's uncertainty ("[I]t is not known / Whether for east or west" [1.2.9–10]), Aufidius, whether because he has other spies[55] or because of his own military judgment, is "more" than certain that "[s]ome parcels of their power are forth already / And only hitherward" (1.2.31–33). Instead of the Volscians quickly conquering Roman towns, the Romans are already headed for Corioles itself. The invaders have become the invaded.[56]

Accepting the revised strategy and taking his leave, Aufidius tells what he and Martius have sworn: "If we and Caius Martius chance to meet, / 'Tis sworn between us, we shall ever strike / Till one can do no more" (1.2.34–36). The men have sworn to fight each other to the death. Unlike Martius, however, Aufidius does not praise his sworn enemy. Nor does he welcome the war just so he can fight him. Whereas Martius would "make / Only my wars with him"

(1.1.233–34), Aufidius will fight him to the death "[i]f [they] chance to meet." The private duel—the contest of virtue—is not all that matters to him. When the senators wish him the gods' assistance ("The gods assist you!" [1.2.36]), Aufidius accepts their wish. In contrast to Martius, Aufidius has no objection to the gods' assistance. Fittingly, "[a]ssist" will be his final word (5.6.154).

Act One, Scene Three

1.

The third scene, in contrast to the first two, is emphatically private and domestic. Martius's mother and wife sit indoors on low stools, sewing, awaiting his return from war. Only three scenes in the play (1.3; 3.2; 4.5) take place in a private house, only the first two of them in Rome, and only the first without the presence of Roman senators. Scene 3 is the only domestic scene in the play and the only one without words from a man.[57]

Virgilia is unhappy and afraid because Martius has gone to war. Volumnia is rejoicing. For Volumnia, public honor is superior to a lover's love. "If my son were my husband," she tells Virgilia, "I should freelier rejoice in that absence wherein he won honour, than in the embracements of his bed, where he would show most love" (1.3.2–5). In Rome, the private realm is subordinate to the public. The highest private goods are attached to the city's public good. The affections as well as the interests of individuals lie chiefly with their country. "I do love / My country's good," Cominius will impassionedly declare,

> with a respect more tender,
> More holy and profound, than mine own life,
> My dear wife's estimate, her womb's increase
> And treasure of my loins.

(3.3.111–15)

Cominius subordinates every private good of his, however precious, to Rome's public good. And just as he speaks of his wife's honor or reputation ("estimate") and of their children ("her womb's increase / And treasure of my loins"), but not of his wife herself, so, more generally, romantic love is mostly missing from Rome. A city in which men pride themselves on rising above bodily desires, Rome is generally a city of austerity as well as of valor. Not only does Coriolanus praise Valeria for being "chaste as the icicle / That's curdied by the frost from purest snow / And hangs on Dian's temple" (5.3.65–67). The only time he kisses his wife—the only erotic moment in the play—he affirms that "[his] true lip / Hath virgin'd [the kiss] e'er since" he carried it from her (5.3.47–48). To be chaste is to remain a virgin—a noun that Shakespeare coins, here, as a verb.[58] Men's strongest passions in Rome pertain to public honor rather than to private love, to the battlefield rather than to the bedroom.[59] The martial always trumps the marital.[60] Hegel captures Volumnia's quintessential Roman thought when he wittily describes the city's doubly metonymic name:

> The city of Rome had besides its proper name another secret one, known only to a few. It is believed by some to have been 'Valentia,' the Latin translation of 'Roma' ['strength' in Greek]; others think it was 'Amor' ('Roma' read backwards).[61]

"Roma" is, at once, strength read forward and love read backwards. And it is the one because it is the other.

Volumnia, explaining why Virgilia should welcome his going to war, describes Martius when he was just a boy. Indicating that he has been in the public eye since childhood, she says that when "youth with comeliness plucked all gaze his way" and she would not for anything give up an hour of her "beholding" him, she,

> considering how honour would become such a person—that it was no better than picture-like to hang by th'wall, if renown made it not stir—was pleased to let him seek danger where he was like to find fame.

> (1.3.7–8, 9, 10–14)

Volumnia emphasizes what is "becom[ing]." Her standard is seemliness, not beauty. Where in Greece the noble is associated with the beautiful, in Rome it is associated with the decorous (*decorus*). The Greek word for what the Romans mean by "noble" is not *to kalon*, but *to prepon*.[62] Accordingly, even while the word "noble" (with its variants) occurs more frequently in *Coriolanus* than in any other Shakespeare play (eighty-six times), neither "beauty" nor "beautiful" is ever mentioned.[63] In Rome, the noble implies the suitable and the seemly—what is appropriate and how one appears to others.[64] It befits a life of public duty, lived in constant public view.

Like most Romans, but unlike her son, Volumnia sees no tension between honor and virtue. Honor, she says, becomes a comely person. Just as the desire for public honor spurs noble action, public honor confirms noble virtue. The two principal senses of honor—virtue and office—reflect each other. Indeed, the Romans have the same word, *honestas*, for both virtue and reputation. The good citizen is the citizen held to be good. Since what is honorable will be honored by other good men, the city's recognition attests to one's virtue. For Volumnia, virtue is thus always citizen virtue, courage always citizen courage.[65]

Volumnia describes Martius when he first went to war. Although Roman youths normally began military service at seventeen,[66] Shakespeare will stress that Martius was only "sixteen" (2.2.87), and still without a beard (". . . with his Amazonian chin he drove / The bristled lips before him" [2.2.91–92]), when he fought his initial battle.[67] Volumnia, moreover, did not merely "let him seek danger where he was like to find fame." Although "yet he was but tender-bodied" (1.3.5–6), she "sent" him to "a cruel war" (the battle of Lake Regillus, against the Tarquins [2.1.148–49; 2.2.87–89, 94–95]), from which he returned crowned with leaves of oak.[68] "I tell thee, daughter, I sprang not more in joy at first hearing he was a man-child, than now in first seeing he had proved himself a man" (1.3.15–18). The Romans have only one word for virtue—*virtus*. Coming from the Latin word for man (*vir*), the word identifies virtue, in general, with manliness or valor. "[I]n those days," Plutarch writes,

> valiantness was honored in Rome above all other virtues, which they call *virtus*, by the name of virtue [it]self, as including in the general name all the other special virtues besides.[69]

The Romans not only see courage as the highest virtue but, taking the part for the whole, give to all the virtues the name of the one which they think outshines the rest. Virtue is valor. Valor, however, must be "proved," and it must be proved in battle. Thus, as joyful as she was in hearing that her newborn was a "man-child," Volumnia was certainly no less joyful in first seeing "he had proved himself a man." "Man" is a term of distinction. A male is not necessarily a man. One is born a male but makes oneself a man. The former is a matter of birth; the latter, of virtue or action.

When Virgilia, avoiding the word "war," asks what she would have thought if Martius had died "in the business" (1.3.19), Volumnia answers, "Then his good report should have been my son, I therein would have found issue" (1.3.20–21). The son's fame would have been the mother's son. His good account would have been her child. By remaining alive in the memory of Romans, Martius would have remained alive for Volumnia as her son. In winning fame for his noble death, he would not perish. Volumnia, whose own name—literally, "book," in Latin—alludes to fame,[70] suggests that she would have preferred her son's death to his obscurity. It is not clear, however, that she quite means what she suggests. Intending to underscore her point, she declares:

[H]ad I a dozen sons, each in my love alike, and none less dear than thine and my good Martius, I had rather had eleven die nobly for their country, than one voluptuously surfeit out of action.

(1.3.22–25)

Volumnia, speaking as a stern Roman matron, intends her declaration to be unequivocal. She "profess[es] sincerely" (1.3.21–22) that she would rather have her sons die nobly for their country than have one live a soft life of sensual pleasure. Volumnia, nevertheless, lets something slip. She speaks of having "a dozen" sons, but of only "eleven" dying nobly. She holds one back. She unwittingly confesses that she would not want all to die. Despite herself, Volumnia's patriotism and material pride yield to her maternal love. Fame only partly compensates for death.

Volumnia elevates the public over the private not just in what she intends to say, but in how she says it. Although addressing her daughter-in-law in private, she speaks as though she were delivering a public oration, using a variety of rhetorical tropes appropriate to public speech, particularly intensifying comparisons,[71] her most characteristic figure of speech throughout the play. Even her most private moment seems largely public.

When a waiting-gentlewoman announces that Lady Valeria has come to visit, and Virgilia then asks to leave, Volumnia refuses to let her go and, instead, describes what she imagines she sees Martius doing and hears him saying in battle. Volumnia's imaginary depiction of Martius dealing out death in war is the closest the play comes to presenting poetry in Rome. While leading up to a description of Hecuba and Hector (and thus specifically recalling Homer's poetic portrayal of Troy), it breaks into blank verse and, using a variety of tropes,[72] imitates Martius's imagined action and speech: "Methinks I see him stamp thus, and call thus . . ." (1.3.32). Volumnia's poetry is a distinctly Roman form of poetry. Aristotle distinguishes between poetry and rhetoric. In addition to writing separate works on each, he argues that each art has its own purpose, though they share some features. The purpose of poetry is wonder and therefore understanding, while the purpose of rhetoric is persuasion and therefore action.[73] The distinction between the two arts rests on the distinction between thought and action. Rome, however, is a city of action, not of thought. Hence, as Roman writers of a much later age make plain, poetry in Rome is not so much distinguished from rhetoric as made a part of it. Instead of keeping the two arts distinct, the Romans develop a single art of speech, whose diction is poetic but whose purpose is rhetorical. Poetry becomes an instrument of moral instruction or persuasion—and hence of action—an instrument, furthermore, addressed, as here, to specific audiences to produce specific effects.[74] Poetry becomes poetic moralizing.[75] Volumnia had at least implicitly suggested the Roman view of poetry when she said that comeliness was "no better than picture-like to hang by th'wall, if renown made it not stir." Whatever fails to lead to action is wanting. Here, in portraying Martius's dishonoring and defeating Aufidius, she goes further. Earlier, she described Martius's comeliness "pluck[ing]" all gaze his way. Now, she tells of his "pluck[ing]" Aufidius down by the hair (1.3.7, 30). The incongruous echo of a young boy's comely looks in soldier's bloody deed brings out what she meant when, voicing the Roman bias in favor of action, she denigrated comeliness which lacks a spur to warlike deeds.

In describing Martius's imagined actions, Volumnia uses two similes. The first likens the Volscians fleeing Martius to children fleeing a bear: "As children from a bear, the Volscians shunning him" (1.3.31). The second likens Martius to a farm laborer who must cut down all the field or else not be paid:

> His bloody brow
> With his mail'd hand then wiping, forth he goes
> Like to a harvest man that's task'd to mow
> Or all, or lose his hire.
>
> (1.3.34–37)

Both similes, like the previous intensifying comparisons, emphasize sharp contrasts: children and a bear, all or nothing. Moreover, each appears in the context of Martius fighting alone against all the Volscians. Yet, the similes themselves seem unheroic. Notwithstanding her disparagement of peace and her praise of war, Volumnia seems to recognize that war—particularly heroism in battle—needs to be explained by peace. While a simile explains the unfamiliar by the familiar, war is unfamiliar, but peace is known to all. Thus, even while—or precisely because—Martius seems at home in war rather than in peace, Volumnia, although inspired by war to eloquence, glosses war by the more ordinary, more natural world of peace.

Virgilia, swearing by the tutelary god of Rome, is horrified by Volumnia's mention of Martius's bloody brow ("His bloody brow? O Jupiter, no blood!" [1.3.38]). But Volumnia, dismissing her as a fool, proclaims, "[Blood] more becomes a man / Than gilt his trophy" (1.3.39–40). A man's spilled blood, speaking immediately for his deeds, most becomes him, because it is direct evidence of his valor. Volumnia thus compares Hecuba and Hector. "The breasts of Hecuba / When she did suckle Hector," she says, mingling a mother's milk and a warrior's blood, "look'd not lovelier / Than Hector's forehead when it spit forth blood / At Grecian sword contemning" (1.3.40–43). A man spilling blood from his head in contempt of the enemy that struck him looks lovelier than his mother suckling him. Disdaining death is more lovely than nurturing life. The exclusive emphasis on manliness, while deprecating everything female, seems ultimately to imply the supremacy of death over life.

When Virgilia entreats the heavens to protect Martius against Aufidius, Volumnia confidently corrects her: "He'll beat Aufidius' head below his knee, / And tread upon his neck" (1.3.46–47). Just as she associates Hector's honor with his scornful, bleeding head, Volumnia, exemplifying the anatomy of honor, associates Aufidius's dishonor with Martius's beating his head to the ground, as she did when she first described their fighting ("See him pluck Aufidius down by th'hair" [1.3.30]) and as Martius himself did when he vowed to "strike at Tullus' face" (1.1.239). It is interesting though perhaps not surprising that although she suggests that she would rather Martius die in battle than lack fame, Volumnia always imagines him triumphant. Martius may be wounded, but he is never killed.

If Hecuba suckled Hector with a mother's milk, Volumnia suckled Martius with the blood of war (cf. 3.2.129). Martius is Volumnia's only son (1.3.6; 4.1.33), and she is a widow who raised and educated him from an early age by herself. She has been both mother and father to him. Owing to the large number of Roman deaths in battle, many widowed Roman mothers brought up sons who, having been bred by their mothers for their family's glory, became prominent Romans. Along with Volumnia, Cornelia, mother of Gracci, Aurelia, mother of Caesar, Atia, mother of Augustus, and Procilla, mother of Agricola, are celebrated examples.[76] Indeed, the most admired Roman mothers were widows. But although not unique, Volumnia is nevertheless extreme. While taking the place of Martius's father (whom Shakespeare never even mentions[77]), she tries to suppress everything female in herself and to instill wholly unmoderated manliness in her son. Rather than tempering the Roman identification of manliness and virtue, she has only intensified it. Not so much both mother and father to Martius as a mother who wishes to be his father, she has, in effect, turned herself into a man, leaving no mother to mitigate a father's authority. Menenius will call Martius his son and call himself his father (5.2.62, 69–70[thrice]). He will also report that Martius called him father when Cominius went to plead with him not to attack Rome (5.1.3; see also 5.3.10). It was customary in Rome that, when a young boy was left fatherless, the widow chose a family friend to act as his male advisor.[78] But the soft, sensual Menenius could hardly fill in, especially in Volumnia's eyes, for Martius's natural father. Volumnia's would-be transformation from mother to father, from woman to man, while increasing her son's excessive spiritedness, illustrates spiritedness's characteristic tendency to take a part as the whole and then to absolutize it. To be human is to have a mixed nature—to be born of both mother and father, as Volumnia will later acknowledge (4.2.16–18). But, in raising her son, Volumnia has rejected man's mixed nature. Like her son, she has wanted to make the masculine side of human nature the only side. From his days as a young boy, she has tried to act as though Martius never had a mother—as though he had never been generated. She, of course, does not see that her high praise of her son's bloody brow implies his repudiation of her as his mother.

2.

A moment ago, just after declaring that Hecuba's suckling breasts never looked lovelier than Hector's forehead contemptuously spitting forth blood at his foe, Volumnia, in her very next breath, ordered the waiting-gentlewoman to "[t]ell Valeria / We are fit to bid her welcome" (1.3.43–44). Volumnia seemed to suggest that her celebration of bloody warfare and death suited her greeting of Valeria. And, much later, as previously noted, when the women come to beseech him not to attack Rome, Coriolanus will describe Valeria admiringly in the most austere terms (5.3.64–67). But Valeria hardly seems to match what either Volumnia or Coriolanus suggests about her. Rather than being warlike or severe, she is merry, playful, warm, sociable, and even irreverent. She banters, plays on words, seeks mirth and treats with witty, even whimsical, humor the story of Penelope (1.3.82–86), the *locus classicus* of the faithful wife awaiting her husband's return from war. Where Volumnia solemnly refers to Homer's account of war, Valeria jokingly refers to his account of marriage. And where Volumnia detracts from birth in favor of war, Valeria visits a woman expecting a child while her city is fighting a war. Valeria, moreover, seems to have an immediate effect on Volumnia, who, suddenly speaking of sweetness and mirth, greets her as "[s]weet madam" (1.3.49) and concludes that they should leave without Virgilia, because "she will but disease our better mirth" (1.3.103–4). It is easy to think that there is nothing cheerful or sweet about the haughty, harsh, and hard Volumnia. But just as she greets Valeria as "[s]weet madam," Valeria's final words call her "good sweet lady" (1.3.106).

Shakespeare's presentation of Valeria seems to show, on the one hand, how Coriolanus's spirit exaggerates and distorts what it sees, so that it sees what it wants to see, and, on the other hand, that Volumnia has a side which is at odds with the spirited one that she has always shown her son and encouraged in him. As Martius simplifies Valeria, Volumnia simplifies herself. Volumnia, the widowed mother, is not all there is to Volumnia, the woman. Volumnia is not as denatured as she most often appears. Notwithstanding her grim words about Hector and Hecuba, she gladly goes with Valeria to visit the expectant mother.

Valeria, who is charmed by Martius's young son's youthful spirit, describes watching the boy at play. With a determined look on his face, she says, he ran

> after a gilded butterfly, and when he caught it, he let it go again, and after it again, and over and over he comes, and up again, catched it again; or whether his fall enraged him, or how 'twas, he did so set his teeth and tear it. Oh, I warrant how he mammocked it!

> (1.3.60–65)

Valeria's account of the boy, who is interested only in becoming a soldier (1.3.55–56), describes the self-defeating tendency of spirited ambition. The splendor of the gilded butterfly sets the boy's ambition in motion. But as soon as he catches the butterfly, it loses its worth. What matters is the catching, not the having. The brilliance sets a challenge for the boy, but once he meets it, the challenge loses its meaning. And so the boy lets the butterfly go, and tries to capture it again. And again, and again. Satisfaction is impossible. Success deprives the challenge of worth.[79] And so in his frustration, the boy cruelly tears the butterfly to pieces. Valeria fails to understand what she reports. She is unsure whether the boy became enraged because he fell or for some other reason (". . . or whether his fall enraged him, or how 'twas . . ."). In fact, the boy punishes the butterfly for letting him catch it. The success of his ambition causes him to become angry and take revenge on what aroused his ambition. For the boy, gaining his goal is as empty as losing it. Like his father, whom he perfectly resembles ("O'my word, the father's son!" [1.3.57]; "One on's father's moods" [1.3.66]), the boy needs an enemy as distinguished from a conquest. All spirit, he is always in need a fresh enemy to conquer.

Valeria brings news that "the Volscians have an army forth, against whom Cominius the general is gone," and Martius and Lartius "are set down before their city Corioles" (1.3.95–96, 98). Earlier, Brutus stated that the second in command can better attain fame than the first (1.1.260–71). After the battles, Cominius will be extremely grateful and gracious to Martius. But we might wonder whether he takes the battle for himself and leaves the braver, less cautious fighters behind to lay siege to Corioles, in an effort to protect his own glory. Valeria says that Martius and Lartius are confident that they will win and that the war will be brief (1.3.98–99), but not until Martius unexpectedly enters and captures Corioles does anyone—including the Volscians and Martius himself (1.2.25–30; 1.4.1–12)—seem to consider the siege as anything more than a secondary operation.

Act One, Scene Four

1.

Shakespeare frames the play's only battle scenes with two episodes depicting Roman magnanimity. Here, Martius and Lartius are before the city of Corioles. When they see a messenger approaching, Martius offers a wager that Cominius's army has begun fighting. Lartius accepts the bet, pledging his horse to Martius's, and Martius agrees. Martius, however, quickly loses, as the messenger reports that the two armies have not yet begun to fight. "So, the good horse is mine," Lartius says (1.4.5). Having lost the wager, Martius offers to buy back the horse, but Lartius refuses. "No, I'll nor sell nor give him: lend you him I will / For half a hundred years" (1.4.6–7). Spirited men want to appear magnanimous. In particular, they want to give, for giving is a sign of independence and strength, and therefore of superiority. At the same time, they want others to be indebted to them, while they remain indebted to no one, for indebtedness implies dependence and therefore inferiority.[80] Owing to the former concern, Lartius returns the horse to Martius. But, owing to the latter, he will neither sell nor give him the horse, for that would cancel Martius's debt. Instead, he lends Martius the horse, for that keeps his debt alive. Capturing a telling aspect of Roman magnanimity, Lartius's gracious giving conceals his spirited taking. The giving is, in fact, a form of taking. Indeed, what appears most to signify Lartius's generosity—that he will lend Martius the horse "[f]or half a hundred years"—indicates just the reverse. Martius's indebtedness will continue for half a century.

Martius, betting against his own interests, takes the side that he hopes will lose. He loses the wager but wins an opportunity. The opportunity will bring him an even worthier horse (1.9.59–61). Hearing that the other armies lie only a mile-and-a-half away, Martius prays to his namesake: "Now Mars, I prithee make us quick in work, / That we with smoking swords may march from hence / To help our fielded friends" (1.4.10–12). Martius wants to finish his work, here, quickly, so he can have two victories—one here and another to save his friends. While other men pray for victory, Martius prays only for the chance to fight and prove his virtue. Just as he believes that virtue alone should be rewarded in the city, he believes that virtue alone should determine victory in battle.

2.

When the Romans call for a parley, a group of Volscian senators appears on the city's walls. Martius has only one question: "Tullus Aufidius, is he within your walls?" (1.4.13). Martius's stated wish to help his friends in the field seems to be little more than his wish to defeat his personal enemy in the field. Answering Martius's question, a Volscian Senator replies, "No, nor a man that fears you less than he; / That's lesser than a little" (1.4.14–15). The Volscian seems to say the opposite of what he intends. He says that the Volscians in the city all fear Martius at least as much as Aufidius does, but he means that there is not a Volscian in Corioles who fears him more than their greatest warrior does, and that is less than a little, which is to say, nothing at all. By use of the negative, the negation is meant to be doubled, but in fact is canceled.[81] On the spirited Senator's lips, the intensification becomes the cancellation of his boastful taunt.[82]

Hearing the Volscians' drums "bringing forth [their] youth" (1.4.16) in the other battle, the Senator, stirred by the example, vows that those guarding the city will break out of its walls and fight the Romans in the open. Indeed, according to him, the city's gates, though they "yet seem shut," are "but pinn'd with rushes; / They'll open of themselves" (1.4.18–19). Far from being tightly fastened to protect those within the city, the gates were never really fastened, he brags: manly men do not hide behind their city's walls.[83] At the sound of a second alarum from the other battle, the Senator, further aroused, taunts the Romans, "There is Aufidius. List what work he makes / Amongst your cloven army" (1.4.20–21). Speaking of events more than a mile away, the Volscian describes what he cannot see, but only imagine—that the Romans are being cut to pieces. Martius, wishing to be in the other battle, exclaims, "Oh, they are at it!" (1.4.21). And Lartius, taking the noise of that battle with either shame or indignation or both, understands it as a lesson to the Romans to act: "Their noise be our instruction. Ladders ho!" (1.4.22). But before the Romans can mount the walls, the Volscians, making good on the Senator's boast (and altering the Volscians' original battle plan [cf. 1.2.27–30]), charge through the gates and attack them. "They fear us not, but issue forth their city," Martius declares (1.4.23). For Martius, the attack is a sign of the Volscians' contempt for the Romans, whom they do not fear, as the Senator claimed. Accordingly, Martius, considering the battle a contest wholly of courage, urges the Romans to show that their strength lies in their hearts rather than in their weapons. "Now put your shields before your hearts, and fight / With hearts more proof than shields," he exhorts his men (with a chaismus for emphasis) (1.4.24–25). The Romans should prove that their hearts are more impenetrable than their shields, that they carry within themselves their strongest weapon. Valor should be their only weapon. Thus, urging "brave Titus" to "[a]dvance" (1.4.25), Martius makes explicit that the Volscians insult the Romans by their deeds as well as with their words. They show their scorn by leaving the protection of the city's walls and fighting the Romans in the open: "They do disdain us much beyond our thoughts, / Which makes me sweat with wrath" (1.4.26–27). The Volscians' scorn enrages Martius. And his outrage, eclipsing at least for the moment his desire to duel Aufidius, sparks his heroic effort to conquer Corioles. Wrath kindles his courage.

Martius, while urging on his men, threatens to kill any Roman who withdraws or falls back: "I'll take him for a Volsce, / And he shall feel mine edge" (1.4.28–29). In his rage at the Volscians, Martius considers a Volscian any Roman who frustrates the satisfaction of his wrath. Even before the armies meet, his fury at the one army leads to his fury at the other. Owing to his rage, he cannot tell the armies apart—or does not think it matters. All that matters is the satisfaction, not the object, of his wrath.

Notwithstanding Martius's threat, the Romans are driven back to their trenches. Martius, exploding with fury, curses them as pusillanimous. Just as his first words to the people described them as loathsome sores (1.1.163–65), he now would punish them by plastering their bodies with boils and plagues, so that they would be smelled before they are seen and infect one another even against the wind (1.4.30–33). Their bodies would be as disgusting as their souls. What they are outwardly would reveal what they are inwardly. Accordingly, Martius, like his mother imitating him (1.3.32–34), taunts his soldiers, saying they have "the souls of geese" though they "bear the shapes of men" (1.4.34, 35). They are only superficially or externally men. Inwardly, they are worse than apes, having "run / From slaves that apes would beat" (1.4.35–36). Martius's curse and invective have a specific cause: "All hurt behind, backs red, and faces pale / With flight and agued fear!" (1.4.37–38). Brave men get wounded in the front. They face the enemy, even in retreat. These shameless "shames of Rome" (1.4.31), however, turned their backs and took fearful flight. Their backs rather than their faces red with blood, they were cowardly in retreat.

Martius, calling upon them to "[m]end and charge home" (1.4.38), gives his men another chance, though, again, he threatens to "leave the foe / And make war on [them]" (1.4.39–40) if they fail. Offering them encouragement for the first time,[84] he declares, "If you'll stand fast, we'll beat them to their wives, / As they us to our trenches" (1.4.41–42). Outraged by the Volscians' insults and the Romans' faint-heartedness, Martius charges toward the city, exhorting his men to "Follow me!" (1.4.42). Martius credits Fortune with opening the city's gates. He means that good fortune favors those in pursuit, not those in flight: "'Tis for the followers Fortune widens them, / Not for the fliers" (1.4.44–45). Having good fortune is having the chance to fight to the death. Entering Corioles, Martius cries, "Mark me, and do the like!" (1.4.45). No one, of course, does. "Foolhardiness! Not I," the First Soldier exclaims (1.4.46). Such hardiness is foolhardy, to the troops. As the Volscians withdraw into the city, only Martius pursues them, and he is immediately shut in. Everyone assumes that he has been or soon will be killed. "[H]e is himself alone, / To answer all the city" (1.4.51–52), the Soldier says, stressing Martius's solitariness. Martius is "alone" against "all."

His soldiers certain that he will be cut to pieces like meat for cooking ("To th'pot, I warrant him" [1.4.47]), Martius's chances of staying alive seem so slim that Lartius immediately offers a eulogy. Lartius, the only Roman soldier Martius ever calls "brave" or "valiant" (1.4.25; 1.5.11) and the only one he seems to respect, first compares him to his sword: "Oh noble fellow! / Who sensibly outdares his senseless sword, / And when it bows, stand'st up" (1.4.52–54). Like other men but unlike his sword, Martius is capable of feeling pain. Yet, he is braver than his sword. After his sword is bent, he still stands upright. Lartius, implying that Martius competes even with ("outdares") his sword, suggests that, like a sword, Martius is unsparing of himself and indifferent to the object of his slaughter. In battle, he comes to resemble the weapon he should wield[85] and proves himself yet firmer and truer. Lartius then compares Martius to a flawless gem as large as he. "A carbuncle entire, as big as thou art," he continues, "Were not so rich a jewel" (1.4.55–56). In Lartius's eyes, the blood on Martius's body is transmuted into the fiery, red transparency of a jewel, and Martius becomes richer than a precious ruby his size would be. For Lartius, however, Martius is not "fierce and terrible / Only in strokes" (1.4.57–58). Apostrophizing him (while referring to him in the past tense), Lartius says, "Thou wast a soldier / Even to Cato's wish." Terrible in his strokes, Martius was terrible also in the grimness of his countenance and the thunderous sound of his voice. Just the sight and sound of him would make his "enemies shake, as if the world / Were feverous and did tremble" (1.4.56–61).[86] Lartius's praise, fusing together the inanimate and the animate, the instrumental and the cosmic, compares Martius first to his weapon, then to a perfect gem his size, and finally to an implacable force of nature. Lartius's eulogy leaves it difficult to decide whether Martius, in going beyond himself, becomes more or less than human.

Martius, covered with blood but still fighting, appears on the wall, assaulted by the enemy. Whereas, earlier, the Roman soldiers thought it foolhardy to follow him into the city, now they follow Lartius and rush in to rescue Martius or to share his fate ("Oh, 'tis Martius! / Let's fetch him off, or make remain alike" [1.4.62–63]). Martius's heroism inspires their courage. A hero whose soldiers often exceed themselves (see 4.6.76–80, 91–96, 102–6), Martius perfectly embodies the Romans' customary reliance on their leaders rather than on their troops in battle.

Lartius compares Martius to Cato the Elder, who fought in the Second Punic War against Hannibal, nearly three centuries after the events in *Coriolanus*. Shakespeare's glaring anachronism (the first of several in the play) seems to capture an important aspect of the character of written history—and hence of political life—in early Rome. Just as reading and writing are always connected in the play to current action and lasting fame,[87] the Roman annals were concerned with both. They were, as their name suggests, a chronicle of the year's political and military events. They included magistrates, battles, laws, treaties, priests, prodigies, fires, floods, famines, and so on.[88] Thus Menenius will remind the tribunes that Rome's "gratitude / Towards her deserved children is enroll'd / in Jove's own book" (3.1.288–90), Volumnia will warn Martius about how his "chronicle [will be] writ" (5.3.145), and Martius will taunt the Volscians that, "If you writ your annals true, 'tis there, / That like an eagle in a dove-cote, I / Flutter'd your Volscians in Corioles" (5.6.113–15). The annals, however, described not only the year's occurrences, but also the lives and characters of Romans of outstanding glory and fame. They served not merely as records of events, but as examples of virtue, written chiefly for future generations of readers to imitate.[89] Performing the function of a "noble memory" (5.6.153), they served both to remember and to remind (Varro, *On the Latin Language*, 6.49). The annals thus chronicled ceaseless change; yet, linking the future to the past by tying the latter particularly to the gods ("enroll'd / in Jove's own book"), they rested on and sustained the view that the noble past should guide the future. Pointing at once to the past and the future, they encouraged the Romans to believe in, and act for, the greatness of Rome's future. Timeless *exempla* were thus the core of Rome's written history. While the noble past was always present, the future mirrored the past, just as the past foreshadowed the glorious future. Cato can therefore provide an example of virtue for Martius, just as Martius can furnish one for him.[90] Anachronism is of the essence of Rome's own written history.

Act One, Scene Five

Even while their fellow citizens are still fighting (1.5.8), the Romans fall to plundering. While particularly disgusted by the worthlessness of the cheap booty the soldiers value, Martius understands that rewards generally measure an action's merit: "See here these movers, that do prize their hours / At a crack's drachma!" (1.5.4–5). Prizes prize deeds. The prizes that the doer accepts indicate his estimation of his action's worth. They delimit his deed.[91]

Imagining that the sound of the other battle is that of Aufidius piercing the Romans, Martius hurries off to fight him, "the man of [his] soul's hate" (1.5.10), despite his own nearly fatal wounds. He says that Lartius is to take enough Romans to hold the city, while he, Martius, "with those that have the spirit" (1.5.13), will hasten to Cominius's aid. In the opening scene, Martius, needing soldiers for the war, begrudgingly praised their spirit (1.1.249–50). Now, his need more urgent, he praises them again, this time without insult or mockery. In the next scene, preparing to march against Aufidius, he will openly flatter the soldiers (1.6.67–85).

Lartius tries to dissuade Martius from fighting a second battle: "Worthy sir, thou bleed'st; / Thy exercise hath been too violent / For a second course of fight" (1.5.14–16). As Lartius recognizes, Martius feasts on fighting. His second battle ("second course") would be his banquet's main dish ("second course"),[92] to which the battle in Corioles was merely an appetizer. Martius takes Lartius's words of caution as praise: "Sir, praise me not" (1.5.16). He understands the mention of his bloody wounds as praise, for the wounds display his valor (see 1.3.39–40). Martius denies, however, that he yet deserves the praise: "My work hath yet not warm'd me" (1.5.17). While his spilled blood renews his strength rather than weakens him (". . . is rather physical / Than dangerous to me" [1.5.18–19]), he will not deserve praise until "[t]o Aufidius thus" he appears and fights (1.5.19).

Lartius, no longer trying to restrain Martius, calls upon "the fair goddess, Fortune," to "[m]isguide" his opponents' swords (1.5.20, 22). Fortune is to affect the outcome of the fight. Martius, bidding farewell, wishes only that Fortune be no less a friend to Lartius than to those she most favors. Just as when he entreated Mars solely for the opportunity to fight (1.4.10–12) and when, entering Corioles, he credited Fortune with opening the city's gates (1.4.44–45), Martius is silent about Fortune favoring his own victory. Notwithstanding his strong respect for Lartius, what is good enough for Lartius is not good enough for himself. Where Lartius looks to Fortune as well as to courage, Martius looks only to his virtue.

Act One, Scene Six

The Romans in the field are being driven back. Cominius expects them to be attacked again. Urging them to rest and commending them for having fought well ("Breathe you, my friends; well fought" [1.6.1]), he tells his troops that they have disengaged "[l]ike Romans, neither foolish in our stands / Nor cowardly in retire" (1.6.2–3). Romans, according to Cominius, combine prudence and bravery. They are prudent in attack and brave in retreat. Their bravery is not divorced from some calculation of ordinary interest. On the other hand, their calculation does not degenerate into cowardice. Reconciling conflicting virtues, the Romans are, at once, courageous and cautious, brave and moderate.

Cominius is in many ways Martius's opposite. Where Martius knows only to charge, Cominius knows also to retreat. Where Martius curses his troops for pulling back, Cominius commends his for retiring. And as he is moderate, so Cominius is largely deaf to what arouses Martius's spirit. While the sound of Cominius's battle inspired Martius to attack (1.5.9–12, 21), "hav[ing] heard / The charges of our friends" (1.6.5–6) has not prevented Cominius from withdrawing. Caution governs his action. So, too, does the concern for favorable outcomes. Seeking divine support, Cominius invokes "[t]he Roman gods" to determine ("lead") the "successes" of "both [Roman] powers" (1.6.6, 7, 8). While the troops' victories would in one sense be "[their] own" (1.6.7), in another they would not. The Romans would owe the gods "thankful sacrifice" (1.6.9) for the victories the Romans could claim.

Like the Volscians in Corioles, Aufidius has disregarded the Volscians' battle plan. Instead of bringing his army back to Corioles to raise the siege (1.2.27–23), he has kept it in the field. We might wonder whether the imagined glory of his expected victory has caused him to neglect the plan. Whatever the case, he will be surprised and furious to hear that the Volscians have lost the city (1.10.1–7).

Edward Gibbon's description of Alaric the Visigoth aptly describes Martius: "[His] indefatigable ardor . . . could neither be quelled by adversity nor satiated by success."[93] Although it takes a messenger more than an hour to get from Corioles to the second battle (1.6.10–21), Martius, having fought his way against deadly odds, arrives in almost no time at all. So bloody from head to foot that he looks as though he were "flay'd" (1.6.22), he is hardly recognizable. But just as Lartius praised him for his grim looks and thunderous sound in battle (1.4.58–61), Cominius recognizes him by his bloody looks and thunderous sound (1.6.22–27). Martius's only concern is that he has come too late to fight. "Come I too late?" he asks twice (1.6.24, 27).

"Ay," Cominius answers, "if you come not in the blood of others, / But mantled in your own" (1.6.28–29). Where Martius, echoing Volumnia, seeks praise in his being covered in his own blood (1.5.16–20; cf. 1.3.34–43), Cominius seeks Martius's safety in his being covered in the blood of others.

Martius understands Cominius's answer to mean that the fighting is not yet over, that he has not come too late. Enraptured by the prospect of battling Aufidius, Martius compares his present desire and joy to those of his wooing his wife and of their wedding night. "Oh! Let me clip ye," he exclaims, "In arms as sound as when I woo'd; in heart / As merry as when our nuptial day was done, / And tapers burn'd to bedward" (1.6.29–32). Like his mother's describing him in battle (1.3.31, 34–37), Martius explains war by peace, killing by love, the spirited by the erotic. As he embraced his beloved when he wooed her, Martius embraces Cominius when asking to fight. And just as he was joyous on his wedding night when the candles indicated that it was time for bed, he is joyous now when told that the time to fight his greatest enemy is at hand. Where Volumnia explained the actions of war by actions of peace, Martius explains the passion of war by the passion of peace. Glossing his love of war by his love of his wife, he suggests that war is his true love, his real bride. Martius is, literally, a war-lover. While his heart's desire is his standard, his greatest love is victory in combat.

After reviling his own troops, again, for cowardice, Martius rebukes his commander for pausing in battle: "Are you lords o'th'field? / If not, why cease you till you are so?" (1.6.47–48). No pause is permissible, for Martius. When Cominius explains that he pulled his forces back because they were fighting at a disadvantage and the retreat was merely tactical, Martius, thinking ahead, asks on which side the Volscians have placed their best fighters ("their men of trust" [1.6.52]). Cominius tells that they have placed in the vanguard the Antiates, "their best trust" (1.6.54), who are commanded by Aufidius, "[t]heir very heart of hope" (1.6.55). Martius then triply entreats Cominius—by "all the battles" they have fought, by "th'blood" they have shed together, and by "th[eir] vows" of friendship (1.6.56–58)—to set him directly against Aufidius and his Antiates, and let him and his men "prove" (1.6.62) themselves without delay. The combination of Martius's impetuous speed and Cominius's cautious delay has, ironically, permitted Martius to pursue his second victory—the one Cominius evidently sought for himself. Cominius, explicitly wishing to do otherwise (1.6.62–64), can do nothing but allow Martius to have his way: "[Y]et dare I never / Deny your asking" (1.6.64–65). Having rebuked his commander, Martius finally commands him.

When Cominius offers him his choice of soldiers, Martius singles out those "[t]hat most are willing" (1.6.67). Needing soldiers, he flatters those who have just been forced to retreat. Instead of berating them for cowardice, he declares it would be a "sin to doubt" (1.6.68) that any of them loves the blood in which Martius is smeared, fears for his life less than a bad reputation, thinks a brave death outweighs a bad life and loves his country more than himself. The solicitation succeeds: *They all shout and wave their swords*" (s.d. 1.6.75). Although Martius called only upon "him alone, or so many so minded" (1.6.73) to volunteer, all the soldiers show their eagerness. By a mixture of flattery and shame, his appeal succeeds beyond his expectations. Martius flatters the men by affirming while appealing to their spirit and shames them by forcing those who refuse to fight to "express" (1.6.74) publicly what he says would be a "sin to doubt."[94] He flatters and shames their pride.

The soldiers do more than shout and wave their swords. "*They take [Martius] up in their arms, and cast up their caps*" (s.d. 1.6.76). Surprised and delighted, Martius cries out, "O me alone! Make you a sword of me!" (1.6.76). Whereas Lartius had suggested that Martius resembles his sword in battle (1.4.52–54), Martius suggests that the soldiers turn him into his sword. Taking him up in their arms, they transform him from a swordsman into a sword. Singled out by his soldiers ("me alone"), he becomes his army's single weapon. He becomes, in his own eyes, nothing but his weapon. The result, ironically, of his blatant flattery of the soldiers, this is Martius's happiest moment in the play. Nowhere else does Martius openly express such pleasure. Nor does he anywhere else permit commoners to touch him.

This is also the only time Martius offers his soldiers (or any Roman commoners) genuine thanks: "[T]hanks to all" (1.6.80–81).[95] Martius, however, needs fewer soldiers than have volunteered. He says that he ("I" [1.6.81]) must select a certain number from all and promises the rest the opportunity to take part in another fight, as occasion demands. He does not, however, select the soldiers himself: "[F]our shall quickly draw out my command, / Which men are best inclin'd" (1.6.84–85).[96] Delegating the invidious task to others, Martius deflects and divides the blame. This is his most politic moment among the Romans.

Where Martius speaks solely of the soldiers' honor, Cominius prudently if uninspiringly obscures their reward. "Make good this ostentation," he promises, "and you shall / Divide in all with us" (1.6.86). He leaves unclear whether "all" includes plunder, honors or both.

Act One, Scene Seven

Lartius is concerned about winning the battle in the field. Not only are he and some troops to join Cominius and Martius, but his lieutenant is also to dispatch a large number of troops ("[t]hose centuries" [1.7.3]) to the other battle, if Lartius sends for them. "[I]f we lose the field, / We cannot keep the town" (1.7.4–5). Corioles is the prize, but the countryside is indispensable to holding it. While the Volsces foolishly opened the city's gates (1.4.16ff.), the Romans need only keep them shut and guarded in order to hold Corioles at least in the short run (1.7.1, 6). Lartius's assessment draws attention, again, to Cominius's decision to fight the other battle with neither of his two best fighters.

Act One, Scene Eight

Martius finally has the duel he has sought. Before Aufidius and he begin to fight, they hurl their most contemptuous insults at each other. Mixing personal abuse and respect, they duel with words before swords. Martius says that he will fight with none but Aufidius because he hates him "[w]orse than a promise-breaker" (1.8.2). Martius hates promise-breakers, because breaking one's promise is breaking one's word of honor. Virtue is at stake in keeping promises (see 1.1.237–38). Aufidius, declaring that the hate is mutual, matches Martius's insult: "Not Afric owns a serpent I abhor / More than thy fame and envy" (1.8.3–4). As Martius compares Aufidius to a promise-breaker, Aufidius compares Martius to the most abhorrent African snake. According to ancient legend, the most loathsome African snakes sprang from the blood of the female monster, Medusa (Ovid, *Metamorphoses*, 4.614–20). Where Martius taunts Aufidius with lacking honor, Aufidius taunts Martius with being low, unmanly and monstrous. Aufidius says he abhors Martius's "envy and fame." The phrase is ambiguous. On the one hand, Martius's "envy and fame" are his malice ("envy") toward Aufidius (see 1.1.229) and his renown ("fame") as a warrior, particularly as the warrior who has beaten him many times (1.10.7–10; 4.5.122–23, 182–89). On the other hand, taken as a hendiadys, they are his "envied fame." The phrase's twin meanings are really the same. Aufidius hates Martius's envied fame, for while he seeks such fame for himself, much of Martius's comes from his repeated victories over him.

Fixing their feet to fight, the two men announce what is at stake in the combat. Both describe chiefly what it means to lose rather than to win. Martius says that the first to flinch should die the other's slave and be doomed by the gods after death. Aufidius says that if he, Aufidius, flees, Martius should hunt him down like a hare. Living as a slave or being killed as a timid beast seems a fitting fate for a fleeing coward. Martius had previously said that the blood covering him was his own and, understanding its mention as his praise, said that he would not deserve the praise until he appeared "[t]o Aufidius thus" and fought (1.5.19). Now, however, defiantly calling Aufidius by his personal name ("Tullus" [1.8.7]) and taunting him with the news that within the last three hours "[a]lone I fought in your Corioles walls, / And made what work I pleas'd," he declares, "'[T]is not my blood / Wherein thou seest me mask'd" (1.8.9–10). Trying to provoke his wrath, Martius wants to fight Aufidius when Aufidius is at his best. To enhance his victory and fully deserve his praise, he must increase Aufidius's vengeful rage: "For thy revenge, / Wrench up thy power to th'highest" (1.8.10–11). Answering, Aufidius declares that if Martius were Hector—"the whip of your bragg'd progeny" (1.8.12)—he would not escape him here. No Roman, and not even the most illustrious of Rome's legendary ancestors, would get away.

Aufidius, however, is mistaken. The two men fight. And Martius nearly cuts Aufidius to pieces, as we soon learn (1.10.7–10; 4.5.182–94), when some Volscians come to Aufidius's aid and are themselves *driven in breathless* (s.d. 1.8.13). Aufidius angrily curses the men for the shaming assistance: "Officious, and not valiant, you have sham'd me / In your condemned seconds" (1.8.14–15). Aufidius will soon state that he would stop at nothing—that he would violate all honor and trust—to kill Martius (1.10.12–27). And, much later, his rivalry having turned entirely to bitter resentment (4.7; 5.6.10–60), he will treacherously kill him. But for now he seems still to regard his fight to the death with Martius as a contest of virtue whose rules of honor must be fully obeyed, lest a fighter dishonor himself.

Act One, Scene Nine

1.

The Romans have won the field and command the day. With a flourish heralding the victors, Cominius and his army enter on one side and Martius, with a wounded arm, on the other. Cominius, saying that not even Martius himself would believe his deeds, describes how four groups of Romans will take his report of them. Of the first three groups, he describes their silent gestures; of the fourth, their spoken words. Senators, he says, will "mingle tears with smiles" (1.9.3); great patricians will listen, at first disbelieve ("shrug"), but "[i]'th'end admire" (1.9.4–5); women will be "frighted," but, "gladly quak'd," will want to "hear more" (1.9.5, 6); and

> the dull tribunes,
> That with the fusty plebeians hate thine honours,
> Shall say against their hearts, "We thank the gods
> Our Rome hath such a soldier."

(1.9.6–9)

Cominius, punning on the word "dull," depicts the dumb ("dull") tribunes as gloomy ("dull") at the news. Knowing that Rome, indeed, is fortunate to have such a soldier, but hating the honors that Martius's actions bring, the tribunes are forced to say what they hate to say. This is the first time anyone describes them and the only time anyone other than the tribunes themselves mentions their "hearts." The tribunes will mention their own hearts twice, once publicly and once privately. Although they will publicly declare that their hearts are inclined to Martius's election (2.2.54–57), they will privately speak of their hearts as hostile to it and will wish to keep their hearts hidden from public sight (2.1.266–68). While the silent gestures of the others reveal their silent thoughts, the spoken words of the tribunes, here, as elsewhere, conceal and even contradict their unspoken thoughts.

Cominius uses the same metaphor of dining for Martius's fighting as Lartius used. Lartius said that the battle in Corioles was merely an appetizer to the main dish ("second course") of Martius's battle with Aufidius (1.5.16). Cominius reverses the dishes. "[T]his feast" of victory, he says, was but "a morsel" compared to the great dinner of Corioles which Martius had already eaten ("Having fully din'd before" [1.9.10–11]). While both men underscore Martius's great appetite for war, each sees the other's battle as more glorious than his own. Each graciously derogates from the victory that he might at least partly claim for himself.

Lartius, arriving from Corioles, enters and begins to praise Martius for his actions there. "Here is the steed, we the caparison," he announces (1.9.12), likening Martius to a horse and everyone else to its mere trappings. The comparison seems especially apt, for a horse is most like a spirited soldier, is most pleasing to Mars,[97] and particularly resembles Martius in Corioles: "The virtue of a horse makes him both run quickly and abide the enemy" (Aristotle, *Nicomachean Ethics*, 1106a19–21). When Lartius, continuing, begins to describe what Cominius would have thought had he "beheld" Martius (1.9.13), Martius interrupts and stops him: "Pray now, no more. My mother, / Who has a charter to extol her blood, / When she does praise me, grieves me" (1.9.13–15). Volumnia said that the ambition for renown is a necessary spur to noble action (1.3.9–14). But Martius, saying that he does not want even his mother's praise (cf. 1.1.37–38; 3.2.107–8), denies that he wants anyone's. Praise pains him, he says. Instead of explaining why or of saying nothing, Martius insists that he does not deserve praise. He has done, he says, only what he could, as others have; and he did it for his country, as others have, as well. In fact, he continues, revising his comparison of himself to the others, whoever did his best achieved more than he ("He that has but effected his good will / Hath overta'en mine act" [1.9.18–19]). Whether or not intended, Martius's ostensible modesty serves to magnify his merit. In effect claiming what he professes to disclaim, Martius suggests that his intention was not fully accomplished and he could have done still better. As unbelievable his achievements were, he might have achieved even more.

Fundamentally ambivalent toward praise and honor, Martius must hide his desire for them from himself as well as from others. He would like to think, and have others think, that, for him, virtue is its own reward, that "[h]e . . . / . . . rewards / His deeds with doing them" (2.2.126–28). Just as he wants his virtue to depend on nothing outside himself, he wants to believe that he practices it entirely for its own sake. Wholly self-sufficient, his virtue, he wishes to believe, is unconditional in its end, as in its origin. But virtue is not enough for Martius. Like any Roman, Martius needs to have others recognize what he does and what he deserves. He is ambitious for noble distinction. Loving victory, he loves renown. But, as also with honor, praise tends to impugn the very virtue which it seems to confirm. Praise is only as good as those who give it. As Martius has already said, the people's praise is as worthless as the people themselves (1.1.181–83). Strictly speaking, not even Aufidius could adequately praise him for victory. Coming from someone Martius has defeated, the praise would come from an inferior. Paradoxically, Martius wants to prove himself the very best, but his being the very best would deprive him of anyone worthy of praising him. In addition, praise could easily be seen as mercenary. In welcoming it, Martius's reason for acting might seem to be not the excellence that he achieves, but the external reward that it brings—"[a] bribe to pay my sword," as he will call the war's spoils (1.9.38). His virtuous actions would then seem to be not their own end, but simply a means to another. Moreover, to be ambitious for praise is to be dependent on those who give it and therefore to deny the self-sufficiency that Martius seeks to claim. It amounts to his allowing others to be the arbiter of his worth and ultimately to seeing himself through their eyes. Furthermore, as Martius has already pointedly observed (1.5.4–5), any reward measures the worth of the deed. Because it is meant to be commensurate with the deed, praise tends to delimit the deed which it extols. Just as praise, on the one hand, is only as good as those who bestow it, the deed, on the other hand, is only as good as the praise it receives. No praise can therefore do justice to what most deserves praise. However much Martius seeks recognition and distinction, his desire for praise and honor transforms itself—or at least tries to transform itself—into a disdain for honor and praise. Forced by its own claim to merit, it seeks to rise above itself and come to scorn what it desires in order truly to deserve it.

Cominius tries to address Martius's concerns. Declaring that Martius's merits should not be cast into oblivion ("You shall not be / The grave of your deserving" [1.9.19–20]), he says that it would be a crime—worse than a theft and no less than a slander—to hide Martius's actions, the very highest praise of which would seem too modest. It is not Martius, however, but Rome who must hear his praise. Martius claimed to have acted for Rome, "for my country" (1.9.17). As though taking him at his word, Cominius answers on Martius's grounds. "Rome must know / The value of her own," he replies, appealing to the city's good (1.9.20–21). Martius must hear his praise, for Rome needs to know his merit. Rather than Martius gaining recognition, Rome would gain knowledge. The city would come to know her own. "Therefore I beseech you—," Cominius continues, "In sign of what you are, not to reward / What you have done—before our army hear me" (1.9.25–27). The praise is to be a sign to Rome of what Martius is, not Rome's reward to him for what he has done. Martius can listen without compromising himself or his virtue.

Martius, however, again objects. "I have some wounds upon me, and they smart / To hear themselves remember'd," he says, separating himself from his wounds and personifying them (1.9.28–29). Martius cannot be praised without mentioning his wounds, and his wounds are pained at being remembered. What pains him is not his having received the wounds, but his hearing them mentioned. Yet, Martius's remonstrance, far from stopping the stream of praise, only increases Cominius's effort to render him his due. Cominius attempts to justify his continuing against Martius's apparent wishes. Were Martius's wounds not remembered, he says, they well might "fester 'gainst ingratitude, / And tent themselves with death" (1.9.30–31). No longer warning of Martius's becoming the grave of his deserving, Cominius warns that Martius's wounds, indignant at not hearing themselves remembered, might reject all remedy but death. Cominius, evidently aware of Martius's deep ambivalence, seems to recognize that Martius desires the recognition that he refuses. Although he had said that Rome, not Martius, must hear it, he now states that Martius must hear the praise. Rome may need to know the value of her own, but Martius needs to know the value that Rome places on him.

Cominius thus offers Martius his choice of a tenth of all the horses and of all the large booty won in the field and in the city. But Martius once more refuses: "I thank you, general; / But cannot make my heart consent to take / A bribe to pay my sword: I do refuse it. . . ." (1.9.36–38). Even as he tries to speak univocally, Martius implicitly divides himself. Much as he has just done when speaking of his smarting wounds, he now describes himself as one thing, his heart as another. He ("I") cannot compel his heart ("my heart") to agree with him ("consent") to take a bribe to pay his sword. Reflecting the spirited war within his soul, Martius uses a synecdoche to refer to himself by a part ("my heart"), which he separates from himself and personifies as though it had its own will. He attempts to maintain his wished-for integrity by identifying himself with one of his soul's warring parties—the potentially ignoble one—while placing the virtuous party—his incorruptible heart—outside himself. He removes his soul's inner conflict by alienating one of its clashing parties. And he defends his soul's purity by isolating his soul from the party that might succumb to the ignoble temptation. By identifying himself with the potentially corruptible party, he shows or suggests that his soul's purity lies in its denying himself an impure reward.[98] Martius's self-denial is his self-affirmation. The victory of his spirit is its victory over itself—the victory of virtue over the spirited ambition for external rewards for virtue.

Martius, insisting that he deserves no praise, had said that others who carried out their intentions surpassed his actions (1.9.18–19). Now, however, saying that he will accept only an ordinary share of the spoils, he describes the same soldiers, not as those who fought in battle with him, but as those who "have beheld the doing" (1.9.40; cf. 1.9.13). They were simply spectators of his heroic deeds. Even as he claims indifference to honor and praise, Martius suggests that his fighting was a public performance for all to behold. His scene of battle was a theater of war in the theatrical as well as the military sense.[99]

At Martius's refusal to take more than a common soldier's share, the soldiers sound "*[a] long flourish. They all cry, 'Martius! Martius!', cast up their caps and lances*" (s.d. 1.9.41). The soldiers understand Martius's refusal as an expression of his modesty. If they see his indifference to gain as indicating his spiteful insolence toward them in the disputes about their debts, they see it as indicating his acknowledged equality with them in the distribution of spoils.

Martius becomes furious at the flourish and not only demands that it be ended, but wishes that the drums and trumpets never be sounded again: "May these same instruments, which you profane, / Never sound more!" (1.9.41–42). Because he regards instruments of war to be profaned when used to salute a hero, he wishes that the drums and trumpets never summon men to battle again. Martius would rather give up war than have its instruments acclaim a hero, for he fears that the salute will corrupt the city. "When drums and trumpets shall / I'th'field prove flatterers," he continues,

> let courts and cities be
> Made all of false-fac'd soothing! When steel grows
> Soft as the parasite's silk, let him be made
> An overture for th'wars! No more, I say!

(1.9.42–46)

Martius fears that the soldiers' praise of the hero on the battlefield will lead to the hero's flattery of the people in the city. The soldiers' praise is nothing more than flattery, since those who give it lack judgment. In this case, they mistake Martius's expression of pride for an expression of humility. Despite its worthlessness, however, the praise will lead the hero to flatter the people in the city. He will flatter them in order to keep their flattery. If victory in battle is a prelude to election in the city, elections, Martius seems to warn, amount to mutual flattery between the hero and the people, turning the hard conduct and weapons of war ("steel") into the soft flattery and clothing ("silk") of a parasite. Praise on the battlefield will corrupt the hero and hence the city.

The unstated premise of Martius's angry imprecation is that the hero is ambitious for honor and praise. Not surprisingly, Martius immediately denies the premise. Making light of both the blood on his face ("For that I have not wash'd my nose that bled" [1.9.47]) and his achievements ("Or foil'd some debile wretch" [1.9.48]), and repeating his contention that he did only what many others have done unnoticed, he insists, again, that the praise is undeserved:

> [Y]ou shout me forth
> In acclamations hyperbolical,
> As if I lov'd my little should be dieted
> In praises sauc'd with lies.
>
> (1.9.49–52)

To permit the praise is to suggest that he desires it. Or, as Martius says, combining a metaphor of eating with a conditional, the soldiers shout as if he loved that his small merits should be fattened upon praises spiced with exaggeration and hence with lies.[100] The conditional is meant to be a denial.

Before the second battle, Martius first rebuked and then commanded his commander (1.6.47–48, 55–65). Now, preventing his commander from doing his duty to praise him, he tries to show himself superior to, rather than grateful for, the praise. "Too modest are you," Cominius gently rebukes him, tactfully reminding Martius that he is speaking to his general,[101] "More cruel to your good report than grateful / To us that give you truly" (1.9.52–54). Martius's professed rejection of praise has the effect, intended or otherwise, of heightening the reward that it disavows. Where Martius rejected having his first pick of all the horses as well as the other treasure won in battle, Cominius now announces, not only "to us, [but] to all the world," that Martius "[w]ears this war's garland: in token of the which, / My noble steed, known to the camp, I give him, / With all his trim belonging" (1.9.58–61). Martius wins what Lartius had likened him to (1.9.12). Although he refused his pick of the horses won in battle, Martius is able to accept the consul's horse, because it is a "token," not a reward or measure, of his accomplishment. Indeed, it is the token of a token—a "token" of the "war's garland," Cominius says. Twice removed and entirely symbolic, it does not mark the limits of Martius's merit.

In addition to the war's garland and the consul's horse, Martius wins a new name:

> [A]nd from this time,
> For what he did before Corioles, call him,
> With all th'applause and clamour of the host,
> Martius Caius Coriolanus!
>
> (1.9.61–64)

The Romans are ambitious for their names. "[S]eek[ing] danger where [they are] like to find fame" (1.3.13–14), they live and die for their names.[102] Martius, however, becomes named for his vanquished enemy. Like spiritedness itself, he becomes defined by what he opposes and defeats. Paradoxically, seeking to depend on nothing but his virtue, Martius, in consequence of that virtue, becomes identified, externally and negatively, by what he conquers. His spirited self-sufficiency negates itself as it fulfills itself. While adding the surname "Coriolanus" (whose felicitous root is Latin for "heart"), Cominius at the same time reverses Martius's personal and family names: "call him . . . / Martius Caius Coriolanus!" The name that Martius wins for his victory eclipses his family name and even reduces it to less than a personal name.[103]

Martius does not refuse the name. Although he rejected the shout of "Martius" and a flourish, he accepts the shout of "Coriolanus" while permitting a "*[f]lourish*" of "*[t]rumpets . . . and drums*" (1.9.66 and s.d.). One might say, as Plutarch suggests while discussing the surname "Coriolanus," that it is impossible to refuse a surname, for a surname is what others choose to call you (Plutarch, *Coriolanus*, 11.2–4). But Martius accepts the name as well as the horse and flourish with no reluctance, though apparently with some embarrassment. "I will go wash," he says, "And when my face is fair, you shall perceive / Whether I blush or no" (1.9.66–68). If Martius is blushing (as seems likely), the blush would seem to show the combination of his pleasure in being praised and his concern that his pleasure can be seen, betraying his desire for the praise. But embarrassed by his apparent embarrassment,

Martius conceals behind his bloody face whether or not he blushes. He conceals the outward sign of his pleasure beneath the outward sign of his valor. What is on his face covers what is in his face. Martius finally offers Cominius his thanks ("howbeit, I thank you" [1.9.68]) and graciously promises to ride his new horse and try always to bear his surname as becomingly as he can. This is, however, the last time he ever thanks a Roman.

2.

The episode concerning the poor man is the counterpart of Martius and Lartius's wager in 1.4. The two episodes, dealing with magnanimity, frame Martius's action in battle. Martius, describing his predicament as "[t]he gods begin[ning] to mock me" (1.9.77), says that having refused most princely gifts, he must beg his general for something. He must beg for the freedom of a poor man who was once his kind host in Corioles but is now a prisoner of Rome. The man, he says, cried to him, "[b]ut then Aufidius was within my view, / And wrath o'erwhelm'd my pity" (1.9.84–85). Cominius gladly approves: "Were he the butcher of my son, he should / Be free as is the wind" (1.9.86–87). But when Cominius asks the man's name, Martius cannot remember it. "By Jupiter, forgot!" he swears, by the god of hospitality (1.9.88).[104] Martius blames his forgetfulness on his tiredness. No doubt he is tired: this is one of only two times that he ever asks for wine (1.9.90; 5.3.203). However, as we have seen, men like Martius would much rather confer benefits than receive them. The one is the mark of a superior, the other of an inferior. Such men therefore do not enjoy being reminded of their debts. Hence, Martius is apt to have a good memory for benefits he has conferred but a bad one for those he has received. While making him eager to benefit, pride makes him quick to forget. Unable to bear owing a debt to anyone, Martius is unable to return a kind favor.[105]

Just as it spurred his courage at Corioles, Martius says that "wrath" overwhelmed his pity when Aufidius came into view. Aristotle distinguishes between acting from courage and acting from wrath. In the case of courage, the action is performed because of the noble; in case of wrath, because of pain (Aristotle, *Nicomachean Ethics*, 1116b23–17a9). Martius wants to believe, and wants others to believe, that he fights for the sake of the noble. Yet, he says, or perhaps admits, here, that he fought Aufidius out of wrath. Even when not seeking revenge—even when fighting "a lion / That [he is] proud to hunt" (1.1.234–35)—he fights from rage. We might wonder whether he is able to distinguish between courage and rage, virtue and passion. His spirit may shroud the difference.

Act One, Scene Ten

Aufidius, learning that Corioles has been taken but reassured by a soldier that it will be returned on good terms ("good condition" [1.10.2]), becomes furious at the thought that it has been lost. Shifting the sense of "condition" from "terms" to "quality" or "situation," he angrily answers, "Condition! / I would I were a Roman, for I cannot, / Being a Volsce, be that I am" (1.10.4–5). Where Martius would switch sides in order to face the severest test (1.1.230–35), Aufidius would do so in order to avoid being of the defeated party. Unable to be himself ("be that I am") in defeat, he would rather be a victorious Roman than a defeated Volscian.[106] Winning outweighs loyalty. Thus, combining the two senses of "condition," Aufidius continues, "Condition? / What good condition can a treaty find / I'th'part that is at mercy?" (1.10.5–7). To be in another's power is to be defeated.

If Aufidius cannot be a Volscian so long as the Romans have defeated Corioles, neither can he be honorable so long as Martius has defeated him. After saying that Martius has beaten him each of the five times they have fought and would do so, he thinks, if they fought as often as they eat, Aufidius swears that the next encounter will be their last: "By th'elements, / If e'er again I meet him beard to beard, / He's mine, or I am his" (1.10.10–12). But Aufidius no sooner envisions a manly contest in which either might kill the other than he explicitly discards honorable restraint. "Mine emulation / Hath not that honour in't it had," he says;

> for where
> I thought to crush him in an equal force,
> True sword to sword, I'll potch at him some way,
> Or wrath or craft may get him.

(1.10.12–16)

Aufidius's sense of rivalry has lost its sense of honor. Owing to his mortifying defeats, Aufidius will now stop at nothing to kill Martius. His loss of battle has led to his loss of honor. Unable to defeat Martius in combat, Aufidius will now do whatever it takes to destroy him.

And having said that wrath or craft may get him, Aufidius goes on to explain that while Martius is "[b]older" than the devil, he is "not so subtle" (1.10.17). Prowess is his strength; lack of guile, his weakness. Martius may not be beaten in open battle, but he can be defeated by clever deceit.

Aufidius thus casts off not only his sense of honor, but his courage, as well: "My valour's poison'd / With only suff'ring stain by him: for him / Shall fly out of itself" (1.10.17–19). Aufidius's valor, having been disgraced or eclipsed ("suff'ring stain") by Martius alone, has become poisoned and will desert its own nature completely ("fly out of itself"). Just as he cannot be defeated and still be a Volscian or be honorable, Aufidius cannot be defeated and still be valorous. He will become an assassin, instead. Aufidius lists eight possible impediments to wrath—"[e]mbarquements all of fury" (1.10.22)—which he says shall not "lift up / Their rotten privilege and custom 'gainst / My hate to Martius" (1.10.22–24). The restraints involve physical vulnerability or weakness ("Nor sleep . . . / Being naked, sick" [1.10.19–20]), on the one hand, and the sacred ("nor sanctuary, / . . . nor fane, nor Capitol, / The prayers of priests, nor times of sacrifice" [1.10.19–21]), on the other. Rather than allowing them to stop him, Aufidius would take advantage of the one and violate the other. Aufidius then adds the law of hospitality:

> Where I find him, were it
> At home, upon my brother's guard, even there,
> Against the hospitable canon, would I
> Wash my fierce hand in's heart.
>
> (1.10.24–27)

As Martius's debt to the poor man in Corioles for his kindness indicates (1.9.80–85), the law of hospitality, reconciling the opposite senses of "host"—"hostile" and "hospitable"[107]—serves to moderate the harsh condition of endless warfare. Protected by the gods, who consider its violations violations against themselves, the hospitable canon regards the obligation to defend foreign guests as even more sacred than the obligation to defend kin.[108] Aufidius, however, would violate the canon and kill Martius in Aufidius's own home, under the protection of Aufidius's own brother. He would kill him anywhere, at any time, in any way.

Aufidius speaks of the "hate" caused by his envy, frustration, and mortification. Unlike anger, which characteristically claims to be in the right, bitter hatred is compatible not only with admitting that the other person deserves what he possesses, but with announcing one's own vicious intent. Instead of claiming justice, it can expressly renounce virtue and even decency entirely. Yet it is not clear that Aufidius means all that he shamelessly proclaims. While anger characteristically causes people to exaggerate their claims to justice, such hatred may cause them to exaggerate their unscrupulousness. Wanting destruction, they will boast of their willingness get it at any cost. Aufidius will, of course, plot treacherously against Coriolanus and "potch" him, but not before trying to use him rather than destroy him, and not before Coriolanus shames him yet again.

Aufidius, always prompt to act, is already preparing to reverse the Volscians' defeat. Concluding act 1, he discloses that he is awaited at a certain grove south of the city. And while not wanting to be left behind by the speed of events (". . . that to the pace of it / I may spur on my journey" [1.10.32–33]), he sends a soldier to spy upon the Romans in Corioles and learn how the city is held and who are held prisoner. As these words end act 1, act 3 will begin with the news that Aufidius has quickly raised a fresh army, which has forced Lartius to come to terms sooner (and presumably less favorably) than expected with the city of Corioles, and that Aufidius is set to attack Rome, again.

Notes

1. The doubleness of the grievances is both echoed in and obscured by the Citizen's pun on "poor" ("We are accounted poor citizens" [1.1.14]) and his bitterly sarcastic pun on "dear" ("they think we are too dear" [1.1.18]). "[P]oor" means both impoverished and worthless; "dear" means both expensive and worthy.

2. E.g., "[R]ather to die than to famish," "We . . . poor citizens, the patricians good," "surfeits on . . . relieve us," "we might guess . . . , but they think," "[our] leanness . . . their abundance," "our sufferance . . . [their] gain," "pikes . . . rakes," "hunger for bread, not . . . thirst for revenge" (1.1.3–4, 14–15, 17–18, 19–20, 21, 22, 23–24).

3. On "very" placed before substantives, see E. A. Abbott, *A Shakespearian Grammar* (London: Macmillian, 1870: reprint, New York: Dover, 1966) §16; Alexander Schmidt, *Shakespeare-Lexicon*, 2 vols. (Berlin: Georg Reimer, 1902; reprint, New York: Dover, 1971), s.v. Very. For "very" in this sense, see also 1.4.49; 1.6.55; 2.1.83, 110, 184, 197; 4.5.230; 4.6.71; 5.2.39.

4. Tacitus, *A Dialogue on Oratory*, 36; Cicero, *Brutus*, 21–22. See further Jan H. Blits, *The End of the Ancient Republic: Shakespeare's "Julius Caesar"* (Lanham: Rowman and Littlefield, 1993), 34–37.

5. Besides copulative verbs, only "can" (including "cannot" and "could"), "come," "do," "have" (including its use as an auxiliary verb), "let," and "make" occur more often.

6. In addition, "tell" appears forty-three times, "cry" fifteen times in the dialogue and once in the stage directions, and "shout" eight times in stage directions and five times in the dialogue (including one "unshout"). Note also "themes / For insurrection's arguing" (1.1.219–20).

7. Robert S. Miola, *Shakespeare's Rome* (New York: Cambridge University Press, 1983), 181.

8. See, e.g., Polybius, *The Histories*, 6.52.10–55.4; Sallust, *Catiline Conspiracy*, 7.3; *Jugurthine War*, 1.3, 4.5–6; Diodorus Siculus, *Library*, 31.6.

9. Cicero, *De partitione oratoria*, 26.91–92; Livy, 10.9.6.

10. Plutarch, *Comparison of Alcibiades and Coriolanus*, 3.1; *North's Plutarch*, 8 vols. (1579; reprint, London: David Nutt, 1895), 2:193.

11. Plutarch, *Coriolanus*, 15.5, 17.1.

12. Apart from the fact that all Roman men would be expected to fight, the only indications of Menenius's military experience are his saying that he can scarcely bear to put on his armor (3.2.35) and his referring, boastfully and perhaps with considerable exaggeration, to "us o'th'right-hand file" (2.1.21–22), a term originally referring to the place of honor given to the best military men; cf. 3.1.241–42. On the term, see J. W. Fortescue, "The Army: Military Service and Equipment," in *Shakespeare's England*, eds. S. Lee and C. T. Onions, (London: Oxford University Press, 1916), 2 vols., 1:114.

13. Charles Cowden Clarke, *Shakespeare Characters* (London, 1863 [New York, AMS Press, 1974]), 479; Mungo MacCallum, *Shakespeare's Roman Plays* (London, 1910 [London: Macmillian, 1967]), 560–63; Cantor, 30–31.

14. See, e.g., Hobbes, *Leviathan*, ch. 17–18; *De Cive*, 5.9.

15. Adrian Poole, *Coriolanus* (New York: Harvester, 1988), 3. On the sacred quality of the Senate, see Livy, 6.41.

16. See Jan H. Blits, *The Soul of Athens: Shakespeare's "A Midsummer Night's Dream"* (Lanham: Lexington Books, 2003), 151.

17. See, e.g., 1.1.22–23, 71–73; 1.4.10–12; 1.5.20–22; 1.6.6–9; 1.8.6; 1.9.8–9; 2.1.1, 100, 104, 120–21, 139, 169–70, 178, 217; 2.3.56, 110, 133–35, 155; 3.1.85, 140–41, 231, 287–91; 3.3.32–37, 72–74, 143; 4.2.11–12, 45–48; 4.1.136; 4.6.20–25, 36–37, 154; 5.2.75–77; 5.3.46–48, 70–75, 104–9, 166–68, 183–85; 5.4. 31–35, 56; 5.5.2. For augurs, divines, and priests, see 1.10.21; 2.1.1, 83, 211; 2.3.60; 5.1.56. See also Cicero, *De Natura Deorum*, 2.8; Varro, *The Latin Language*, 6.16; Virgil, *Georgics*, 1.340–50; Plutarch, *Numa*, 14, Pliny, *Natural History*, 18.2.

18. Livy, 1.19–21; Plutarch, *Numa*, 8.3; Machiavelli, *Discourses*, 1.11.

19. Livy, 1.8; Plutarch, *Romulus*, 13.1–4.

20. Dionysius of Halicarnassus, *Roman Antiquities*, 6.36.1.

21. Shakespeare combines parts of two separate popular uprisings in Rome: the secession of the people to the Sacred Mount, which led to the establishment of the tribunate, and the sedition of the people because of the famine, which was caused by their absence from their farms during the secession; see Dionysius of Halicarnassus, 6.22–90, 7.1; Livy, 2.23–34; Plutarch, *Coriolanus*, 5–7.1, 12.

22. Sir Phillip Sidney, *An Apology for Poetry (or The Defense of Poesy)*, ed. R. W. Maslen (Manchester: Manchester University Press, 2002), 96. On the tale's "old and harsh kind of eloquence [of] those days," see Livy, 2.32.8; tr. Philemon Holland (1600), *The Romane Historie* (London: Gabriel Bedell, 1659), 54.

23. Quintilian, *Institutio oratoria*, 5.11.19.

24. Erasmus, *De Copia*, in Craig R. Thompson, ed., 84 vols., *Collected Works of Erasmus* (Toronto: University of Toronto Press, 1978), 24:632–33.

25. See, e.g., Cicero, *De inventione*, 1.79, 87.

26. "To leave the meal and take the bran." M. P. Tilley, A *Dictionary of Proverbs in England in the Sixteenth and Seventeenth Centuries* (Ann Arbor: University of Michigan Press, 1950), M785.

27. E.g., 1.1.189; 2.3.58, 76; 3.1.83, 87; 3.3.67, 84; 5.6.87, 104, 112. For the trope of metastasis or retortion, see Henry Peacham, *The Garden of Eloquence* (1577; reprint, Menston: The Scholar Press Limited, 1971), s.v. Metastasis.

28. E.g., 1.1.164–66, 183–87, 195; 1.6.48; 2.1.175–76; 2.3.51–52, 58; 3.1.29, 32–36, 49, 87–88, 90–96, 129–31; 3.2.14–15, 99–101; 3.3.58–61, 84; 4.1.2–3. For the trope of percontatio or epiplexis, see Quintilian, 9.2.6–16.

29. Ever since at least George Steevens, editors have generally interpreted Martius's difficult sentence to say (with minor variations), "Your virtue is to speak well of him whom his own offenses have subjected to justice, and to rail at those laws by which he whom you praise was punished." George Steevens in *The Johnson-Steevens Edition of the Plays of William Shakespeare*, ed. Samuel Johnson and George Steevens, 12 vols. (1773; reprint London: Routledge/Thoemmes Press, 1995), 7:338. Besides overlooking Martius's defining need for an enemy to oppose (as well as some serious syntactical difficulties), Steevens's gloss is at odds with the tone of the speech as a whole. While the gloss assumes that Martius uses the word "worthy" sarcastically, the speech is conspicuously forthright and outspoken, saying exactly if brutally what he means. Moreover, with just one possible, brief exception (1.6.42), Martius never uses sarcasm when he is free to be forthright. For his sarcasm, see, e.g., in context, 1.1.249–50; 3.3.33–37; for his sarcastic use of "worthy," see 2.3.80, 136. For his reference elsewhere to demotic "virtue," see 2.3.59–60.

30. See also, e.g., 1.1.248; 1.4.31, 34; 3.1.32, 88, 92, 138, 237–38; 3.3.120; 4.1.1–2.

31. The antitheses and inversions are intensified, moreover, by their terseness ("nor . . . nor" [1.1.168]; "foxes, geese" [1.1.171]), parallel phrasing ("The one . . . / The other" [1.1.168–69]; "Where . . . / Where" [1.1.170–71]; "find you . . . , finds you" [1.1.170]; "upon the ice, / Or . . . in the sun" [1.1.172–73]; "deserves . . . , / Deserves" [1.1.175–76]), transposed thoughts ("him noble that was now your hate, / Him vile that was your garland" [1.1.182–83]), and paradoxical or self-canceling pairings ("who desires most that / Which would increase his evil" [1.1.177–78]; "swims with fins of lead, / And hews down oaks with rushes" [1.1.178–79]).

32. Clarita Felhoelter, *Proverbialism in Coriolanus* (Washington: Catholic University of America Press, 1956); Cantor, 109.

33. See *Oxford English Dictionary*, s.v. Emulation, 1 and 3.

34. The people's caps, which are frequently mentioned in *Coriolanus*, often in the context of their political power (1.1.211; s.d. 1.6.75; s.d. 1.9.40; 2.1.68; 2.2.265; s.d. 3.3.137; 4.6.132, 136), are a symbol of their liberty. When a slave was freed in Rome, he was given a felt cap. From this ritual arose the proverbial metaphor of calling a slave to his "cap of liberty," by which was meant offering his freedom or raising a popular rebellion by exorbitant promises; see, e.g., Livy, 30.45; Valerius Maximus, *Memorable Deeds and Sayings*, 5.2.5; Seneca, *Letters*, 1.47.18; Plutarch, *Sayings of Romans*, 196E (the Elder Scipio, 7).

35. See *OED*, s.v. Generosity, 1 and 3.

36. MacCallum, 525.

37. The establishment of the tribunate marks the first time in Western history that an aristocracy is forced to share power with officers of the people. The Spartan ephorate, although sometimes likened to the tribunate (e.g., Cicero, *Republic*, 2.33.57–58; *Laws*, 3.7.15–16), represented not the commoners alone but the political community as a whole and may actually have functioned as an aristocratic office curbing the royal power; see Xenophon, *Constitution of the Spartans*, 15.7.

38. Livy, 2.33; Dionysius of Halicarnassus, 6.87.2–3.

39. See Aristotle, *Politics*, 1297b6–10; also Livy, 2.21, 23.

40. Polybius, 6.10; Plutarch, *Lycurgus*, 5–6.

41. See 1.2.10–13; 4.3.13–19; Livy, 2.25; Plutarch, *Coriolanus*, 5.3.

42. See 1.9.66–68; 2.1.55–56, 61–62; 4.5.61–62, 157–59. Note also 4.6.116–18.

43. See also, e.g., 1.3.46–47; s.d. 1.6.76; s.d. 1.9.40; 2.1.68, 104, 262–65; 2.2.26–27; 2.3.16–34, 97–98, 167; 3.1.92; 3.2.10, 73, 77–78; s.d. 3.3.137; 4.5.198–99; 4.6.130–37; 5.6.91. Note also 2.2.88; 3.1.1.

44. Plutarch, *The Roman Questions*, 283a.

45. Dionysius of Halicarnassus, 6.49.5–51.3.

46. William Rosen, *Shakespeare and the Craft of Tragedy* (Cambridge: Harvard University Press, 1960), 185.

47. Cicero, *Letters to his Brother Quintus*, 1.1.38.

48. The original sense of "demerit" is the same as "deserts" or "merit"; see *OED*, s.v. Demerit, 1.

49. Cantor, 43.

50. Cantor, 43, 45.

51. See also Dionysius of Halicarnassus, 6.70ff.; Livy, 2.33.1–3.

52. Cantor, 61–62.

53. J. Patrick Coby, *Machiavelli's Romans: Liberty and Greatness in the "Discourses on Livy"* (Lanham: Lexington Books, 1999), 28.

54. According to Livy, the Volscians' "wonted nature" is to prepare for war "secretly [and] underhand[edly]." Livy, 2.22; Holland, 45.

55. For his other spies, see 1.6.18–19; 1.10.27–29; 4.3.

56. Miola, 173.

57. A silent male attendant ushers in Valeria when she enters (s.d. 1.3.47).

58. See *OED*, s.v. Virgin, v.

59. See Blits, *Ancient Republic*, 4–6.

60. See, e.g., 1.6.29–32; 4.5.107–19.

61. Hegel, *The Philosophy of History*, trans. J. Sibree (New York: P.F. Collier and Son: 1901), 376; also Plutarch, *Romulus*, 1.1.

62. Cicero, *De officiis*, 1.93.

63. The words "beauty" and "beautiful" are absent from no other Shakespeare tragedy and from only two other Shakespeare plays (*Timon of Athens* and *Henry the Fourth, Part 2*). For "becomes" in the sense of "being suitable" or "being comely,"

note, further, "[Blood] more becomes a man" (1.3.39); "the wounds become him" (2.1.122); "This palt'ring becomes not Rome" (3.1.58); "Your dishonour . . . / . . . bereaves the state / Of that integrity which should becom't" (3.1.158); ". . . such as becomes a soldier" (3.3.56). Also: "We are fit to bid her welcome" (1.3.44); "I mean . . . / To undercrest your addition" (1.9.89–90); "When what's not meet, but must be, was law" (3.1.166); "Let what is meet be said it must be meet" (3.1.168); "A goodly city is this Antium" (4.4.1); "A goodly house" (4.5.5); "a happier and more comely time" (4.6.27); ". . . that curtsy . . ." (5.3.27); ". . . and unproperly / Show duty as mistaken . . ." (5.3.54–55); "Show'd . . . any courtesy" (5.3.161). Although "lovelier" is mentioned once, it is synonymous with "more becoming" (1.3.39–41). See also 2.2.85; note that "dignifies" (*dignitas*) is linked etymologically with *decorum*.

64. Cicero, *De officiis*, 1.93–141.

65. Aristotle, *Nicomachean Ethics*, 1116a16–b2; Polybius, 6.54.

66. Gellius, 10.28.1.

67. Plutarch does not mention his age but describes Martius as a "stripling" (Plutarch, *Coriolanus*, 3.1; North, 2:145).

68. In addition to emphasizing his young age, Shakespeare heightens Martius's achievement and glory. In Plutarch's account, Martius wins the crown of oak for saving a fellow Roman's life (Plutarch, *Coriolanus*, 3.2). In Shakespeare's, he wins it for proving himself the "best man in the field" (2.2.97; see also 1.9.59; 2.1.123–24).

69. Plutarch, *Coriolanus*, 1.4; North, 2:144; for the derivation of *virtus* from *vir*, see Cicero, *Tusculan Disputations*, 2.43.

70. Cf. 3.1.287–90; 5.2.14–16; 5.3.68–70, 140–48; 5.6.113–15.

71. Besides the explicit comparisons ("more comfortable" [1.3.2]; "freelier rejoice in . . . than in . . ." [1.3.3–4]; "no better than" [1.3.11]; "not more joy at . . . than . . . in" [1.3.16–17]; "each . . . alike" [1.3.22]; "no less dear" [1.3.23]; "I had rather . . . than . . ." [1.3.24–25]), nearly every word involves an implicit comparison: e.g., "son" / "husband" (1.3.2); "absence" / "embracements" (1.3.3, 4); "honour" / "love" (1.3.4, 5); "most love" (1.3.5); "but tender-bodied" (1.3.6); "only son" (1.3.6); "all gaze" (1.3.7); "a day of kings' entreaties" / "an hour from [a mother's] beholding" (1.3.8, 9); "seek danger" / "find fame" (1.3.13–14); "I sent him" / "he returned" (1.3.14–15); "first hearing" / "first seeing" (1.3.16, 17); "man-child" / "man" (1.3.17, 18); "good report" / "son" (1.3.20); "eleven die nobly for their country" / "one voluptuously surfeit out of action" (1.3.24, 25). Other tropes include anaphora ("When . . . ; when . . . ; when . . ." [1.3.5–8]), epiphora (". . .man-child" / ". . . man" [1.3.17, 18]; ". . . son" / ". . . issue" [1.3.20, 21]), chaismus ("had I" / "I had" [1.3.22, 24]), simile ("picture-like" [1.3.11]), alliteration (e.g., "where he would show most love" [1.3.5]; "kings' entreaties" [1.3.8]; "find fame" [1.3.13–14]; "his brows bound with oak" [1.3.15]; "love alike" [1.3.22]), and symmetrical structure ("in that . . . wherein" / "in the . . . where" [1.3.3, 4–5]).

72. The tropes include anaphora ("Methinks . . ." / "Methinks . . ." [1.3.29, 32]), antistrophe ("stamp thus"/ "call thus" [1.3.32]), antithesis ("in fear" / "in Rome" [1.3.33, 34]; "Or all, or lose his hire" [1.3.37]), symmetrical structure ("Methinks I hear" / "Methinks I see" [1.3.29, 32]; "you were got in" / "you were born in" [1.3.33,

34]), alliteration ("hear hither" [1.3.29]; "bloody brow" [1.3.34]), and anachronism ("mail'd-hand" [1.3.35]). On the similes, see below.

73. Aristotle, *Poetics*, 1452a4, 1460a11–18, *Metaphysics*, 982b11–19, *The Art of Rhetoric*, 1355b26–35.

74. Horace, *Ars Poetica*, 114ff, 153ff.

75. See Blits, *Deadly Thought*, 144–45.

76. Tacitus, *Dialogue on Oratory*, 28.6; *Agricola*, 4.2; Plutarch, *Tiberius Gracchus*, 1.4–5; *Sertorius*, 2.

77. Cf. Plutarch, *Coriolanus*, 1.2.

78. Gaius, *Institutes*, 1.150ff.; Ulpian, *Rules*, title 11.

79. Seth Benardete, *Achilles and Hector: The Homeric Hero* (South Bend: St. Augustine Press, 2005), 73.

80. Aristotle, *Nicomachean Ethics*, 1124b10–14.

81. Alexander Schmidt, in Furness, 102.

82. Cf. 1.4.55–56, where Lartius's high praise of Martius inverts less and greater.

83. Plutarch, *Sayings of Kings and Commanders*, 190a; *Sayings of Spartans*, 212e, 215d, 230c.

84. Previously, the closest he came to offering encouragement was to preface his first threat by urging them on with the cry, "Come on, my fellows" (1.4.27).

85. Benardete, 73.

86. See Plutarch, *Coriolanus*, 8.3; *Cato the Elder*, 1.6; see also Plutarch, *Sayings of Kings and Commanders* (Cato, 7, 23), 198e, 199c.

87. See 1.2.3–17; 1.9.72–73; 2.1.107–15, 126–27, 132–36; 2.3.233–43; 4.3.10–12; 5.1.67–69; 5.2.14–16, 87–89; 5.3.145–47; 5.6.1–8, 62–63, 81–84, 113–15.

88. Cicero, *De oratore*, 2.51–64; Quintilian, 10.1.31; Gellius, 2.28.6; Servius, *ad Aeneid*, 1.373; Macrobius, *Saturnalia*, 3.2.17.

89. Sallust, *Jugurthine War*, 4.5–6; Cicero, *De oratore*, 2.36; Livy, Preface, 10; Tacitus, *Annals*, 4.32–33.

90. See Virgil, *Aeneid*, 6.752–892; 8.626–731. For Martius explicitly as a Roman *exemplum*, see, e.g., Livy, 2.54.6; 7.40.12; 28.29.1; 34.5.9.

91. Charles Mitchell, "Coriolanus: Power as Honor," *Shakespeare Studies*, 1 (1965), 206.

92. For the pun on "course," see *OED*, s.v. Course, 5 ("The rush together of two combatants in battle or tournament") and 26 ("Each of the successive parts or divisions of a meal").

93. Edward Gibbon, *The Decline and Fall of the Roman Empire*, 3 vols. (New York: Modern Library, n.d.), 2:172.

94. On the importance of the public situation, see Cantor, 36.

95. Cf. 1.1.163; 2.3.168. Martius will twice thank Cominius (1.9.36, 68) and once a citizen in Antium (4.4.11).

96. Although the Folio reads "four," most editors, either to avoid his apparent contradiction or else on the grounds that Martius is not the man to delegate such a choice, alter the text to read "I"; see Furness, 132–35.

97. Xenophon, *On the Art of Horsemanship*, 9.2; Plato, *Phaedrus*, 253d3–e1; Plutarch, *Roman Questions*, 97.

98. For the psychology, see Ronna Berger, "The Thumatic Soul," *Epoché*, 7 (2003), 156–57.

99. For Martius's actions as theatrical acting, see also 2.2.96; 3.2.15–16, 109–10; 5.3.40–42, 183–85.

100. On the distinction between lies and the exaggeration (or attenuation) of hyperbole, see Quintilian, 8.6.74–76.

101. John Dover Wilson, ed., *The Tragedy of Coriolanus* (Cambridge: Cambridge University Press, 1960), 169.

102. Blits, *Ancient Republic*, 86–89.

103. For the Roman nomenclature, see Plutarch, *Coriolanus*, 11.2–4. Until now, Martius's personal and family names have been mentioned only in their proper order (1.1.6, 25–26, 222, 240; 1.2.34; 1.9.58). From now until Martius goes to Antium, they will always be mentioned in reversed order (1.9.64, 66; 2.1.163, 164; 2.2.46; see also 2.1.171–73). Once he goes to Antium, they will be mentioned, again, only in their proper order (4.5.66, 183; 4.6.29, 76; 5.6.88).
Although most modern editors immediately give Martius his new name, the honor, strictly speaking, comes not from Cominius or the army, but from the city or the Senate, and so the Folio does not invest Martius with the name until he arrives in Rome and the city proclaims and confirms the honor. See 2.1.194–96 and Richard Grant White, in Furness, 160.

104. For Jupiter as the god of hospitality, see Virgil, *The Aeneid*, 1.731; Cicero, *De Finibus*, 3.66; Ovid, *Metamorphoses*, 10.224; Pliny, 36.34.

105. Aristotle, *Nicomachean Ethics*, 1124b10–18. Shakespeare underscores the point by transforming a "wealthy man" in Plutarch (*Coriolanus*, 10.3; North, 2:154) to a "poor man" in the play (1.9.81). On Coriolanus as "an imperfect, and typically Roman, misunderstanding of what it means to be great-souled," see John Alvis, "Coriolanus and Aristotle's Magnanimous Man," *Interpretation*, 7 (1978), 6.

106. MacCallum, 584, 585.

107. See, e.g., Livy, 1.58.8; 6.26.3; 23.33.7.

108. For the sacredness of the law of hospitality and religious sanctions for its violation, see Ennius, *Hecuba* (Valhen), 211; Cicero, *Verrine Orations*, 2.2.1110; Livy, 1.9.13, 32.21.23; Ovid, *Metamorphoses*, 5.45; Lucan, *Civil War*, 9.131; Curtius, *History of Alexander*, 5.2.15. For the obligation to defend foreign guests as even more sacred than the obligation to defend kin, see Diodorus Siculus, 20.70.3-4; Gellius, 5.13.5.

ACT TWO

~

Act Two, Scene One

1.

Act Two opens with Menenius and the tribunes. Notwithstanding their mutual antagonism, the men often appear together. They will enter together when Coriolanus has completed his allotted time to campaign for the people's votes (s.d. 2.3.136); Menenius will negotiate with them to bring Coriolanus to trial to answer their charges by a lawful form (3.1.261–331); the tribunes will taunt Menenius that all is going well in Rome following Coriolanus's banishment (4.6.10–19); Menenius will blame them for Rome's desperate situation after hearing that Coriolanus is leading the Volscian army against the city (4.6.96–99, 118–19, 122–25, 147– 8); the tribunes will persuade him to go to Coriolanus to plead for mercy (5.1.31–62); and Menenius will be with Sicinius when the news arrives that the women's plea has prevailed (5.4). Commentators often point out that Menenius—a patrician who pursues pleasures of food and drink—and the tribunes—the most spirited and ambitious of the plebeians—form a link and mediate between Rome's two classes.[1] The link, however, is entirely new. In the play's opening scene, Menenius dealt directly with the people (1.1.50–162). Now, following the establishment of the tribunate, he must deal with the tribunes, and only through them with the people. His influence with the people is now mediated by the people's own officials.

Unlike in the opening scene, when he flattered the people and tried to beguile them with a pretty tale, Menenius, rather than trying to soothe his listeners, openly derides and reviles the tribunes, becoming angry, rude, abusive, and ever more loquacious, while the tribunes, for their part, become ever quieter and little more than impatient, and only mildly remonstrate with him. The difference between Menenius in the two scenes, and between him and the tribunes here, seems to stem from his expecting good news soon from the battlefield. In the opening scene, the people were mutinous, and the patricians, feeling weak, thought they had to pacify or compromise. But now that at least the augurer says the Romans will have news of Martius's victory "tonight" (2.1.1–4), even the mostly moderate Menenius can take the upper hand.

News that the Volscians were in arms mitigated the civil strife in Rome. Each party recognized its need of the other. Now, with the end of the war in sight, civil strife—or at least civil sparring—returns. Just as the war put an end to the strife, the end of the war brings back the strife. When Brutus asks whether the augurer's news will be good or bad, Menenius replies, "Not [good] according to the prayer of the people, for they love not Martius" (2.1.3–4). Menenius might have spoken of good news for Rome. Instead, he speaks of bad news for one of its parties. He immediately translates the war news into partisan terms. Because it is won by Martius, Rome's victory is the people's loss. Sicinius, appealing to nature (and likening the people to beasts), tries to defend the people's not loving Martius. "Nature teaches beasts to know their friends," he says (2.1.5). Menenius, rather than replying that nature should teach the people to know that Martius is their friend in war, asks, "[W]ho does the wolf love?" (2.1.6). While Sicinius appeared to mean that nature teaches beasts to love their friends and hate their enemies, Menenius takes him to mean that it teaches them to love their enemies as prey. Love in politics is nothing more than predatory appetite, as Sicinius's answer seems to confirm: "The lamb" (2.1.7). One loves one's enemy if one can devour him: "Ay, to devour him, as the hungry plebeians would the noble Martius" (2.1.8–9; cf. 1.1.84–85; 3.1.288–91; 4.5.77; also 4.5.191–94). Brutus, deflecting the issue of appetite by twisting Menenius's metaphor, claims that Martius is "a lamb indeed, that baes like a bear" (2.1.10): lacking the strength that he claims to have, Martius does not even sound like the beast he pretends to be (cf. 1.4.56–61; 1.6.25–27). The issue is not the people's predation but Martius's pretension. Menenius, hardly more plausible, reverses Brutus's wild claim: "He's a bear indeed, that lives like a lamb" (2.1.11). To his enemies, Martius is a weak animal who tries without effect to frighten his enemies. To his friend, he is a strong beast who lives a gentle life. At least when sparring with or baiting each other, both sides see Martius on the outside contrasting with Martius on the inside. To the one, he shams his strength; to the other, he hides it.

Menenius, turning the conversation largely to the tribunes themselves and their own pretensions, shifts the topic from knowing one's friends and enemies to knowing oneself. Describing the tribunes, sarcastically, as wise men ("old men" [2.1.12]), he asks what fault mars Martius's character that they themselves do not have in abundance. Going beyond the First Citizen, who exempted him from at least one vice (1.1.41–45), Brutus says that Martius has every fault, but then Sicinius quickly adds that he is stocked "[e]specially in pride" (2.1.18), and Brutus, going further, adds, "[a]nd topping all others in boasting" (2.1.19). Martius's greatest fault is not simply to be proud, but to brag. It is hard to be sure whether the tribunes are only trying to malign Martius or whether they recognize his ostensible modesty as ostentatious display. Whatever the case, finding the accusation "strange" (2.1.20), Menenius asks whether the tribunes know how the nobles judge them. When asked to be told, Menenius initially hesitates: "Because you talk of pride now—will you not be angry?" (2.1.24–25). Menenius seems to think that the tribunes, proudly expecting to be held in high regard, will be insulted and hence angered at hearing the patricians' low opinion of them. Menenius, however, proceeds, explaining that in any event it takes very little to anger the tribunes: "Why, 'tis no great matter; for a very little thief of occasion will rob you of a great deal of patience" (2.1.27–28). Menenius appears to be mistaken. The tribunes are very seldom genuinely angry or indignant. While in private always calculating and never angry or indignant, in public they put on shows of anger or indignation purely for political effect.[2] Their spirit is divorced from indignation, though not from resentment or ambition. Menenius, accordingly, modifies what he just said: "Give your disposition the reins, and be angry at your pleasures; at the least, if you take it as a pleasure to you in being so" (2.1.29–32). Recognizing that anger contains and conceals a pleasure—the pleasure of prospective revenge[3]—Menenius, punning on the word, corrects his apparent mistake: the tribunes may be angry as they wish ("at your pleasures"), if they enjoy being angry ("take it as a pleasure"). As is emphasized by his qualifying phrase ("at the least") and his conditional "if," Menenius does not take their anger seriously. It is nothing but show.

Menenius restates the tribunes' charge: "You blame Martius for being proud" (2.1.31–32). And when Brutus tries to strengthen it by adding to the number of accusers ("We do it not alone, sir" [2.1.33]), Menenius contorts his augmented charge into a confession:

I know you can do very little alone, for your helps are many, or else your actions would grow wondrous single: your abilities are too infant-like for doing much alone.

(2.1.34–37)

Where Martius acts "alone," the tribunes act only with the help of others. What they might do by themselves ("single") would be insignificant ("single"). Coming back then to the charge of pride, Menenius aims it against the tribunes themselves:

> You talk of pride. O that you could turn your eyes toward the napes of your necks, and make but an interior survey of your good selves. O that you could!

> (2.1.37–40)

The tribunes are proud because they lack self-knowledge. They are always looking away from themselves, never reflecting on themselves or seeing what is inside themselves. For good reason, Menenius does not compare the tribunes to Martius in this regard. If they did see themselves, he continues, they would discover a pair of "unmeriting, proud, violent, testy magistrates (alias fools) as any in Rome" (2.1.42–44).

When Sicinius, trying to parry the charge by turning it back upon him, says that Menenius is "known well enough too" (2.1.45), Menenius describes what others know of him. A self-deprecation that is meant to be disarming, the self-description—the most extensive self-characterization in the play—is rhetorical in purpose. Reporting what others know or think of him, Menenius describes himself as an un-patrician patrician. He says that he is known to be a whimsical patrician, to love strong wine undiluted by water, to be inclined, when on the bench, to take the side of the party who first presents his case, to become angry quickly for a trivial cause, to stay up late at night and sleep late in the morning, and to say what he thinks: "What I think, I utter, and spend my malice in my breath" (2.1.52–53). Menenius describes himself as a blunt, not a clever, speaker. His bluntness, he cleverly suggests, guarantees his honesty and good will (cf. 1.1.50–53). Although Menenius says hardly anything in public about the people or the tribunes that Martius does not also say, the people trust him, while they hate Martius. As we see here, Menenius openly confesses his plebeian manners and taste. Not only the manners and taste themselves, but his confession of them, helps to make him agreeable to the people, for such a confession, incompatible with patrician pride, seems to reflect a lack of martial spirit. Indeed, Menenius himself suggests that he is all talk. Once he has had his say, he says, his malice is fully spent. Nothing about him need frighten the people.

Supposedly to demonstrate that he says whatever he thinks, Menenius describes himself when meeting the tribunes. His description of himself thus quickly reverts to his disparagement of them, since it purports to show that he candidly utters exactly what he thinks of them. Yet, rather than speaking plainly, Menenius speaks largely over the tribunes' heads, describing them with a baffling mixture of directness and sarcasm, open insults and apparent compliments, frequent puzzling puns and obscure metaphors. He begins by saying that his face is an open book ("[I]f the drink you give me touch my palate adversely, I make a crooked face at it" [2.1.55–56]), and then he lists what he can or cannot say in the tribunes' favor. He can call them "weals-men," but not "Lycurguses" (2.1.54). He can say that they speak well when he finds "the ass in compound with the major part of [their] syllables," that is, using pompous legal phrases beginning "whereas" and having something asinine to say. He must put up with those who call them "reverend grave men," that is, dignified and dead. Yet, they "lie deadly," that is, excessively and like the dead, who say they have "good faces," that is, honest and hand-some (2.1.57–61). Menenius then asks darkly, twice echoing Sicinius's last words ("Menenius, you are known well enough, too" [2.1.45]),

> If you see this [self-description] in the map of my microcosm, follows it that I am known well enough too? What harm can your bissom conspectuities glean out of this character, if I be known well enough too?

(2.1.61–65)

The second question is meant to answer the first. The tribunes can see in his face ("the map of my microcosm") what Menenius says about, or shows of, himself, but they are nevertheless still blind ("your bissom conspectuities") to him. They see only what he wants them to see: his transparency is a mask.

When Brutus protests, "Come, sir, come, we know you well enough" (2.1.66), Menenius denies that the tribunes know anything ("You know neither me, yourselves, nor any thing" [2.1.67]) and then attacks them for their petty ambition and base actions. They are "ambitious for poor knaves' caps and legs," he says (2.1.68): they seek to have the commoners bow and scrape before them. And, ambitious for the plebeians' obeisance, they take too seriously—or seriously in the wrong way—any trifle brought to them for judgment. They give petty disputes endless hearings, become vexed by mi-nor nuisances, and make worse rather than resolve the disputes before them, sending the cases away only more confused. Wanting to appear im-portant in their own eyes by appearing important in the eyes of their fellow plebeians, the tribunes possess a high and solemn view of low and small things. They ape the patricians they attack.[4] We might note in this context Dionysius of Halicarnassus's explanation of Brutus's adopted name: "He had the same name, Lucius Junius, as the man who had overthrown the kings, and desiring to make the similarity of their names complete, he wished also to be called Brutus," by which he, in fact, made himself a laughingstock to many people "because of his vain pretentiousness."[5]

Menenius ridicules the tribunes, saying, "I cannot call you Lycurguses" (2.1.54). The insult, though accurate, is unfair. No Roman can be called a Lycurgus, for, as we have seen, Rome's political institutions come about largely by chance in response to exigencies as they arise (see 1.1.207–20). More especially, Menenius himself, who, besides telling of his enjoying sleep and wine, suggests that he would enjoy chests of gold (2.1.130–31), could hardly be called a Spartan, let alone a Lycurgus, who, in framing Sparta's regime, forced the Spartans "to leave their gold and silver, to forsake their soft beds" and "to give up banqueting and feasting."[6] What makes Menenius like a plebeian makes him altogether unlike a Spartan. Fittingly, Brutus, answering his scorn, says that Menenius is "well understood to be a perfecter giber for the table than a necessary bencher in the Capitol" (2.1.80–82). Unlike the austere, laconic Spartan, the sensual, glib Menenius is more accomplished as a humorous dinner companion than as a senator dealing with the country's affairs.

Menenius, changing tactics, derides the tribunes' dignity or worth. Stressing the reversal of reverence into mockery, he says, "Our very priests must become mockers, if they shall encounter such ridiculous subjects as you are" (2.1.83–84). The tribunes' pretensions are so ridiculous that they would make even priests scoff at the Senate's sacred quality. Menenius next ridicules the tribunes' ability as public speakers. Again emphasizing opposites, he says that even when the tribunes

> speak best unto the purpose, it is not worth the wagging of [their] beards; and [their] beards deserve not so honourable a grave as to stuff a botcher's cushion, or to be entombed in an ass's pack-saddle.
>
> (2.1.85–88)

Despite what their political success has led the tribunes to believe, their words do not deserve even the lowest honor. Menenius's mention of what the tribunes' speech is "worth" and what their beards "deserve" returns his derision of them to his indignation at their attack on Martius:

> Yet you must be saying Martius is proud: who, in a cheap estimation, is worth all your predecessors since Deucalion, though peradventure some of the best of 'em were hereditary hangmen.
>
> (2.1.89–92)

Neither the tribunes' pride in their success nor their criticism of Martius's pride is deserved. Thus, flinging a final insult, Menenius takes his leave, saying that "[m]ore of [their] conversation would infect [his] brain, being the herdsmen of the beastly plebeians" (2.1.93–95). The tribunes' success with the people is no reason for their having pride, for the people are little more than beasts, as Sicinius himself has admitted (2.1.5). Though they think they are statesmen, the tribunes are nothing more than herdsmen.

In attacking the tribunes, Menenius overlooks the vast political advantages to Rome of what he criticizes. The tribunes' tendency to magnify both themselves and their office helps to satisfy their ambition to appear important among the Roman people ("ambitious for poor knaves' caps and legs"). As previously noted, the office gives the most ambitious plebeians a stake in the regime and will make them its defenders rather than its enemies. In addition, the paltriness of the matters with which the tribunes deal ("a cause between an orange-wife and a faucet-seller . . . of threepence" [2.1.70–71]), while beneath the dignity of a patrician, allows someone to look after issues that are important to the people involved. What Menenius sees as a despicable disparity between the tribunes' pettiness and their overweening self-estimation provides an opportunity for the satisfaction of their ambition, on the one hand, and of the people's ordinary or daily concerns, on the other. Menenius also seems to underestimate the tribunes in at least one crucial respect. They may not know themselves, but they know something important. Their political scheming will show that they know how to manipulate both Coriolanus and the commoners, and use each against the other—a knowledge indispensable to the workings of the mixed regime.

2.

Volumnia, who, along with Virgilia and Valeria, is hurrying to catch sight of the returning Martius, stops to tell Menenius that "my boy Martius approaches . . . with most prosperous approbation" (2.1.99–100, 102). While the heroic warrior is still "[her] boy," his wounds and honors will confirm his superlative success ("with most prosperous approbation"). In contrast to the tone of Menenius's exchange with the tribunes, the mood immediately becomes both celebratory and reverent. After Menenius, greeting the women decorously, compares them to Diana ("the moon, were she earthly, no nobler" [2.1.96–97]), Volumnia joyfully urges him to join them "for the love of Juno" (2.1.100), and Menenius, hearing that Martius is returning with proof of the greatest success, flings his cap to "Jupiter" in "thank[s]" (2.1.104). As the private is subordinate in Rome to the public, personal joy is inseparable from invoking and thanking Jupiter and Juno, the city's divine defenders.[7]

Menenius no sooner throws his cap to Jupiter in joyous thanks for Martius's victorious return than he elevates Martius to something more than human. When Volumnia says she thinks there is a letter from Martius to him, Menenius vows to "make my very house reel tonight" (2.1.110). But, then, when Virgilia confirms the letter, he exclaims:

> A letter for me! It gives me an estate of seven years' health; in which time I will make a lip at the physician. The most sovereign prescription in Galen is but empiricutic, and, to this preservative, of no better report than a horse-drench.

> (2.1.113–17)

The source of death for many on the battlefield becomes the source of health for Menenius in the city. Lartius, thinking Martius had been killed fighting alone in Corioles, compared him to a jewel his size and found him richer (1.4.54–56). Menenius, thinking Martius victorious in battle and gracious to him, compares him to the best medicine in the world and finds the medicine mere quackery. Where Lartius spoke of death and heroic nobility, Menenius speaks of life and bodily heath. Each speaking entirely in character, both men see Martius as more than a mortal. Soon, others will explicitly call him a god or say that others see him that way.

Martius, although he refused his general's praise (1.9.13ff.), has written to the Senate ("the state" [2.1.107]) as well as to his mother, wife, and Menenius, presumably telling of his achievements. The letter to the Senate seems superfluous. "The senate has letters from the general," Volumnia will soon report, "wherein he gives my son the whole name of the war: he hath in this action outdone his former deeds doubly" (2.1.132–35; see 1.9.72–73; 2.1.126–27). Martius, however, may see a fundamental difference between self-praise and praise from another. Self-praise closes the gap between the merit of the praiser and the merit of the praised. The praise is as good as he who receives it. Such praise also keeps the praised dependent on no one but himself. The praise's self-reflexiveness guarantees both the value of the praise and the independence of the man who is praised. Nevertheless, the praise also shows the need or desire of the man praised for public recognition.

Menenius and Volumnia begin a long, detailed discussion of Martius's wounds, both old and new, which ends only with the flourish announcing his triumphal entry (2.1.117–55). Menenius, saying that Martius "was wont to come home wounded" (2.1.118), asks whether he is wounded. And Volumnia is not only certain but thankful that he is: "Oh, he is wounded; I thank the gods for't" (2.1.120). "The wounds," as Menenius says, echoing what she had said earlier, "become him" (2.1.122; cf. 1.3.39–43). Immediately and directly equated with his actions, they show that he not only killed the enemy—"every gash was an enemy's grave" (2.1.154–55)—but endured the enemy, as well (cf. 1.4.37; 3.3.110–11). Those who see them will see proof of his bravery. Volumnia thus declares, "[T]here will be large cicatrices to show the people when [Martius] shall stand for his place" (2.1.146–47). She takes for granted that he will show the people his scars in order to win their votes.

At the sound of a shout and flourish, heralding his entry, Volumnia describes Martius as carrying death in his arm:

> These are the ushers of Martius: before him he carries noise, and behind him he leaves tears:
> Death, that dark spirit, in's nervy arm doth lie,
> Which, being advanc'd, declines, and then men die.
>
> (2.1.157–60)

Volumnia, who has spoken in verse only to depict Martius and Hector in bloody battle (1.3.29–47), breaks into verse to delineate Martius delivering death.[8] While portraying with a gruesome antithesis the triumphal sounds before him and the mournful tears behind, Volumnia describes with a couplet—virtually her only rhyme in the play—how, the dark spirit of death lying in his strong arm, Martius need only raise and then lower his arm to cause men to die. She at once personifies death and dehumanizes her son. His arm the instrument of death, he becomes an unstoppable, unfeeling, lifeless killing machine.

3.

Julius Caesar begins with a Roman triumph for Caesar which is "universal" in scale and scope (JC, 1.1.30–51). Martius's entry to Rome—the triumph Cominius may have wanted for himself—presents, on a local scale, the ritual that was the highest honor the republic bestowed for victory and the most impressive manifestation of a Roman's glory. "There is nothing among the Romans more stately and magnifical than [a] triumph" (Livy, 30.15.12; Holland, 605).[9]

Volumnia told of Martius's receiving "the whole name of the war" (2.1.133–34), by which she meant the full credit for the victory. Now, making her metaphor literal, a Herald, while echoing Cominius's transposition of Martius's personal and family names when declaring his surname (1.9.64–66), announces Martius's new name and the reason for it:

> Know, Rome, that all alone Martius did fight
> Within Corioles gates: where he hath won,

> With fame, a name to Martius Caius. These
> In honour follows Coriolanus.
> Welcome to Rome, renowned Coriolanus!

And the Romans respond, "Welcome to Rome, renowned Coriolanus!" (2.1.161–66). Martius has won the "renown" and "fame" that his mother thought should arouse men to action (1.3.12, 14). Coriolanus, however, again refuses the acclaim. "No more of this; it does offend my heart. / Pray now, no more" (2.1.167–68). What his mother sees as spurring and rewarding action, he sees as offending "[his] heart." As when he refused praise and spoils on the battlefield (1.9.28–29, 36–38), Coriolanus uses a synecdoche to refer to himself by a part ("my heart"), which he then personifies as though it had a mind of its own. He divides himself and identifies himself with one of his soul's warring parties in order to maintain the single-mindedness that he seeks.

Coriolanus appears with his mother only four times and with his wife only three times in the play.[10] Like much else in Rome, all the occasions occur in public and are witnessed by others. Coriolanus never has a private moment with any family member. And although he is always gentle toward his wife, he hardly ever exchanges a word with her. In this scene, Virgilia—"my gracious silence" (2.1.174)—says not a word to him. On the second occasion, again saying nothing to him, she will twice cry out in anguish ("O heavens! O heavens!"; "O the gods!" [4.1.12, 37]). And, on the last occasion, she will finally speak to him, though merely four lines (5.3.37, 39–40, 125–27). The four family scenes mark the essential steps in Coriolanus's career. In the first, having captured Corioles "alone" (2.1.161), Coriolanus celebrates his triumph and is reunited with his family. In the second, wishing his virtue to be unconditional or "absolute" (3.2.39), he initially refuses to be "[f]alse to [his] nature" (3.2.15), but finally gives in to his mother. In the third, having been convicted of treason, he is banished from Rome and, "go[ing] alone / Like to a lonely dragon" (4.1.29–30), leaves his family and city to join Rome's enemy. In the fourth, ready to attack Rome, he is beseeched by his family, and, unable to "stand / As if a man were author of himself / And knew no other kin" (5.3.35–37), abandons Rome's enemy and is, at once, reunited with and permanently separated from his family.[11]

Guided by Cominius ("Look, sir, your mother" [2.1.168]), Coriolanus greets his mother first and then his wife. Honoring Volumnia by kneeling to her, he speaks of her reverence for the gods, while demonstrating his own for her: "Oh! / You have, I know, petition'd all the gods / For my prosperity" (2.1.168–70). Coriolanus assumes that his mother would pray for a victory that he would not pray for. Unlike him, she would wish for the gods' assistance. Much later, when entreating him not to attack Rome, Volumnia will say that she can no longer pray to the gods for his victory (5.3.104–9). We, in fact, never see her pray for his victory, but, instead, see her thanking the gods for his wounds (2.1.120). In her mind, the two may be the same: his wounds are equivalent to his victories.

Volumnia greets her son with a confusion of names. Calling him "my good soldier," she rehearses his three names: "My gentle Martius, worthy Caius, and / By deed-achieving honour newly nam'd— / What is it?—Coriolanus, must I call thee?" (2.1.170–73). Volumnia first speaks in oxymora. Martius is, as his name itself suggests, anything but "gentle." Nor he is "worthy" as Caius, but rather as Martius or Coriolanus (1.1.235; 1.5.15; 4.3.22–23; 4.5.127). Volumnia then characterizes Coriolanus as having been newly named "[b]y deed-achieving honour." In keeping with her view that the desire for honor should stir noble actions and noble actions should bring the sought-for honor, her phrase means both "honor that achieves or spurs deeds" and "honor achieved through deeds." Honor and deeds are, reciprocally, cause and effect. Each implies the other. The circularity that Coriolanus seeks in virtue, Volumnia finds in honor. Volumnia, however, asks whether she must call her son "Coriolanus." In fact, she will call him by his surname only once. That will be in the Volscian camp when she means not "conqueror of Corioles," but "man of Corioles"—the betrayer of his family and country (5.3.170). Not surprisingly, Volumnia already appears to have trouble with the name.[12] For while "Martius" ties her son to his birth, "Coriolanus" lifts him above or apart from his maternal origins. The name recognizes his deeds, but ignores his family.

Turning to Virgilia, Coriolanus jests gently at her tears, while at the same time clearly acknowledges that his virtue implies the destruction of the family:

> Wouldst thou have laugh'd had I come coffin'd home,
> That weep'st to see me triumph? Ah, my dear,
> Such eyes the widows in Corioles wear,
> And mothers that lack sons.

> (2.1.175–78)[13]

Coriolanus knows tears of sorrow, but not of joy. If one cries at joyous news, one would laugh at sorrowful news. Menenius, by contrast, mixes rather than opposes laughter and tears: "I could weep, / And I could laugh, I am light and heavy" (2.1.182–83). Where Coriolanus sets laughter and tears against each other, Menenius combines them. Joy ("light") and sadness ("heavy") may be opposites, but laughter and tears are not.

Menenius, in his delight, welcomes Coriolanus, Cominius, and Lartius, adding a curse upon the hearts of those not glad to see them (2.1.184–85). Although "Rome should dote on [them], yet . . . / We have some old crab-trees here at home that will not / Be grafted to your relish" (2.1.186–88). Menenius, at once indignant and contemptuous, attributes the tribunes' distaste for its heroes to their natural stock. Dismissing them, he says that they cannot help being foolish: "We call a nettle but a nettle, and / The faults of fools but folly" (2.1.189–90). The tribunes cannot help being the fools that they are. Their folly is inborn, and placing them in their new office will not graft them to a better stock. Cominius and Coriolanus enjoy Menenius's barb. To Cominius, Menenius is always right ("ever right" [2.1.190]); to Coriolanus, he is always himself ("Menenius, ever, ever" [2.1.191]). In the glow of victory, not even Coriolanus takes the tribunate seriously or sees the tribunes as a danger.

Holding the hands of his mother and his wife—a gesture he will repeat when he leaves Rome (4.1.57) and again when he capitulates to Volumnia (s.d. 5.3.182)—Coriolanus says that before going to "our own house" (2.1.193) he must visit the patricians from whom he has received new honors. The public comes before the private. Coriolanus also confirms what one might have surmised from 1.3: although a husband and a father, "Martius, thinking all due to his mother that had been also due to his father if he had lived, never left his mother's house" (Plutarch, *Coriolanus*, 4.4; North, 2:147). And as Coriolanus lives with his mother, so Volumnia lives through her son. Their dependence is mutual, though different. For Coriolanus, it is based on filial reverence and duty; for Volumnia, on maternal pride and opportunity. His success, as she paradoxically if ambiguously puts it, provides her inheritance: "I have liv'd / To see inherited my very wishes, / And the buildings of my fancy" (2.1.196–98). Coriolanus's success gives shape and substance to her dreams and desires. The realization of her wishes, however, is not yet complete: "[O]nly / There's one thing wanting, which I doubt not but / Our Rome will cast upon thee" (2.1.198–200). Volumnia has lived long enough to see her dreams nearly come true. All that remains is Coriolanus's election as consul. Volumnia sees no conflict between Coriolanus's virtue, which belongs to war, and her highest ambition, which belongs to peace. She has no doubt, as she asserts with an intensifying triple negative, that anything would prevent "[o]ur Rome" from electing its heroic warrior.

Coriolanus's response points to a fundamental inversion inherent in elected rule. "Know, good mother," he answers, "I had rather be their servant in my way / Than sway with them in theirs" (2.1.200–2). Coriolanus would rather serve Rome in his way than rule Rome in Rome's way. To serve in his way is not really to serve but to rule, and to rule in Rome's way is not really to rule but to serve. An elected leader must accommodate himself at least to some degree and in some respects to the citizens' wishes, fears, tastes, desires, and even foolishness. He must compromise with those he rules and therefore be ruled by them rather than properly rule them (cf. 3.2.90). As Coriolanus clearly realizes, strictly speaking, an elected ruler can never really rule.

3.

The tribunes remain behind, as the others leave, and discuss what to do about Coriolanus. All the people talk of him, Brutus says, and they drop everything else and do whatever they can, at all costs, to see him. "Such a pother, / As if that whatsoever god who leads him / Were slily crept into his human powers, / And gave him graceful posture" (2.1.216–19). The Romans take Coriolanus for a god—the god of war. As though he were transformed into the god that leads him, they see Martius as Mars.

When Sicinius says he is sure that the people will quickly elect Coriolanus consul, Brutus states the political consequence that he fears: "Then our office may, / During his power, go sleep" (2.1.220–21). If elected consul, Coriolanus would render the tribunes' new office idle or inefficacious. The people, Brutus fears, would follow their hero rather than the tribunes, whose political power rests on their protecting the people against the nobles in general and Coriolanus—"chief enemy to the people" (1.1.6)—in particular. In order for the tribunes to keep their power, the people must fear and hate the city's heroes. They must think of their great heroes not as their leading champions, but rather as their chief enemies. Sicinius, suddenly more confident, recognizes Coriolanus's inability to keep the people's favor: "He cannot temp'rately transport his honours / From where he should begin and end, but will / Lose those he hath won" (2.1.222–24). Unable to moderate or restrain himself as he moves from his honors on the battlefield to those in the city, Coriolanus not only will fail to win new honors, but will lose those he has already won. Although war undercuts the tribunes' new office, military success, Sicinius explains, can only temporarily overcome the people's fear and hatred. "Doubt not / The commoners, for whom we stand," he reassures Brutus, "but they / Upon their ancient malice will forget / With the least cause these his new honours" (2.1.224–27). Owing to their long-standing class hostility, the people will forget Coriolanus's military honors if given the slightest provocation. And, Sicinius continues, he has as little doubt that Coriolanus will provoke them as that he will be proud to do it. Coriolanus's proud hatred of the people and their fearful hatred of him will combine to spoil his honors and lose him the people's favor.

Brutus, supporting Sicinius's conclusion, says he has heard Coriolanus swear that, were he to stand for consul, he would never "[a]ppear i'th'market-place" (2.1.231), never wear "[t]he napless vesture of humility" (2.1.232), nor, "showing (as the manner is) his wounds / To th'people," ever "beg their stinking breaths" (2.1.233–34). Rome's customary election procedures consist in formal rituals or gestures. The marketplace is the stronghold of the people's political power. The plebeian counterpart of the patricians' Senate, it is where the tribunes go to meet with the people and candidates for the consulship go to solicit the people's votes, and where the people will try Coriolanus (2.2.159; 3.1.30, 111, 329; 3.2.93, 104, 131). "The napless vesture of humility" is a threadbare woolen garment—"a poor gown . . . without any coat underneath."[14] While the gown itself symbolizes that the office-holder serves the people, its simplicity is meant to stress the candidate's humility, as its name plainly suggests. And by showing his wounds while soliciting the people's votes, the candidate shows evidence of his service to Rome and his courage in fighting Rome's wars. He asks for future service as the reward for his past service. Under Roman custom, a candidate seeking the city's highest office must preform certain gestures which, ostensibly overturning the principle of aristocracy, reverse high and low, superior and inferior, command and obedience, ruling and serving, ruler and ruled. Through the gestures, the noble candidate must, in effect, "beg" the commoners for what he deserves.

Coriolanus, however, has said that he would rather forego the consulship than obtain it in any way other than being asked by the patricians to take it. "It was his word. Oh, he would miss it rather / Than carry it but by the suit of the gentry to him / And the desire of the nobles" (2.1.235–37). Sicinius wishes nothing better than for Coriolanus to keep his word. By doing that, he says, Coriolanus would serve the tribunes' interests ("as our good wills") and his own "sure destruction" (2.1.240, 241). The two outcomes are the same: "So it must fall out / To him; or our authority's for an end" (2.1.241–42). Coriolanus must be destroyed or else the tribunes' authority will be destroyed. But as unbeatable as he is in war, Coriolanus is easily defeated in politics. The tribunes' strategy is twofold. The tribunes, who have themselves likened the people to beasts (2.1.5), are to insinuate ("suggest" [2.1.243]) to the people how much Coriolanus has always hated them and, in particular, that, to the full extent of his power, he would have made them beasts of burden, silenced their pleaders, and taken away their liberties,

> holding them,
> In human action and capacity,
> Of no more soul nor fitness for the world

Than camels in their war, who have their provand
Only for bearing burthens, and sore blows
For sinking under them.

(2.1.246–51)

The insinuation suggests both insult and injury. It is intended to provoke both anger and fear. Because he thinks they lack human souls (cf. 1.4.34–35), Coriolanus will treat the people not as humans, but as beasts. Because he thinks they care only for food, he will give them only food. And because he thinks they lack reason or judgment, he will rule them with blows rather than with words. The strategy's second part involves the timing. The tribunes must make these suggestions "[a]t some time when [Coriolanus's] soaring insolence / Shall teach the people" (2.1.252–53). Coriolanus's insolence will confirm the tribunes' suggestions in the people's minds. His actions will verify their words and incite the people. And it will not be difficult to arrange such a time. On the contrary, "that's as easy / As to set dogs on sheep" (2.1.254–55). The people are to be the dogs; Coriolanus, the sheep (cf. 2.1.10). Coriolanus's soaring insolence, Sicinius confidently concludes, "will be his fire / To kindle their dry stubble; and their blaze / Shall darken him for ever" (2.1.255–57). Coriolanus's insolence will easily ignite the people's anger and fear, and their anger and fear will consume him in their blaze.

A messenger arrives and, reporting that Coriolanus is expected to be consul, describes his reception in the city, saying that he has never seen anything like it. Like Brutus, he describes the city thronging to see and hear Coriolanus rather than Coriolanus returning to the city. To the tribunes and their messenger, the focus of concern is not Coriolanus but his effect on Rome. Where Brutus described "all" Romans of all sorts ("[w]ith variable complexions"), from "prattling nurse" and "kitchen malkin" to "[s]eld-shown flamens" and "veil'd dames" (2.1.203–16), pressing to see him, the messenger describes not only matrons flinging their gloves and ladies and maids alike throwing their scarves and handkerchiefs, but even "dumb men throng[ing] to see him, and / The blind to hear him speak" (2.1.260–61). And where Brutus told of the crowd taking Coriolanus for Mars, the messenger tells of the nobles bowing to him "[a]s to Jove's statue" (2.1.264). All of the Romans celebrate and deify him. But while to the crowd he embodies the divine in himself, to the nobles he points beyond himself to something still higher—to an idealization of Jove himself (cf. 5.4.21–22). Leaving for the Capitol, Brutus says that Sicinius and he should "carry with us ears and eyes for th'time, / But hearts for the event" (2.1.267–68). They should observe what happens, but keep their hearts hidden and hungry for Coriolanus's destruction.

Act Two, Scene Two

1.

Two officers are preparing for the meeting in the Capitol at which Cominius, the current consul, is to deliver an encomium of Coriolanus. The meeting comes between the nomination and election of the next consul. Although there are three candidates, everyone expects Coriolanus to win (2.2.1–4; also 2.1.258–59).[15] According to Roman procedure, the Senate nominates and the people elect. The people's voting power, dating from the first consuls,[16] was their principal institutional strength before the establishment of the tribunate. Just as Romulus created a kingship that shared at least some power with a senate,[17] after the kings' expulsion the Senate created a consulate which, while retaining the powers and even the insignia of the king,[18] shared some power with the people. In a certain sense, Rome had a mixed regime before the establishment of the tribunate, but a very imperfect one. Although the people had the power to elect consuls, their vote did not protect them from the nobles' abuse.[19]

The two officers have contrary views of Coriolanus. When the First Officer characterizes Coriolanus as "a brave fellow; but . . . vengeance proud, and [one who] loves not the common people" (2.2.5–6), the Second Officer defends his not loving them. Many great men have flattered the people without loving them, he says, and the people have loved many without knowing why. The people's love and hate are thus equally worthless: "So that if they love they know not why, they hate upon no better a ground" (2.2.10–11). No one, then, should care about winning the people's love or avoiding their hate.

> Therefore, for Coriolanus neither to care whether they love or hate him manifests the true knowledge he has in their disposition, and out of his noble carelessness lets them plainly see't.
>
> (2.2.11–15)

Knowing their sentiments for what they are, Coriolanus lets the commoners see his contempt for them, because he is scornfully indifferent to their opinion of him. His patrician "carelessness" shows that he does not care what they think of him.

The First Officer denies Coriolanus's indifference. If Coriolanus did not care about having or not having their love, he says, he would waver indifferently between doing the people good and harm. "[B]ut he seeks their hate with greater devotion than they can render it him, and leaves nothing undone that may fully discover him their opposite" (2.2.18–21). As he himself has suggested (1.1.175–76), Coriolanus seeks the people's hatred and does everything he can to demonstrate his hatred of them. He seeks their opposition in order to be seen completely as their opposite ("fully discover him their opposite"). Their adversary ("opposite"), he is their contrary ("opposite").[20] Defined by opposition, he is unable to be indifferent. As his new name indicates, he can have no detachment from what he opposes. "Now to seem to affect the malice and displeasure of the people is as bad as that which he dislikes, to flatter them for their love," the officer explains (2.2.21–23). To think that the people are worthless and then flatter them for their favor is disgraceful. But it is no less disgraceful to offend and injure them just to show that he will not flatter them. The First Officer's judgment comes directly from Plutarch and reflects Plutarch's own judgment. "[H]e is less to be blamed that seeks to please and gratify his common people," Plutarch writes,

> than he that despises and disdains them and therefore offers them wrong and injury because he would not seem to flatter them to win more authority. For as it is an evil thing to flatter the common people to win credit, even so is it besides dishonesty and injustice also to attain to credit and authority for one to make himself terrible to the people by offering them wrong and violence.[21]

Spiritedness leads Coriolanus to think of himself as the Second Officer describes him—as superior to caring what the people think of him. But it also forces him to be as the First Officer describes him—as defined by being their opposite. Coriolanus's understanding of himself as wholly independent of the people depends, incongruously, on their hateful opposition to him. He depends on them for his putative independence of them. Far from not caring about the people, as the Second Officer says, he cares too much. He does not despise them enough not to care. Owing to his spirited pride, however, Coriolanus must hide this central truth from himself. He must let the mutual hatred blind him to his need. If, as Plutarch says, Coriolanus's offering the people wrong and violence is dishonest and unjust, the injustice is to the people, but the dishonesty is primarily to himself.

The Second Officer, switching from Coriolanus's disposition toward the people to the people's obligation to him, declares that Coriolanus has "deserved worthily" (2.2.24) the people's votes. Arguing that it would be "a kind of ingrateful injury" (2.2.31–32) for the voters to reject him, the officer implicitly connects what makes the people hostile to him and what makes him worthy of election. While others have done nothing more than to go hat-in-hand to the people to win their support, Coriolanus's "ascent is not by such easy degrees" (2.2.25). Instead of being "supple and courteous to the people"

(2.2.26–27), he has been fierce and victorious in battle. Fierceness, however, breeds fear, and fear breeds hate. People hate what they fear, because they fear it. And so what deserves the people's love and gratitude arouses their hate and ingratitude, instead. Nevertheless, the ingratitude would be indefensible. "[Coriolanus] hath so planted his honours in their eyes and his actions in their hearts," the officer continues,

> that for their tongues to be silent and not confess so much were a kind of ingrateful injury. To report otherwise were a malice that, giving itself the lie, would pluck reproof and rebuke from every ear that heard it.

> (2.2.29–34)

There can be no decent or creditable reason not to elect Coriolanus. Any reason given to refuse him would display a pure maliciousness that would turn back on itself and accuse the accuser.

Despite their sharp disagreement, the two officers seem judicious and temperate. They seem strangely out of place in fiercely partisan Rome. Their combination of birth and office may account for this. As minor Senate officers, they are, presumably, in sympathy by birth with the commoners and by office with the nobles. Thus, even while the First Officer is critical of Coriolanus and the Second of the people, they avoid the extremes of either side.[22] "No more of him; he's a worthy man" (2.2.35), the First Officer genially replies.

2.

At the sound of a sennet, the patricians and tribunes enter, "[l]ictors before them" (s.d. 2.2.36). The stage direction is ambiguous. The ambiguity points to the ambiguity of the tribunes' authority. Lictors are magisterial attendants. Dating from the time of the kings, they walk before their magistrate in public, carrying the fasces whose rods symbolize the magistrate's authority, particularly his penal power of life and death.[23] According to Plutarch, the tribunes have no lictors, because, their authority consisting largely in blocking a magistrate's power, their office is an opposition to magistracy rather than a magistracy itself (Plutarch, *Roman Questions*, 81). The stage direction, however, leaves it unclear whether the tribunes are to be thought of as a magistracy or as a check on magistracy, an ambiguity Shakespeare will soon repeat when Sicinius refers to the meeting as "our assembly" (2.2.57) but the stage direction reads, "*Sicinius and Brutus take their places by themselves*" (s.d. 2.2.36).

Menenius, indicating that the Senate has just decided matters concerning the Volscians, announces that the purpose of the present meeting is to reward ("gratify" [2.2.40]) Coriolanus's noble service in defense of his country. Menenius then asks the senators, whom he addresses as "Most reverend and grave elders"—a term of address he had ironically granted the tribunes (2.2.42; cf. 2.1.60)—to request

> The present consul, and last general
> In our well-found successes, to report
> A little of that worthy work perform'd
> By Martius Caius Coriolanus, whom
> We met here, both to thank and to remember,
> With honours like himself.

> (2.2.43–48)

Coriolanus not only receives all the honor from the day's battles ("the whole name of the war" [2.1.133–34]), but is to receive it from his general. The honor flows away from, rather than to, the general, contrary to what Cominius seemed to want. Menenius wishes Cominius to report "[a] little" of what Coriolanus achieved. The First Senator, however, cannot hear enough. "Speak, good Cominius," he urges; "Leave nothing out for length, and make us think / Rather our state's defective for requital / Than we to stretch it out" (2.2.48–51). The nobles should think that they lack the means rather than the will to reward Coriolanus properly. Their intention should be beyond doubt.

The Senator, continuing, says too much. Evidently counting on their compliance, he tells the tribunes, in only slighted veiled terms, that the senators expect them to use their influence with the commoners to gain their approval for Coriolanus's election ("We do request your kindest ears, and after / Your loving motion toward the common body, / To yield what passes here" [2.2.52–54]). Where Coriolanus sees the establishment of the tribunate as a concession to the people, other nobles seem to see it as a more effective way to rule them. While the tribunes can control the people ("Masters o'th'people" [2.2.51]), the Senate can control the tribunes. The Senate can thus rule the people better by ruling them indirectly through their own officers. The Senator's request, however, quickly miscarries. When Sicinius answers that the tribunes' "hearts [are] / Inclinable to honour and advance / The theme of our assembly" (2.2.54–57), Brutus immediately and explicitly adds a stipulation:

> Which the rather
> We shall be bless'd to do, if he remember

> A kinder value of the people than
> He hath hereto priz'd them at.
>
> (2.2.57–60)

A deliberate provocation, Brutus's condition sets a price and gives a warning. By a "kinder" value, Brutus, echoing the Senator's word, means both that Coriolanus must be friendlier to the people and that he must regard them more as being of the same kind as himself (cf. 2.3.75). The Senator's ill-timed request has, in effect, opened public negotiations on what Coriolanus must do to get the tribunes'—and hence the people's—support. Menenius, apparently recognizing the danger, rebukes Brutus for his impertinence ("That's off, that's off!"), adding, "I would you rather had been silent. Please you / To hear Cominius speak?" (2.2.60–62). But Brutus again warns, while at once outwardly agreeing with and openly correcting Menenius: "Most willingly; / But yet my caution was more pertinent / Than the rebuke you give it" (2.2.62–64).

Menenius, this time, replies to the substance of Brutus's demand: "He loves your people, / But tie him not to be their bedfellow" (2.2.64–65). Menenius seems to take Brutus's demand at face value. Neither here nor anywhere else does he or any other senator suggest that the tribunes are disingenuous, let alone duplicitous, in their cry for Coriolanus's better treatment of the people. Only Volumnia will do that (4.2.33). Instead, Menenius suggests that a leader should not get into bed with the people. The republic, like the tribunes's own office, rests on not only distance but animosity between the people and the city's heroes. The great danger to Rome is the return of monarchy. While the nobles do not want to be ruled by an equal, the people do not want to be ruled harshly. Although the people hated the last Tarquin king, they hated him not because he was king, but because he "behav[ed] himself not like a king, but like a cruel tyrant."[24] Thus, Junius Brutus's first act as Rome's first consul was to make the people swear a solemn oath never to permit another king in Rome:

> And first above all other things, while the people were yet greedy of this new freedom, for fear lest they might any time after be won by entreaty or moved by gifts on the [former] king's part, he caused them to swear that they would never suffer any to be king at Rome.[25]

The wishes and interests of the people, unlike those of the nobles, are not necessarily or even fundamentally at odds with monarchy. As the tribune Brutus has already indicated, the people want to be treated kindly, and a king can readily do that. Indeed, it is frequently in his interest to gratify them.

The Roman kings, who often sided with the people against the nobles, sought to curb the patricians' ambitions by courting the people's favor. Thus, just as the people supported and the patricians opposed Romulus, it was the patricians, not the people, who finally expelled the kings.[26] While ambition and envy keep the nobles from welcoming another king, only fear of the gods—and of Rome's heroes—suffices to keep the people from doing so. And, at least while the Tarquins were alive, the nobles were never quite confident that pious fear would suffice.[27] It is certainly no coincidence that Caesar's monarchy, while avoiding the title of king, will come to power in the name of the people.[28] Nor is it insignificant that the Second Officer talked of demagogues in Rome flattering the people (2.2.7–11, 25–28)[29] or that the First Citizen described the city as having a "kingly crown'd head" (1.1.114). Because the danger to the regime is a monarchy supported by, and in support of, the people, Coriolanus's contempt of the commoners contains a necessary condition for the preservation of Rome's republican regime. On the one hand, it prevents Coriolanus from stooping to win their favor, as Caesar will do, while, on the other hand, combined especially with his courage in battle, it causes them to fear and distrust him. It keeps Rome's two parties apart. Paradoxically, while the nobles must moderate their treatment of the people, the people must continue to fear their noble heroes.

3.

When Menenius bids Cominius to speak his praise, Coriolanus gets up to leave. Thrice before he goes, Coriolanus states his opposition to hearing himself praised. All three times, he contrasts speech and action. First, when a senator tells him never shame to hear his noble deeds, Coriolanus, implicitly slighting the pain of wounds while emphasizing that of praise, declares, "I had rather have my wounds to heal again / Than hear say how I got them" (2.2.69–70). Then, when Brutus, with mock concern, says that he hopes his words did not drive him from his seat, Coriolanus replies, "No, sir; yet oft, / When blows have made me stay, I fled from words," adding that Brutus "sooth'd not, therefore hurt not" (2.2.71–73). The pain of praise makes Coriolanus flee, while that of blows makes him stay. Finally, after Menenius interrupts Coriolanus's sudden harangue of the people ("[B]ut your people, / I love them as they weigh—" [2.2.73–74]), Coriolanus contrasts even indolent activity following a call to arms with hearing his praise: "I had rather have one scratch my head i'th'sun / When the alarum were struck, than idly sit / To hear my nothings monster'd" (2.2.75–77). Performing actions is real; hearing them praised is idle. Coriolanus objects that praise distorts his deeds by turning them into unnatural marvels ("my nothings monster'd"). It is true that encomium involves amplification, if not exaggeration.[30] Yet, as when Cominius tried to praise Coriolanus on the battlefield (1.9.15–19), Coriolanus's rejection of praise, here, magnifies his deeds while ostensibly slighting them. His exaggerated understatement of his deeds—"my nothings"—conspicuously belies itself, thus calling attention to his heroic courage and action. In a word, Coriolanus's public rejection of praise amounts to his implicit self-praise, while at the same time seemingly demonstrating his superiority to praise. Coriolanus does not so much reject praise as seek it so that he might reject it.[31]

When Coriolanus leaves, Menenius, evidently still trying to deflect Brutus's demand that Coriolanus treat the people more kindly, attempts to turn his departure to his advantage. Flattering the tribunes ("Masters of the people" [2.2.77]), as the First Senator had done, he asks, How can Coriolanus flatter the people "when you now see / He had rather venture all his limbs for honour / Than one's on's ears to hear it?" (2.2.79–81). Coriolanus is no more hostile to the people than to himself. He cannot hear himself praised any more than he can flatter them. As though having ended the matter, Menenius, not giving the tribunes a chance to reply, directs Cominius to proceed.

Cominius's praise, delivered by Rome's highest official, is the play's most extended example of epideictic or laudatory oratory. Closely modeled on the rules of classical rhetoric, it consists of a brief *exordium* or introduction (2.2.82–83), a narrative, stating the case (2.2.83–87), a long proof, confirming it (2.2.87–126), and a brief *peroration* or conclusion (2.2.126–29).[32] After introducing the speech by briefly stating his inability to match Coriolanus's deeds with words ("I shall lack voice: the deeds of Coriolanus / Should not be utter'd feebly" [2.2.82–83]), as is common in encomia,[33] Cominius moves to the narrative, which contains two parts. The first states the speech's major premise: "It is held / That valour is the chiefest virtue and / Most dignifies the haver" (2.2.83–85). The second tentatively states its conclusion: "[I]f it be, / The man I speak of cannot in the world / Be singly counter-pois'd" (2.2.85–87). By narrating and exhibiting his great actions, the proof, which follows, establishes the minor premise that Coriolanus performed the most valorous actions. As with all classical encomium, Coriolanus's noble deeds are used as evidence of his noble character.[34]

The lengthy proof has three parts and a coda. The parts are arranged chronologically and ascend from less to greater deeds.[35] Their most frequent and emphatic trope is comparison, a form of amplification relied upon in all epideictic oratory, for, as Aristotle says, comparison implies superiority, and superiority seems to indicate virtue.[36] Accordingly, borrowing Aristotle's three specific examples of comparison, Cominius tells how Coriolanus acted alone and did what he did better than anyone else, how he greatly surpassed expectations, and how he has often achieved such things.[37] Cominius also omits mention of Coriolanus's noble ancestry (cf. 2.3.235–43). Although the topic is customary in encomium,[38] he focuses on nothing but Coriolanus himself.

In the opening part, Cominius describes Coriolanus's first battle. He underscores that Coriolanus was younger than normal military age ("At sixteen years" [2.2.87]), the importance of the battle to Rome ("When Tarquin made a head for Rome" [2.2.88]), and Coriolanus's superlative achievement ("[H]e fought / Beyond the mark of others" [2.2.88–89]).[39] Cominius then describes three particular instances of Coriolanus's fighting, offering authoritative witnesses for the first two, and the authority of Coriolanus's opponent himself, as he stresses with "self" as a noun,[40] for the third:

> [O]ur then dictator,
> Whom with all praise I point at, saw him fight,
> When with his Amazonian chin he drove
> The bristled lips before him; he bestrid
> An o'erpress'd Roman, and i'th'consul's view
> Slew three opposers; Tarquin's self he met
> And struck him on the knee.
>
> (2.2.89–95)

Cominius's examples involve multilayered comparisons as well as emphasizing Coriolanus's repeated success. The first, while explicitly comparing young Coriolanus to his fully adult opponents, implicitly compares his manliness to what one could have naturally expected at his age ("[W]ith his Amazonian chin he drove / The bristled lips before him"). The second, while comparing victor to vanquished, Coriolanus to his opponents, as one to three, also compares him to the Roman whom he saved as "bestrid" to "o'erpress'd." Likewise, the third, while comparing the youth with "Tarquin's self," also implicitly compares the standing young soldier with the former king knocked to the ground. Thus Cominius, summing up his initial battle, compares Coriolanus both to what could have been expected at his young age and to all other fighters that day, as well as, more generally, as men compared to women. "In that day's feats," he tells, "When he might act the woman in the scene, / He prov'd best man i'th'field, and for his meed / Was brow-bound with the oak" (2.2.95–98). In demonstrating his superiority to all the others, Coriolanus demonstrated his superiority to himself.

In his proof's second part, Cominius briefly summarizes Coriolanus's seventeen battles between his first and his most recent.[41] With contrasting diction, first compressing words like Coriolanus's compressed age, and then expanding them like his growing victories, he reiterates that Coriolanus entered his youth as a man ("His pupil age / Man-enter'd thus") and, likening him to a rising sea, tells of his robbing all others of the garland: "[H]e waxed like a sea, / And in the brunt of seventeen battles since / He lurch'd all swords of the garland" (2.2.98–101).

In the proof's last part, Cominius recounts Coriolanus at Corioles and in the field. The most important portion of his speech, it constitutes nearly half of the whole. Cominius begins by repeating his inability to speak adequately of Coriolanus's deeds at Corioles ("For this last, / Before and in Corioles, let me say / I cannot speak him home" [2.2.101–3]). Then, he depicts the deeds with his most poetic lines. He first describes a double reversal, one external, the other internal: "He stopp'd the fliers, / And by his rare example made the coward / Turn terror into sport" (2.2.103–5). Next, he portrays the action with a simile: "[A]s weeds before / A vessel under sail, so men obey'd / And fell below his stem" (2.2.105–7).[42] The simile, while pointing up his opponents' feebleness in the face of Coriolanus's prowess, likens the bloody path of his slaughter to the peaceful passage of a ship in water. The comparison of the peaceful and the slaughter at once mitigates and magnifies the slaughter. But, suddenly dropping any hint of peace, Cominius goes on to liken Coriolanus's sword to death's instrument: "[H]is sword, death's stamp, / Where it did mark, it took from face to foot" (2.2.107–8). Like the seal of death, Coriolanus's every stroke was fatal. Accordingly, Cominius characterizes Coriolanus not as a human, but as a "thing." With a suppressed, contrasting metaphor of music and a dancer—the cries of the slaughtered accompanying his motions as music follows a dancer—he identifies Coriolanus as a perpetual instrument of death: "He was a thing of blood, whose every motion / Was tim'd with dying cries" (2.2.109–10). Cominius then describes Coriolanus entering the city alone: "[A]lone he enter'd / The mortal gate of th'city, which he painted / With shunless destiny" (2.2.110–12). Cominius, once more, compares what Coriolanus did with what was to be looked for. The gate through which it seemed deadly for him to pass became the gate upon which he smeared the blood of dying men within the city, unable to flee their fate. What was expected to be fatal to him proved fatal to those who were expected to kill him. And just as he entered "alone," Coriolanus "aidless came off, / And with a sudden reinforcement struck / Corioles like a planet" (2.2.112–14). Painting the city's gate, alone, with "shunless destiny," he acted not like a human but, rather, a superterrestrial power.

Cominius, completing the last part of his proof, speaks of Coriolanus in the day's second battle. With a transition stated in the vivid present ("Now all's his" [2.2.114]),[43] and stressing reversal and doubleness, he first describes Coriolanus internally—what he could sense ("When . . . the din of war gan pierce / His ready sense" [2.2.115–16]) and how his redoubled spirit revived his weary body ("[H]is doubled spirit / Requicken'd what in flesh was fatigue" (2.2.116–17—and then describes his action as though Coriolanus were an inexhaustible hunter enjoying endless slaughter:

> And to the battle came he, where he did
> Run reeking o'er the lives of men, as if
> 'Twere a perpetual spoil; and till we call'd
> Both fields and city ours, he never stood
> To ease his breast with panting.
>
> (2.2.118–22)

While explicitly comparing his fatigued body and his redoubled spirit, Cominius implicitly compares Coriolanus's greatest pleasure with that of other men. Whereas in the earlier parts of his proof he focused on Coriolanus's actions as reflecting his virtue, only here does he hint at Coriolanus's pleasure—the pleasure of a perpetual spoil.[44]

Cominius concludes his proof with a brief coda concerning Coriolanus's austerity. Understanding by "spoil" now not the slaughter of a hunt but the plunder of battle, he reports Coriolanus's rejecting the loot: "Our spoils he kick'd at, / And look'd upon things precious as they were / The common muck of the world" (2.2.124–26). Coriolanus spurns what most men kill and sometimes die for.

Cominius, delivering his peroration, takes Coriolanus's refusal of rewards as showing that he regards valorous action as its own reward, as an end in itself:

> He covets less
> Than misery itself would give, rewards
> His deeds with doing them, and is content
> To spend the time to end it.
>
> (2.2.126–29)

Cominius mentioned Coriolanus's reward or pay (". . . and for his meed / Was brow-bound with the oak" [2.2.97–98]) in all of his battles before the most recent. The city's honor was his reward. But now, as befits a peroration, Cominius amplifies or elevates his subject,[45] proclaiming that Coriolanus never really wanted any kind of reward. He praises Coriolanus just as Coriolanus wishes to be praised. Epideictic oratory often says as much about the speaker as about his subject. This is true of Cominius's speech. Its praise of Coriolanus exhibits Cominius's own character. Cominius, we have seen, evidently hoping to gain glory from the fight against the Volscians, initially assigned Martius and Lartius the task of laying siege to Corioles, while saving the more glorious action for himself. Yet, after Coriolanus's extraordinary single-handed victory at Corioles, he did nothing to prevent him from having a second triumph—the one Cominius seemed to want for himself. And, now, he spares no praise in honoring him, notwithstanding that Coriolanus's triumph has largely eclipsed him in Rome.[46] On the battlefield and in the city, Cominius will not let Coriolanus conceal his own great deeds. Rather, saying that to extol them even "to the spire and top of praises . . . / Would seem but modest" (1.9.24–25), he glorifies the deeds publicly, authoritatively, and emphatically. Generous to his worthiest rival, he praises Coriolanus in Coriolanus's own terms ("[V]alour is the chiefest virtue and / Most dignifies the haver" [2.2.84–85]), focuses entirely on the man himself, unbegrudgingly attributes to him all of the day's success and crowns his praise by adopting Coriolanus's view of himself.[47] Indeed, Cominius's comparisons imply not only Coriolanus's superiority, but his absoluteness: Coriolanus cannot be "singly counter-pois'd," in seventeen battles "[h]e lurch'd all swords," "alone he enter'd" the city and "aidless came off," and "[n]ow all's his." His singularity is unrivaled and unqualified.

Cominius hardly mentions Rome in his praise of Coriolanus. He speaks of it just twice, both times in connection with Coriolanus's first battle as a youth (2.2.88, 93). He says nothing about it in the context of any of Coriolanus's subsequent battles or as his motive for his most recent deeds. Nor does he mention Aufidius. Cominius is silent about Coriolanus's patriotism on the one hand and his private duel on the other. Instead, he tells of Coriolanus's love of slaughter and of his rewarding his deeds with doing them. If Cominius combines prudence with courage in battle, he combines discretion with acclaim in praise.

Although Rome seems to favor generals who take daring chances, the characteristically cautious Cominius is consul. An apparent exception to Rome's usual rule,[48] Cominius, with "years upon [him]" and "full / Of the wars' surfeits" (4.1.45–46; also 3.3.110–11), has served Rome over many years with long, steady, solid service. But just as he seems at least somewhat an exception in Rome, Cominius, although his first love is Rome (3.3.111–15), seems to distance himself from the city's fundamental understanding of virtue. The Romans valorize valor. As noted earlier, they have only one word for virtue, and it is the word for manly valor. Virtue is *virtus*. Cominius states this as his encomium's major premise. But although maxims—general premises concerning human action—are frequent in encomia and often used to provide its major premise,[49] Cominius states his premise as a reported commonplace rather than as a maxim: "It is held that. . . ." And further removing himself from the view, he adds at least a suggestion of doubt as to its truth, in passing from his major premise to his conclusion: "[I]f it be, . . ." Neither introductory phrase is needed. Both could easily have been avoided. Notwithstanding his great admiration for Coriolanus's virtue and his own love of Rome, Cominius seems to disagree with his—and Rome's—view that courage is the sum and substance of virtue.

3.

When Coriolanus returns, Menenius offers him the consulate: "The senate . . . are well pleas'd / To make thee consul" (2.2.132–33). Menenius speaks as though the people have no vote or their having one does not really matter. Unlike the First Senator (2.2.51–54), he does not mention even the tribunes, though they are present. The Senate, he seems to say, chooses the consul. What appears to be Menenius's high-handedness, however, may be his politic effort to mollify Coriolanus and avert the impasse that the tribunes seek. As the tribunes have said, Coriolanus's conditions for election are directly at odds with Roman custom. Although custom requires a candidate to ask for the people's votes and show them his wounds, Coriolanus will accept the consulate if offered by the Senate, but not request it of them and certainly not of the people (2.1.229–37). Menenius may be trying to finesse the difficulty. In the name of the Senate, he first gives Coriolanus what he wants. Unrequested, the Senate offers him the office, which, significantly enough, he graciously accepts: "I do owe them still / My life and services" (2.2.133–34). But knowing full well that the tribunes will insist on maintaining the custom, Menenius then tells Coriolanus that, having the office, he must speak to the people: "It then remains / That you do speak to the people" (2.2.134–35). Menenius seems to think, or hope, that Coriolanus, having already received the office from the Senate on his own terms, will be willing to pretend to ask the people for it, by going through the mere motions. Such a pretense, he seems to think, might serve to placate Coriolanus and the tribunes, alike.

Coriolanus, however, resists. As Brutus had predicted (2.1.229–37), he begs to skip the custom: "[F]or I cannot / Put on the gown, stand naked, and entreat them / For my wounds' sake to give their suffrage" (2.2.136–38). He cannot ask the people for their votes by humbling himself to them and asking them to reward him for his wounds. Sicinius, who "wish[ed] no better"

(2.1.237), insists that the people have their vote ("Sir, the people / Must have their voices" [2.2.139–40]) and that Coriolanus perform every detail of the custom: "[N]either will they bate / One jot of ceremony" (2.2.140–41). Coriolanus "must" do just what he "cannot" and "swore" he "never" would do (2.1.229, 230; 2.2.136, 140). Menenius makes no effort to persuade the tribunes to moderate their demands. Instead, centering his attention entirely on Coriolanus, he cautions him not to press the people too hard and urges him to "fit [himself] to the custom" (2.2.142), reminding him that his predecessors have done so. But Coriolanus still resists, objecting that his going through the formality ("form" [2.2.144]) would be shameful play-acting: "It is a part / That I shall blush in acting" (2.2.144–45). If Menenius tried to assuage Coriolanus by suggesting that he could merely pretend to ask for the people's votes, Coriolanus rejects the pretending precisely because it is pretending. Instead of doing what his predecessors have done, Coriolanus suggests that the custom "might well / Be taken from the people" (2.2.145–46), a suggestion not lost on Sicinius ("Mark you that" [2.2.146]). Coriolanus gives a reason for refusing:

> To brag unto them, thus I did, and thus,
> Show them th'unaching scars which I should hide,
> As if I had receiv'd them for the hire
> Of their breath only!
>
> (2.2.147–50)

Earlier, on the battlefield, Coriolanus, refusing the spoils, said that he could not "make [his] heart consent to take / A bribe to pay [his] sword" (1.9.37–38). Here, he says something different. While he sought, there, to maintain the integrity of his virtue, he is concerned, here, with how the people would understand—or misunderstand—his words and action ("As if I had receiv'd them for the hire / Of their breath only!"). His refusal is meant to deny the conditional. Even while Coriolanus tries to claim indifference to the people's opinion of him, his concern for their opinion stops him.

Telling Coriolanus, again, not to insist upon his refusal, Menenius, turning his attention to the tribunes, finally acknowledges their role and the people's role in the selection of consul: "We recommend to you, tribunes of the people, / Our purposes to them" (2.2.151–52). Then, turning back to Coriolanus, he concludes, "[A]nd to our noble consul / Wish we all joy and honour" (2.2.152–53). As before, Menenius tries to mollify both sides: the people, guided by the tribunes, elect; nevertheless, Coriolanus is already "our . . . consul."

4.

When the others leave, the tribunes remain and briefly discuss what they just saw, what it indicates for the future, and what they should do next. At the end of scene 1, they seemed to take seriously that Coriolanus would never ask the people for their votes. Now, however, they think that he will, though in doing so he will show that he considers it contemptible that the people have the power to give him what he asks them for: "He will require them / As if he did contemn what he requested / Should be in them to give" (2.2.156–58). Whereas they previously thought that Coriolanus would play into their hands by refusing to solicit the people's vote, they now think that he will play into their hands by the way in which he solicits it. His concession to the people will show his contempt for the people. The tribunes, however, need not—and must not—be passive. Since the people may not recognize Coriolanus's scorn, the tribunes must "inform" them of what has happened here so that the people can "perceive's intent" (2.2.156; also 2.2.155). The people will need the tribunes' "lesson[s]" (2.3.175; also 2.3.189).

Act Two, Scene Three

1.

Several citizens, awaiting Coriolanus, are discussing whether to vote for him. At least two are ashamed to be ungrateful to their benefactor. They have "power in themselves" to deny Coriolanus their votes, "but it is a power that we have no power to do" (2.3.4–5). Although they have the political or legal power to do whatever "[they] will" (2.3.3), they have no moral power to be ungrateful to the city's hero. "Ingratitude is monstrous" (2.3.9–10). Nevertheless, the people's obligation to be grateful is not unconditional. Coriolanus must "show [the people] his wounds and tell [them] his deeds. . . . So if he tell us his noble deeds, we must also tell him our noble acceptance of them" (2.3.6–9). The people will respond not to his deeds themselves, but to his telling of them, for the telling amounts to asking, and the asking amounts to begging (cf. 2.1.230–34; 2.3.70–71, 80–81, 115, 157). Coriolanus's obliging speech will obligate them. The people will then reciprocate his "noble deeds" with their "noble acceptance" of them. Asking for their votes by telling of his deeds, Coriolanus will invert the people and himself. He will beg, and they will act nobly.

That is not the only inversion. If Coriolanus shows his wounds and tells his deeds, the Third Citizen says, "we are to put our tongues into those wounds and speak for them" (2.3.6–8). Rather than speaking for themselves as direct evidence of his deeds (cf. 1.5.16; 2.1.154–55), Coriolanus's wounds would acquire the people's "tongues" or "voices" (2.3.1). His deeds would be known by the people's recognition and votes. Their voices would bespeak his deeds. Besides wanting to avoid appearing ungrateful, the people have another reason to vote for Coriolanus. They want to confute his contemptuous view of them as "the many-headed multitude" (2.3.16–17).[50] Where Coriolanus demands "integrity" (3.1.158), the people, both as individuals and as a group, are a many-colored, many-headed monster. Their thoughts, wishes, actions, and desires, as the Third Citizen comically and forgivingly concedes, fly diffusely in different directions. Even by their own account, the people, both separately and together, lack consistency, wholeness, and order.

The Third Citizen, the most voluble of the group, proceeds to offer a series of political opinions. All of them prove at least partly problematic. Presumably intending a humorous truism, the Citizen asks whether everyone is resolved to give his voice, but then adds that it does not matter because "the greater part carries it" (2.3.38). While the Citizen seems to suggest that the election of consul is decided by a majority of the voters, Roman elections are actually determined by a majority of the assigned groups in which the voters cast their votes. Depending on how they are designated, those groups are often skewed against "the greater part," as Shakespeare will later indicate (3.3.8–11). The Citizen thus overstates the importance of the people's collective vote, even while (correctly) minimizing that of their individual votes.

The Citizen, no longer being jocular, next wishes that Coriolanus would take the people's side: "[I]f he would incline to the people, there was never a worthier man" (2.3.39–40). This is, of course, what the tribunes publicly demand as opposed to what they privately seek. It is the people's constant refrain. What would make Coriolanus most worthy to the people would make him most dangerous to Rome. "He that first made banquets and gave money to the common people was the first that took away authority and destroyed commonwealth," Plutarch writes (Plutarch, *Coriolanus*, 14.3; North, 2:159).[51]

The Citizen, then, outlines the Roman campaign procedures. The procedures appear to honor the people. The citizens approach the candidate singly or in groups of two or three, the candidate asks each citizen for his vote, and each citizen announces how he will vote, "wherein every one of us has a single honour, in giving him our own voices with our own tongues" (2.3.45–46). While the people's strength lies in their numbers (see, e.g., 2.3.209–10; 3.1.132–34), the procedures divide them into small groups and force them, furthermore, to declare their votes openly to the candidate. One-on-one and with no secret ballot, the people are easily intimidated and shamed by the candidate. The procedures that flatter the people actually serve to weaken them and work to the nobles' advantage.[52]

The Citizen, who takes it upon himself to direct the others in approaching Coriolanus, underscores what is especially important to the people. "Here he comes," he says of Coriolanus, "and in the gown of humility: mark his behaviour" (2.3.41–42). As already suggested, in Rome's politics of honor and humiliation, the perceived significance of gestures, manners, and symbols is often critical. This will be true of the people's treatment of Coriolanus. It is also true of his treatment of them, for few things are as odious to the people, especially a free people, as to be insulted by a proud man.[53] Hence, the people are to "mark his behaviour," for it will signify his respect or disrespect for them.

Menenius enters with Coriolanus. As though picking up where they left off in scene 2, Menenius is still trying to correct Coriolanus's refusal to seek the people's votes, reminding him that "[t]he worthiest men have done't" (2.3.51), and Coriolanus continues to resist, saying that he cannot bring himself to say what is required:

> What must I say?—
> "I pray, sir,"—Plague upon't! I cannot bring
> My tongue to such a pace. "Look, sir, my wounds!
> I got them in my country's service, when
> Some certain of your brethren roar'd and ran
> From th'noise of our own drums."
>
> (2.3.51–56)

Coriolanus, mortified and indignant, forgets everything about the soldiers in the Corioles battle except their initial retreat and, exaggerating or distorting it, says that they fled not from the enemy but from their own drums. Not the enemy's attack, but simply the call to battle, made them cry and run (cf. 1.4.123ff.). Menenius, with rising concern, swears that Coriolanus must not speak of that but must, instead, ask the voters to think kindly of ("think upon" [2.3.58]) him. Coriolanus, rankled by Menenius's supplicating verb ("Think upon me? Hang 'em!" [2.3.58]),[54] wishes that the people would "forget [him], like the virtues / Which our divines lose by 'em" (2.3.59–60). They should forget Coriolanus, just as they forget the moral lessons the priests waste on them. They should have as little to do with him as they have with even demotic virtue. Menenius, leaving, afraid that Coriolanus will mar all, earnestly beseeches him ("Pray you, . . . I pray you" [2.3.61]) to speak to the citizens in a reasonable ("wholesome" [2.3.62]) manner.

Coriolanus plays on the word "wholesome." Where Menenius meant that Coriolanus should speak to the people in a salutary manner, Coriolanus takes the word to mean that the people should present themselves to him in a sanitary manner: "Bid them wash their faces, / And keep their teeth clean" (2.3.62–63). This is not the first or the last time that he refers to the people as dirty (see, e.g., 1.1.225; 3.1.65; 3.3.121; 4.6.99). Nor is he alone (see, e.g., 4.6.99, 130–33). Sheer patrician prejudice, perhaps as much as anything else, keeps him and other nobles from courting the people.[55] But Coriolanus's explicit disgust rests on an implicit distinction. The filthiness of brave soldiers in battle is one thing; that of commoners in the city is another. The filthiness of soldiers, covering men from head to toe with blood and gore, is noble and healthy, while the filthiness of commoners, resulting from plebeian taste and poor hygiene, is base and disgusting. The former indicates a resistance, the latter a surrender, to what drags man down. The one nobly defies mortality, the other ignobly submits to it. Coriolanus's disgust at the people, a form of his soul's revulsion at mortal decay, is no less moral than physical, no less spirited than sensory.

The first group of citizens approaches Coriolanus. When Coriolanus, taking the initiative, asks whether they know why he is there, the Third Citizen says they know but want him to tell them ("We do, sir; tell us what hath brought you to't" [2.3.65]). The telling would itself be a concession. Coriolanus, however, granting nothing, answers, "Mine own desert, . . . but not mine own desire" (2.3.66–68). Coriolanus wants to be given the office because he deserves it, not because he desires it. When the Citizen presses him on how it is not his desire, Coriolanus replies ironically, as though he were wishing to spare the people rather than himself: "No, sir, 'twas never my desire yet to trouble the poor with begging" (2.3.70–71). To ask the people for their votes is to ask them for something they are too poor to afford.[56] The Citizen, perhaps puzzled, transforms the metaphor of begging into a suggestion of commercial exchange: "You must think, if we give you anything, we hope to gain by you" (2.3.72–73). Instead of saying that what they give Coriolanus would be payment for his past deeds, the Citizen denies that it would be payment for their future gain. While the Citizen's original concern for gratitude is left unmentioned, his reference to commerce, although a denial, points up the important truth that voters often elect candidates not to honor them for their superior virtue but to hire them for their promised service. Candidates compete to show how they can best serve the people, and the people reward those they think will best serve their interests.[57] Elections are typically venal or mercenary on both sides. Accordingly, Coriolanus, who on the battlefield could not take "[a] bribe to pay [his] sword" (1.9.38) and who indignantly recoiled at being thought to have received his wounds "for the hire" of the people's votes (2.2.149), and who, furthermore, could not bear to utter the word "pray" to the people (2.3.52), now, using that word because he needs them,[58] asks the Citizen his "price" for the consulship: "Well then, I pray, your price o'th'consulship?" (2.3.74). "The price is, to ask it kindly," the Citizen replies, echoing Brutus earlier pun (2.3.75; cf. 2.2.59). "[K]indly" means both in a friendly fashion and of the same nature or kind, and it means the former because it means the latter: one should be kind to one's own kind. The price is Coriolanus's showing his recognition that he is of the same kind or nature as the people.

Coriolanus appears to pay the demanded price: "Kindly, sir, I pray let me ha't. I have wounds to show you, which shall be yours in private" (2.3.76–77). Coriolanus seems willing to compromise. Although he will not show his wounds in public, he says what the people require of him. His apparent compromise, however, barely conceals his contempt. While his offer wins the First and Second Citizen's votes, Coriolanus mockingly or self-mockingly describes their votes as "two worthy voices begged" and as "alms" (2.3.80–81) and then brusquely dismisses the men ("adieu!" [2.3.81]). Left confused, the citizens recognize something strange in his conduct. "[T]his is something odd," the Third Citizen says (2.3.82). But the Second Citizen, although partly agreeing ("And 'twere to give again"), quickly makes light of it ("—but 'tis no matter" [2.3.83]). As will now become clearer, Coriolanus has begun to play a part, but he does not so much blush in acting it as show that he is acting it—show that it is not him but simply a part.

When a second group of citizens comes forward, Coriolanus, deriding the people's standard of merit while pretending to adopt it graciously, greets them by asking for their votes on the grounds that he is wearing the right clothing: "Pray you now, if it may stand with the tune of your voices that I may be consul, I have here the customary gown" (2.3.84–85). The people, he scornfully suggests, care only about the most superficial gesture. Where the Third Citizen said nothing about what Coriolanus deserved but only about his manner of asking for the people's votes, the Fourth Citizen, ignoring the fresh insult, says nothing about his manner of asking but only about what Coriolanus deserves. Coriolanus, he says, does and does not deserve nobly of his country. "You have been a scourge to her enemies, you have been a rod to her friends; you have not indeed loved the common people" (2.3.90–92). What Coriolanus sees as perfect consistency, the Citizen sees as self-contradictory: he who hates Rome's enemies should love her commoners. Coriolanus, quibbling on the word "common," ironically if sternly corrects the man: "You should account me the more virtuous, that I have not been common in my love" (2.3.93–94). To love the commoners is to be promiscuous in love. But then, Coriolanus, going beyond his insulting greeting, openly declares that he will flatter the people for their favor. "I will, sir, flatter my sworn brother the people, to earn a dearer estimation of them," he says, referring to the people, with bitter double irony, as his sworn companions in arms to whom he has sworn absolute fidelity: just as they lack the virtue to merit his sworn comradeship, they show that they are unfit for such comradeship by wanting to be flattered. "'[T]is a condition they account gentle," Coriolanus continues,

> and since the wisdom of their choice is rather to have my hat than my heart, I will practice the insinuating nod, and be off to them most counterfeitly; that is, sir, I will counterfeit the bewitchment of some popular man, and give it bountiful to the desirers. Therefore, beseech you, I may be consul.
>
> (2.3.94–102)

Coriolanus announces not only what he will do, but why it will work. The people want to elect those who are gentle toward them, and they mistake flattery for gentleness. Unable to see past outward behavior, they are easily fooled by insinuating gestures, which they take for a loving heart. But even while speaking clear-sightedly of the people's self-deceptive folly, Coriolanus, explaining that he will therefore deceive them, deceives himself. Unwilling to admit to himself that he desires the honor which he deserves but disdains, he says that he will only pretend to desire it. Where the popular man desires an honor which he pretends to deserve, Coriolanus will pretend to desire the honor which he truly deserves. In flattering the people, he will only pretend to be like other men—which is to say, he will pretend to be only pretending, by pretending to be what, in fact, he is.[59] Coriolanus's self-deception—his hiding from himself his desire for the honor he despises—constitutes the core of the brief soliloquy that follows.

When the citizens leave, Coriolanus, reflecting on his situation, and suddenly speaking in couplets, says that it is better to starve, better to die, than to hunger for ("crave" [2.3.113]) the honor which we deserve. What is owed should be freely given and not sought, let alone begged for. Coriolanus, then, punning on the woolen gown of humility, wonders why he should stand there in "this wolvish toge" (2.3.114)—a wolf in sheep's clothing (cf. 2.1.6–11)[60]—to beg of the commoners their needless votes. Why pretend to be what he is not in order to get what is worthless in itself? Answering his own question,

Coriolanus blames custom: "Custom calls me to't" (2.3.116). Coriolanus attacks not just Rome's election custom, but custom or tradition as such:

> What custom wills, in all things should we do't,
> The dust on antique time would lie unswept
> And mountainous error be too highly heap'd
> For truth to o'erpeer.

(2.3.116–20)

Rome's republican order rests on the observance of traditional or customary order. "The Roman state stands upon its ancient customs and men of old" (Ennius, *Annales*, frag. 46). Because Rome's mixed regime is ruled largely in hidden and indirect ways, and, furthermore, because its two major parties bitterly dispute what constitutes the city itself (cf., e.g., 3.1.197–98 and 236–38), the observance of traditional order helps to define the regime in the eyes of the Romans by establishing and manifesting its public order. In the eyes of many Romans, Rome's ancient customs are indistinguishable from the regime itself.[61] Memory, which is inseparable from Roman piety,[62] is the basis of Roman patriotism and identity. But while Rome's republican order tacitly identifies the old or the ancestral with the good (e.g. 2.3.235–43; 3.3.17, 63–64), to follow the old simply because it is old, Coriolanus protests, is to preserve errors. Coriolanus thus rejects the basis for Rome's republican regime in rejecting Rome's election ceremony. He rejects custom in the name of truth, ancestry in the name of virtue. "Rather than fool it so," he continues, "Let the high office and the honour go / To the one that would do thus" (2.3.120–22). But Coriolanus no sooner declares that he will forego the election and let the office and honor go to someone willing to do what he will no longer do, than he abruptly reverses himself, saying that he will continue because the ceremony is half over: "I am half through, / The one part suffer'd, the other will I do" (2.3.122–23). By feigning his weary acceptance of the custom, Coriolanus masks his desire from himself.

Coriolanus is a man without self-knowledge. His lack of self-knowledge seems to be of a piece with his untempered spirit. While spirit tends to simplify the world by seeing things as simple wholes, self-knowledge requires dividing or doubling the self, so that a man is both actor and observer of himself. Introspection requires self-reflection, but self-reflection is at variance with the singleness of a simple whole. Moreover, spirit inclines a man to look away from himself. Essentially reactive or reflexive rather than reflective, it tends to be directed to, as well as determined by, something external. Thus, its outward direction, like its self-unity, is at odds with self-reflection. It is therefore no surprise that Coriolanus has so few lines of soliloquy—a bare three dozen (2.3.111–23; 4.4.1–6, 12–26)[63]—and that they reveal or demonstrate his strong self-deception rather than any real self-examination. Indeed, none of his soliloquies even attempts to understand himself as distinguished from his surrounding circumstances. That which causes Coriolanus to stand "alone" deprives him of self-knowledge.

When a third group arrives, Coriolanus, now determined to dissemble, mockingly insults them with a repeated appeal for their "voices"[64] which, while intended to deceive, confesses what he wishes most to deny. "Here come moe voices," he announces;

> Your voices! For your voices I have fought,
> Watch'd for your voices; for your voices, bear
> Of wounds two dozen odd; battles thrice six
> I have seen and heard of; for your voices have
> Done many things, some less, some more: your voices!
> Indeed I would be consul.

> (2.3.124–30)

Coriolanus's intended deception succeeds perfectly. One citizen says that Coriolanus has "done nobly, and cannot go without any honest man's voice" (2.3.131–32). Another, seconding the first, exclaims, "Therefore let him be consul. The gods give him joy, and make him good friend to the people!" (2.3.133–34). And, leaving, all cry in unison, "Amen, amen. God save thee, noble consul!" (2.3.135), to which Coriolanus responds, "Worthy voices!" (2.3.136). Coriolanus's intended lie to the people is perhaps his most truthful statement of his own ambition. A truth that he intends as a lie to others, it seems to be thoroughly a lie to himself.

Menenius, returning with the tribunes, informs Coriolanus that he has stood his required time "and the tribunes / Endue you with the people's voice" (2.3.137–38). Like the First Senator, Menenius takes for granted that the tribunes' support guarantees the people's. The tribunes control the people. All that remains, Menenius says, is for the Senate to confer the insignia of office. Sicinius seems to agree ("The people do admit you" [2.3.142]), but adds what Menenius omitted: the people still must vote to confirm his election (". . . and are summon'd / To meet anon upon your approbation" [2.3.142–43]). The actual vote, which at the moment seems merely an afterthought, will provide the tribunes the opportunity they seek to block Coriolanus's election. Coriolanus cannot wait to remove his gown and, as he says with unconscious irony, "know . . . [him]self again" (2.3.146). To know himself, he thinks, he need only be without a humbling costume.

3.

Sicinius fears that Coriolanus now has the election and that he is pleased by it ("'Tis warm at's heart" [2.3.151]). Brutus answers, "With a proud heart he wore / His humble weeds" (2.3.151–52). The tribunes will use Coriolanus's proud heart to arouse the people, use the aroused people to thwart and provoke his warm heart, and use his provoked heart, finally, against Coriolanus himself.

The citizens, reentering, say Coriolanus has their votes, but then admit he insulted them. They admit their poor treatment among themselves, but not in front of Coriolanus. Only one citizen, who attributes Coriolanus's behavior to his typical manner of speech, fails to see that they were insulted. The citizens take particular offense that Coriolanus would not show his wounds, "[h]is marks of merit," even though one concedes that he "receiv'd [them] for's country" (2.3.162). His failure to show them in public outweighs the public cause for which he received them. The people's offense at the former cancels their gratitude for the latter.

The Third Citizen, indignantly describing them as mockery, mimics Coriolanus's words and gestures to all the citizens: his promising the First Citizen to show his wounds in private (2.3.164; cf. 2.3.76–77), his doffing his hat to the Fourth and Fifth citizens (2.3.165; cf. 2.3.97–100), his thanking all the citizens for their voices (2.3.169–69; cf. 2.3.77–78, 80–81, 109, 136), and his dismissing the first group abruptly (2.3.170–71; cf. 2.3.81). Since he directed the others in approaching Coriolanus (2.3.47–48), it may not seem surprising that the Third Citizen should know what happened when he was not with them as well as when he was. But it does seem surprising that, although none of the citizens was present, he should know, as he describes in the central of his five examples, with a hypothetical syllogism making explicit Coriolanus's implicit thought, what Coriolanus said in soliloquy: "'I would be consul,' says he; 'aged custom, / But by your voices, will not permit me: / Your voices therefore" (2.3.166–68; cf. 2.3.116ff.). Shakespeare's dramaturgical device—what Aristotle calls an "impossible probable" (Aristotle, *Poetics*, 1460a27)—seems intended to illustrate that Coriolanus, a man without genuine self-reflection, is consequently a man without genuine privacy. Though opaque to himself, he is largely transparent to others. The tribunes exploit the people's belated recognition and humiliation. Sicinius says that the people were either too stupid ("ignorant" [2.3.172]) to see the mockery or, if they did, they are even more stupid ("of such childish friendliness" [2.3.173]) to give Coriolanus their votes. Then Brutus, making clear that the tribunes had previously prompted the people, repeats what they could have told Coriolanus, "[a]s you were lesson'd" (2.3.175). The people might have said that when he had no office Coriolanus was their enemy and always spoke against their "liberties" and their political power ("the charters that you bear / I'th'body of the weal" [2.3.178–79]), and it would be foolish of them to give him "[a] place of potency and sway o'th'state" (2.3.180), if he means to remain a steadfast enemy "to th'plebeii" (2.3.182). Shakespeare has Brutus, here, use the Latin term "plebeii"—the only exclusively Latin word other than proper names in the play—to emphasize the plebeians' political part in the city,[65] as Shakespeare further underscores by referring to them in the stage directions, for the first time, as "plebeians" rather than as "citizens" (s.d. 2.3.152, 253; also s.d. 3.1.178; 3.3.38).[66] Similarly, this is the only time a tribune or any other commoner refers to the "state" (2.3.176, 180) and the first time to the "[common]weal" (2.3.179; cf. 2.1.54). "You should have said," Brutus says, continuing his lesson,

> That, as his worthy deeds did claim no less
> Than what he stood for, so his gracious nature
> Would think upon you for your voices, and
> Translate his malice towards you into love,
> Standing your friendly lord.

> (2.3.183–88)

The people should have said that, as Coriolanus was fully worthy of what he claimed, he should be thankful to the people giving him what he deserved, and he should show his gratitude by offering them his love. He should feel indebted for receiving what he justly claimed.

While Brutus tries to cloak the deliberate provocation by talking of worthiness, graciousness, friendliness, and love, Sicinius attempts to disguise it as a test. To have spoken "as you were fore advised" (2.3.189), he explains, would have been the supreme test of the sort of consul Coriolanus would be. To have spoken that way would have "touch'd his spirit / And tried his inclination," for it would have

> from him pluck'd
> Either his gracious promise, which you might
> As cause had call'd you up, have held him to;
> Or else it would have gall'd his surly nature
> Which easily endures not article
> Tying him to aught; so putting him to rage,

> You should have ta'en th'advantage of his choler,
> And pass'd him unelected.
>
> (2.3.189–97)

Even as he says that Coriolanus's nature cannot endure an express condition tying him to anything, Sicinius, seemingly presenting alternatives ("Either . . . / Or else . . ."), speaks as if the people could demand a "gracious promise" to which they might hold Coriolanus but which might, nevertheless, not gall his nature and provoke his rage. And as Sicinius's purported test is really an instigation—to have "touch'd his spirit" suggests both testing and inflaming it by challenging it[67]—so its predictable result would really be a pretext. By "putting [Coriolanus] to rage," the test would give the people the opportunity to take "th'advantage of his choler, / And pass . . . him unelected."

Brutus strengthens his previous warning by saying that if Coriolanus solicited the people with undisguised "contempt" when he needed their "loves," they should think how "bruising" to them his "contempt" will be "[w]hen he hath power to crush" them (2.3.198, 199, 200, 201). No matter what he says or does now, Coriolanus is not be trusted with power. Then, sounding not unlike Coriolanus himself, Brutus tries to shame the people: "Why, had your bodies / No heart among you? Or had you tongues to cry / Against the rectorship of judgement?" (2.3.201–3). The people, he says, knew better but lacked the spirit, or else their tongues rebelled against the rule of reason. They either were spiritless bodies or had mindless tongues. They lacked either self-respect or proper regard for their self-interest. Sicinius, silently dropping his call for a test, asks whether the people, before now, have ever refused their votes to "the asker" or, on the other hand, ever granted their votes to one "that did not ask but mock" (2.3.204–5). To "ask" is to ask properly—to flatter the people by pretending to love them. To "mock" is to ask improperly—to flatter the people but show that one is just pretending. An offense that goes over their heads is not an offense to their faces.

The appeal succeeds. Some of the citizens, as though they thought it on their own, declare that there is still time to reject Coriolanus: "He's not confirm'd: we may deny him yet" (2.3.207). Even the citizen who initially thought that Coriolanus had not mocked them (2.3.159) is now certain that "[we] will deny him" (2.3.208) and vows to get a thousand other voters and their friends to change their minds. The tribunes, however, are not through. Once again, they try to put words into the people's mouths, coaching them on what to say to their friends. The people may be inconstant and unruly—their opinion may be "giddy censure" (1.1.267)—but they need to think that they have reasons for their choices. They take pride in what they imagine to

be their ability to govern themselves. Brutus, who emphasized that Coriolanus has been an enemy of their liberties and power, instructs the citizens
to tell their friends that, as consul, he would take from the people "[t]heir liberties" and thereby "make them of no more voice" (2.3.213) than dogs kept
to be beaten for barking. And Sicinius, who talked of Coriolanus's spirit and
surly nature and who previously spoke of Coriolanus's mocking the citizens
in suing for their vote, tells them to "[e]nforce his pride / And his old hate
unto you" (2.3.217–18) and reminds them of the "contempt" with which he
wore his humble gown and "scorn'd" them in soliciting their votes (2.3.219,
220). The one tribune stresses the people's political power; the other, their
offended pride. Neither, we might note, even alludes to the issue of food anywhere in the scene.

The Tribunes are still not finished. They need to protect themselves.
Sicinius first suggests that the people explain their reversal by saying that they
were blinded by their grateful affection for Coriolanus ("your loves, / Thinking upon his services" [2.3.220–21]) and did not see how contemptuously he
had treated them. Brutus, seeing an opportunity, corrects him: "Lay / A fault
on us, your tribunes" (2.3.224–25). Rather than say their love blinded them,
the people should say the tribunes spared no effort in urging them to elect
Coriolanus. "Say you chose him," Sicinius urges, "More after our command-
ment than as guided / By your own true affections" (2.3.227–29). The people
should explain that their minds were preoccupied "with what [they] rather
must do, / Than what [they] should," which is to say, with what the tribunes
obligated them to do, even though it went "against the grain" (2.3.230–31).
"Lay the fault on us," Sicinius repeats (2.3.232). Brutus, pressing the people to
"spare us not" (2.3.233), goes so far as to exhort them to say that the tribunes
read them lectures not only on Coriolanus's long history of service to Rome
but on his noble ancestry ("[t]he noble house o'th'Martians" [2.3.236]). The
enemies of the patricians pretend to have extolled patricians in order to pretend to have kept their word with the patricians, and yet avoid Coriolanus's
election as consul. Having it both ways, they protect themselves by having
the citizens pretend to defy them. "Say you ne'er had done't— / Harp on that
still—but by our putting on" (2.3.249–50). If the Second Citizen was sure that
he could round up "five hundred voices" against Coriolanus, and the First Citizen was sure that he could get "twice five hundred, and their friends" to join
them (2.3.209, 210), the people now believe that they already have nearly
everyone's vote: "[A]lmost all / Repent in their election" (2.3.252–53).

Brutus's description of "[t]he noble house o'th'Martians," which closely
paraphrases the opening sentences of North's translation of Plutarch's *Coriolanus*,[68] is conspicuously anachronistic. It places Coriolanus's descendants

among his ancestors. "Ancus Martius, Numa's daughter's son, / Who after great Hostilius here was king" (2.3.237–38), was Coriolanus's ancestor, as Brutus says. But "Censorinus" (Martius Rutilus), although said to be "his great ancestor" (2.3.243), and "Publius and Quintus [Martius]" were, in fact, his distant descendants. Censorinus, "twice . . . censor" (2.3.242), lived some two centuries after Coriolanus,[69] while Publius and Quintus, owing to whom "our best water [was] brought by conduits hither" (2.3.239, 240), followed Censorinus by another hundred years.[70] Indeed, the office of censor was not established until nearly fifty years after Coriolanus's death, and the earliest Roman aqueduct was not built until a century after that.[71] The anachronisms, especially out of the begrudging mouth of a tribune, underscore the glory and longevity of Coriolanus's family. Venerable for its illustrious origin, great accomplishments, and long age, "[t]he noble house o'th'Martians" served Rome for more than half a millennium, from the king who first extended Rome beyond the Tiber to the time of the destruction of Carthage. But precisely by drawing attention to the glory and longevity of his family line, Brutus's words point to the fundamental tension within Coriolanus between virtue and birth. The radical expression of his criticism of custom, Coriolanus's wish to be wholly self-sufficient—to be "author of himself" (5.3.36)—would reject the noble line that Brutus now lauds. If Brutus makes him the descendant of his descendants, Coriolanus would make himself the progenitor of himself.

The tension between virtue and birth, which goes to the heart of his tragedy, also lies at the heart of the aristocratic regime that Coriolanus tries to preserve. Coriolanus spoke of the establishment of the tribunate as breaking the heart of "generosity" (1.1.210). By "generosity," he meant both liberality in giving and the class of well born—excellence both in virtue and in birth. The aristocratic regime tries to keep the two together. As we see throughout the play, "nobility" refers to class and to virtue: "Would the nobility lay aside their ruth"; "I sin in envying his nobility" (1.1.196, 229).[72] Although Coriolanus will finally force the two senses apart, the regime he defends rests on the double identity: the nobles are noble; noble ancestry amounts to noble virtue, as Brutus's laudatory phrase—"[t]he noble house o'th'Martians"—ironically affirms. Or, as Menenius said in his first words to the mutinous people, the Senate's political authority rests on, or is indistinguishable from, its moral authority. Virtue and rank—natural and conventional nobility—imply each other.

Scene 2 began with a paraphrase of Plutarch; scene 3 virtually ends with one. Just as the episodes concerning the wager and the poor man (1.4.1–7; 1.9.77–90), dealing with magnanimity, framed Coriolanus in battle, the two

Plutarchean passages, dealing with his unconditioned virtue, frame his election campaign in Rome. The first (2.2.1–36) explicitly concerned Coriolanus's claim or wish to be indifferent to the voters; the second (2.3.235–43) implicitly concerns his claim or wish to be independent of his birth.

4.

After the citizens go to gather the votes, Brutus and Sicinius yet again discuss their situation. Although recognizing that their ruse runs a risk, Brutus thinks the danger is less than allowing Coriolanus to be elected. Besides, their stratagem contains a particular advantage which improves its chance of success. If the people's refusal sparks Coriolanus's rage, "as his nature is" (2.3.256), the tribunes, both watchful and quick to act, will be able to take "vantage of his anger" (2.3.258). As before, they can use the people and Coriolanus against each other—the people to provoke his anger, and his anger to frighten the people. Manipulating both, they can count on Coriolanus's "nature" to destroy himself.

While Brutus is concerned with how the ambush will work, Sicinius is concerned with how it will look. Concluding act 2, he bids Brutus to go with him to the Capitol, saying that they will be there "before the stream o'th'people" (2.3.259). By the tribunes arriving ahead of the people, "this shall seem, as partly 'tis, their own, / Which we have goaded onward" (2.3.260–61). Separation and indirection supply the tribunes' cover.

Notes

1. See act 1, n13, above.

2. For their calculation rather than indignation, see, e.g., their reaction to Martius's allegedly undeserved honors at Cominius's expense (1.1.265–75). For their feigned indignation, see, e.g., their reminding the people of how Coriolanus scorned them in soliciting their votes (2.3.218–24) and their charging him with treason (3.1.160–62, 170–75). Perhaps their only instances of genuine indignation are their reaction to Coriolanus's resisting their arrest and striking the aediles (3.1.313–16) and their initial anger at the messenger bearing the unwelcome news of Coriolanus's leading Aufidius's army against Rome and their initially accusing the nobles of fabricating the report (4.6.48–49, 60–62, 69–71). Note, however, that the former is quickly replaced by calculation, when the tribunes are warned of bloody consequences (3.1.320–28), and becomes mock indignation when they repeat the charge to the people (3.3.78–83, 96–99), and the latter turns into feigned indignation, when the tribunes finally realize that the news is true (4.6.150–53).

3. Cf., e.g., 1.1.23–24; for the pleasure of anger, see Homer, *The Iliad*, 18.109; Aristotle, *Rhetoric*, 1378b2–9; *Nicomachean Ethics*, 1117a6–9.

4. MacCallum, 535–36; Cantor, 62.

5. Dionysius of Halicarnassus, 6.70.1, trans. Earnest Cary, Loeb Edition, 7 vols (Cambridge: Harvard University Press, 1962), 4:63.

6. Plutarch, *Comparison of Lycurgus and Numa*, 1.3; North, 1:199, 200; also Plutarch, *Lycurgus*, 8–10; for the "severity of [Lycurgus's own] ordinary life," see Plutarch, *Lycurgus*, 11.3; North, 1:132.

7. Plutarch, *Roman Questions*, 92.

8. From now on, she speaks only in verse.

9. The triumphs span the entirety of Roman history. The first, which was the model of those that followed, honored Romulus (Plutarch, *Romulus*, 16.6); the last, more than eleven centuries later, honored the Emperor Honorius (Claudian, *Panegyric on the Sixth Consulship of Emperor Honorius*, 543ff.).

10. With both, 2.1.161–202; 4.1; 5.3.22, 209; with his mother but not his wife, 3.2.6–137.

11. Poole, 33.

12. Janet Adelman, "'Anger's My Meat': Feeding, Dependency and Aggression in *Coriolanus*," in *Representing Shakespeare: New Psychoanalytic Essays*, eds. Murray M. Schwarz and Coppelia Kahn (Baltimore: The Johns Hopkins University Press, 1980), 122.

13. Cf., e.g., 1.4.40–42; 4.4.2–6; 5.6.151; and note the pun on "home" at 1.4.38.

14. Plutarch, *Coriolanus*, 14.1; North 2:158; also *Roman Questions*, 49.

15. Shakespeare disregards that Rome had two consuls; see, e.g., Livy, 2.1; Plutarch, *Publiccola*, 1.4; see also *Coriolanus*, 15.3.

16. Livy, 2.1–3; Plutarch, *Publicola*, 1.4.

17. Livy, 1.9; Plutarch, *Romulus*, 13.1.

18. Livy, 2.1; see s.d. 2.1.36.

19. Livy, 2.21ff.; see Machiavelli, *Discourses*, 1.3.

20. See *OED*, s.v. Opposite, n. 2a and 3.

21. Plutarch, *Comparison of Alcibiades and Coriolanus*, 1.3–4; North, 2:190–91.

22. E. K. Chambers, in Furness, 220.

23. Livy, 2.1.

24. Plutarch, *Publicola*, 1.3; North, 1:249.

25. Livy, 2.1; Holland, 36.

26. On Romulus, see Livy, 1.15.8; Plutarch, *Greek and Roman Parallel Stories*, 32; on the expulsion of the kings, see Livy, 1.59–60. For the alliance of a monarch and the people against the nobles, see, further, Livy, 1.46.1–2.

27. For the nobles' fear of the people's welcoming a return of the Tarquins, see Livy, 2.5.1–2, 2.9.5–8, 2.21.5–6.

28. *Julius Caesar*, 3.2.75ff. See Blits, *Ancient Republic*, 21–37. See also Dionysius of Halicarnassus, 6.74.1–2; Plutarch, *Coriolanus*, 14.3.

29. See also 2.3.100–2, and note 5.4.43–44.

30. Aristotle, *Rhetoric*, 1368a11–39; Quintilian, 3.7.6.

31. Richard S. Ide, *Possessed with Greatness : The Heroic Tragedies of Chapman and Shakespeare* (Chapel Hill: University of North Carolina Press, 1980), 184.

32. Cicero, *De partitione oratoria*, 4, 27; *De inventione*, 1.19; Anonymous, 1.4.

33. Anonymous, 3.11.

34. Aristotle, *Rhetoric*, 1366a23–24, 67b30–33; Cicero, *De partitione oratoria*, 71.

35. Cicero, *De partitione oratoria*, 12, 75; Anonymous, 3.13.

36. Aristotle, *Rhetoric*, 1368a22–24; also Anonymous, 4.59–61.

37. Aristotle, *Rhetoric*, 1368a10–15.

38. Aristotle, *Rhetoric*, 1367b29–30; Quintilian, 3.7.10.

39. Quintilian, 3.7.12–13, 16.

40. Abbott, §20.

41. Anonymous, 1.14.

42. Anonymous, 4.62.

43. Anonymous, 4.35, 51, 68.

44. Anonymous, 4.63–65.

45. Cicero, *De partitione oratoria*, 52. For the brevity of a peroration, see Anonymous, 3.15; 4.41.

46. According to Livy, Coriolanus's glory so completely overshadowed the consul's that no one would have remembered at all that Cominius had fought against the Volscians, had it not been for a record, engraved on a bronze column, of a treaty made at the time with the Latins (Livy, 2.33.9).

47. For Cominius's affection for Coriolanus, see 5.1.2–3.

48. Only Menenius calls him "brave" (5.1.30).

49. Aristotle, *Rhetoric*, 1394a25–28; Anonymous, 4.24.

50. The Third Citizen says that not only Coriolanus but "many" (2.3.18) have called the people many-headed. The phrase, indeed, has a rich history. Socrates, appealing to the spirited Glaucon to distinguish the noble from the base, distinguishes what is noble in a man from the "many-colored, many-headed beast" of the soul's desires (Plato, *Republic*, 588c7–8, 589b1–2). For the phrase describing the Romans, see Horace, *Epistles*, 1.1.76. For Coriolanus's use of it, see 3.1.92, 130, 155; 4.1.1–2; also 3.1.65.

51. Also Dionysius of Halicarnassus, 6.60.2.

52. For the voice vote serving the patricians' interests, and for the fact that the secret ballot was not introduced in Rome until the third quarter of the second century B.C., see Cicero, *Laws*, 3.34–36.

53. Machiavelli, *Discourses*, 3.23.

54. "To 'think upon,' in the mouth of a suppliant, has the special sense of 'to remember *with compassion*.'" H. C. Beeching, in Furness, 249 (his italics); see also 2.3.186, 221.

55. For the continued echo of Coriolanus's words in the decayed republicanism of Casca's contemptuous but complacent description of Caesar and the people in the marketplace, see *Julius Caesar*, 1.2.240–47.

56. This is Coriolanus's only reference to the people as "the poor."

57. Catherine H. Zuckert, "On the Role of Spiritedness in Politics," in *Understanding the Political Spirit* (New Haven: Yale University Press, 1988), 27–28, n.14.

58. Coriolanus uses "pray," here, thrice in eleven lines (2.3.74, 76, 84). The only other time he uses the word in addressing the people is also when he needs them (1.1.250), as is also true of "beseech" (2.3.102).

59. Mitchell, 212.

60. For the wolf as Mars's animal, see Livy, 10.27.8–9; Virgil, 9.566; Horace, *Odes*, 1.17.9; Propertius, *Elegies*, 4.1.55.

61. Blits, *Ancient Republic*, 32–33. In keeping with this, notwithstanding that the substance of Rome's customary rituals shifts over time, the rituals' outward forms and names remain the same, giving the appearance of continuity even when there has been fundamental change. The lictors, for example, were originally attendants to the kings and became attendants to elected magistrates, just as the Senate, in name, goes back to the reign of Romulus and was originally a regal office (Livy, 1.9; Plutarch, *Romulus*, 13).

62. See, e.g., Livy, 27.9.11.

63. "[T]he thirty-six lines of soliloquy in *Coriolanus*—the same number as in *As You Like It*—represent the minimal use of this device in Shakespeare." Charney, 38.

64. Of the forty-eight times the word appears in the play, "voices" occurs twenty-nine times in this scene and seven times in this seven-line speech. See R. B. Parker, ed., *The Tragedy of Coriolanus* (Oxford: Clarendon Press, 1994), 232.

65. Wilson, 193.

66. The word "plebeians" is mentioned in the dialogue at 1.9.7; 2.1.9, 94–95; 3.1.100–1; and 5.4.37—always pejoratively.

67. Parker, 241.

68. Plutarch, *Coriolanus*, 1.1; North, 2:143.

69. Livy, 7.22.7–10.

70. Frontinus, *The Aqueducts of Rome*, 7.

71. Livy, 4.8.2; Frontinus, 5.

72. For the former sense, see, e.g., 2.1.237, 263; 3.1.28, 38; 4.2.2; 4.3.15, 21; 4.5.76; 4.6.58, 133; 4.7.29; for the latter sense, see, e.g., 1.4.52; 2.2.40, 129, 152; 2.3.8; 3.1.152, 253; 3.2.40, 100; 4.2.21; 4.5.107, 117; 5.3.121, 145; 5.6.124, 143, 153.

ACT THREE

~

Act Three, Scene One

1.

Act 1 concluded with Aufidius getting ready to plan a new attack. Act 3 begins with Lartius's news that Aufidius has quickly raised a fresh army whose threat has caused the Romans to come to terms sooner (and presumably less favorably) than they otherwise would have. By his quick action, Aufidius seems to have improved if not entirely altered the terms of the Volscians' defeat (cf. 1.10.1ff.). True to form, Coriolanus, eager to fight Aufidius, offers a bleak view of the military situation, saying that the Volscians are back where they started, ready when the time is right to attack again (cf. 1.1.226–27). Cominius, also in character, disagrees. Offering a sanguine assessment, he predicts that the Volscians are so exhausted that the Romans are unlikely to see them again in their lifetimes. We might wonder whether Cominius's exaggerated correction is at least partly intended to temper Coriolanus's wish for war. It is worthy noting that Cominius already addresses Coriolanus as "lord consul" (3.1.6). He, like all the other nobles, does not for a moment doubt Coriolanus's election.

Coriolanus immediately asks Lartius about Aufidius: "Saw you Aufidius?" (3.1.8). And when Lartius says that he did and that Aufidius cursed the Volscians for surrendering Corioles so shamefully, Coriolanus wants to know whether Aufidius spoke of him and what he said. Lartius reports that Aufidius spoke of how often he had met Coriolanus, "sword to sword" (3.1.13), and

> That of all things upon the earth he hated
> Your person most; that he would pawn his fortunes
> To hopeless restitution, so he might
> Be call'd your vanquisher.

(3.1.14–17)

Hating Coriolanus more than anything else in the world, Aufidius would stake everything to be called his conqueror. Nothing is more important to him than defeating Coriolanus. In the light of what happens later, Coriolanus's reply is rich in irony. Upon hearing that Aufidius is in Antium, Coriolanus responds, "I wish I had a cause to seek him there, / To oppose his hatred fully" (3.1.19–20). And, right away, the tribunes, returning from the marketplace, enter. Not only will Coriolanus have a cause to seek Aufidius in Antium, but the tribunes have already started and will soon do much more to give him that cause. Where act 3 begins with Coriolanus and the other nobles thinking that he is Rome's honored consul, it will conclude with him a dishonored outcast.

2.

When he sees the tribunes approaching, Coriolanus explains that he despises them, "[t]he tongues o'th'common mouth" (3.1.21), because they dress themselves up in authority in a way that no noble can bear ("[T]hey do prank them in authority, / Against all noble sufferance" [3.1.23–24]). Then, as though on cue, the tribunes, in their first words, assert their authority, while pretending to warn Coriolanus of danger: "Pass no further. / . . . / It will be dangerous to go on. No further" (3.1.24–26). All the nobles are taken by surprise. "Hath he not pass'd the noble and the common?" (3.1.28). When he hears that he has not, Coriolanus, asking whether he has received "children's voices" (3.1.29), understands the people's reversal as proving him right in two respects. Unable to keep their word, the people are not to be trusted with political power: "Are these your herd? / Must these have voices, that can yield them now / And straight disclaim their tongues?" (3.1.32–34). And, contrary to what the moderate senators seem to think, the tribunate does no good in controlling the people. The tribunes may speak for them, but they do not restrain their bite. "What are your offices? / You being their mouths, why rule you not their teeth?" (3.1.34–35). Coriolanus sees the people's reversal not simply as their familiar fickleness, however, but as the tribunes' design: "It is a purpos'd thing, and grows by plot, / To curb the will of the nobility" (3.1.37–38). Coriolanus is correct about the tribunes' plot, but he seems to mistake their attempt to protect their new power for their attempt to push for still more. He seems to mistake their defensive action against him, in particular, for their further aggression against the nobility, as a whole. "Suffer't," he warns, "and live with such as cannot rule, / Nor ever will be rul'd" (3.1.39–40). Coriolanus objects that the people can neither rule themselves nor be ruled by others. They are, literally, unruly. What Coriolanus blames as their failing, however, is vital to the republican regime.[1] Were the people able to rule themselves, they would not need the nobles. And were they easily ruled by others, they would not be spirited soldiers. The commoners' combination of incompetence and unruliness keeps them dependent on and useful to the nobles. Like so much else in Rome, their moral faults serve Rome best.

Brutus responds explicitly to Coriolanus's charge of a plot and implicitly to his indictment of the people. Rejecting the charge ("Call't not a plot" [3.1.40]), he attributes the people's reversal to Coriolanus's insulting and malicious behavior, implying that it is Coriolanus's own hostility that is to blame. Passing briefly over his mockery ("The people cry you mock'd them" [3.1.41]), Brutus forcefully renews the old grievance of corn:

> [A]nd of late,
> When corn was given them gratis, you repin'd,
> Scandal'd the suppliants for the people, call'd them
> Time-pleasers, flatterers, foes to nobleness.
>
> (3.1.41–44)

When Coriolanus counters that this was previously known, Brutus, increasingly magnifying his affront, in short order, answers disingenuously ("Not to them all" [3.1.45]), takes feigned offense at his perceived or imagined personal insult ("How! I inform them!" [3.1.46]), and boasts that he would do better than Coriolanus as consul ("Not unlike / Each way to better yours" [3.1.47–48]). In no time at all, Brutus has leveled class distinctions, as Coriolanus clearly sees. "Why then should I be consul?" he indignantly exclaims. "By yond clouds, / Let me deserve so ill as you, and make me / Your fellow tribune" (3.1.49–51). If Brutus could be a better consul, then Coriolanus merits no more than being tribune. The raising of the plebeian implies the lowering of the patrician. Sicinius promptly adds to Brutus's insolence. Rebuking him for "show[ing] too much of that / For which the people stir" (3.1.51–52), he admonishes Coriolanus to proceed "with a gentler spirit, / Or never be so noble as a consul, / Nor yoke with [Brutus] for tribune" (3.1.54–56). Unless he shows a gentler spirit, Coriolanus will never be elected to any office, patrician or plebeian.

While Coriolanus falls momentarily silent, Menenius urges calm, and Cominius, appealing to Roman decorum, declares in dismay, "This palt'ring / Becomes not Rome" (3.1.57–58). While the people have been deceived and incited, he says (tactfully avoiding mentioning the tribunes by name), Coriolanus does not deserve the dishonorable obstacles that have been treacherously thrown in his way. Coriolanus, abruptly ending his brief silence, returns furiously to the issue of corn: "Tell me of corn! / This was my speech, and I will speak't again" (3.1.60–61). Brutus's provocation has worked. Coriolanus's pause was the silence not of restraint but of rage. Even though he perceives that the tribunes are plotting, Coriolanus shows no recognition that they are trying to inflame his frightening fury. He is certain that they manipulate the people, but appears unaware that they are doing the same to him. Or if he is aware, his recognition seems only to add to his anger. Thus, reacting to Brutus's objection to what he had said ("Scandal'd the suppliants for the people, call'd them . . ."), he insists on saying it again. He must say what he thinks. Anger is not only aroused by speech, but issues in speech. Based on a sense of right and wrong, true and false, it listens (if poorly) to speech and then articulates itself through speech. Often shouting to be heard (see, e.g., 1.1.1; 3.3.41, 108; 4.2.13, 38; 5.6.110, 131), it answers what offends it. It insists on telling its side of the story.[2]

Coriolanus thus delivers a long, often-interrupted oration (3.1.63–169), urging the nobles to strip the people of their political rights. His campaign for their votes has suddenly turned into a campaign to revoke their right to vote. It will end with the tribunes' charge of treason (3.1.161–62, 170, 173). Coriolanus's argument against popular suffrage rests on his understanding of the political regime, which in his view is the central political issue. In the name of the regime as such, he attacks not only the desirability but the possibility of a mixed regime.

Despite his rage, Coriolanus's speech follows the rules of classical deliberative oratory. It begins with a brief exordium (3.1.63–67). Most deliberative speeches do not need an exordium, since an exordium seeks to win a receptive or attentive hearing, and the audience already wants to hear what is to be said.[3] In this instance, however, both Menenius and the First Senator, who until now has spoken only to support and praise Coriolanus, try to stop him from speaking (3.1.62). Coriolanus therefore includes an exordium, whose specific purpose is to gain the good will of his listeners by showing his own good will toward them.[4] Now, there are two kinds of exordia—direct and by insinuation.[5] Coriolanus uses both. He first asks ("craves[s]") the "pardons" of his "nobler friends" (3.1.64–65), showing his good will by recognizing their objection. Then, he insinuates that he will benefit "the mutable, rank-scented meinie" (3.1.65) by letting them "behold themselves" (3.1.67) as they truly are, since he does not flatter. Even the commoners, he suggests, should welcome his words, for what he says will provide them with a true reflection of themselves.

The second part of an oration is the narrative. Much as in epideictic oratory, where it summarizes the case, the narrative in deliberative oratory sets forth the question at issue.[6] While brief, clear, and plausible,[7] it should discuss what is either honorable or advantageous, or, preferably, the honorable as the advantageous.[8] Accordingly, Coriolanus, explicitly repeating his earlier speech, proceeds to argue in his narrative (3.1.67–79) that the Senate's actions have been dishonorable and disadvantageous to the Senate. "I say again," he states,

> In soothing [the people], we nourish 'gainst our senate
> The cockle of rebellion, insolence, sedition,
> Which we ourselves have plough'd for, sow'd and scatter'd,
> By mingling them with us, the honour'd number
> Who lack not virtue, no, nor power, but that
> Which they have given to beggars.
>
> (3.1.67–73)

The Senate, which has only itself to blame, has given away both its advantage and its honor in mingling its own power with the people. Coriolanus twice implicitly includes himself among those who are responsible ("we nourish"; "we ourselves have plough'd for . . ."). But he concludes by expressly speaking of "they" who have given power to beggars. His courtesy quickly gives way to accusation.

Menenius and the Senator again try to stop him ("Well, no more"; "No more . . ." [3.1.73–74]), but Coriolanus insists on speaking. "How? No more!," he retorts;

> As for my country I have shed my blood,
> Not fearing outward force, so shall my lungs
> Coin words till their decay, against those measles
> Which we disdain should tetter us, yet sought
> The very way to catch them.
>
> (3.1.74–79)

Coriolanus equates speaking freely and fighting fearlessly. To be less than candid, he says, is to be timid and unpatriotic. In the same way that he never retreats in battle when fighting for his country, he will not remain silent when his country's good is at stake. The Senate's action, as he stresses with a pun similar to his initial insult of the people ("scabs" [1.1.165]), has produced the reverse of what the Senate would want. By "mingling them with us," the Senate will become infected with the vileness ("measles") of the wretched commoners ("measles") whom it scorns.[9] Just as the regime is, at once, the men who rule and the virtues they exemplify, so, likewise, the people are indistinguishable from their vileness. They are identical to the qualities they typify.

When Coriolanus returned in triumph, Brutus described the Romans as believing that a god had crept into his human powers, and the messenger described the nobles as bowing to him as to Jove's statue (2.1.216–18, 264). Now, interrupting, Brutus accuses Coriolanus of thinking that himself: "You speak o'th'people / As if you were a god to punish, not / A man of their infirmity" (3.1.79–81). Coriolanus, in his own eyes, Brutus says, is a god punishing humans for ordinary human weaknesses which he lacks. If spirit causes a man to strive to rise above himself, it seems to urge him, ultimately, to scale heaven and ignore or deny his natural weaknesses. And while inspiring him to seek to exceed his human limitations, it also prompts him to demand a perfectly just world—one in which, everyone getting exactly what he deserves, human weakness is properly punished by the gods, while heroic strength is fittingly rewarded. Spirit, arousing both his ascent and his indignation, causes man to surpass and punish his mortal nature. It causes him to punish in others what he thinks he is superior to in himself.

Since deliberative oratory concerns whether to choose a course of action, the narrative is usually followed by the partition, stating the points agreed upon by both sides and those in dispute. Its purpose is to make the speech clear and perspicuous.[10] Coriolanus, however, is diverted from the partition by the tribunes' next provocation. Nevertheless, his furious response to the provocation sharply delineates the issue between him and the moderate senators, and so serves in place of a partition. When Coriolanus angrily denies that he is speaking from anger ("Choler! / Were I as patient as the midnight sleep, / By Jove, 'twould be my mind!" [3.1.83–85]), Sicinius declares, "It is a mind / That shall remain a poison where it is, / Not poison any further" (3.1.85–87). Sicinius's "shall" is an injunction, expressing an order, as Coriolanus very well understands. "Shall remain!" he cries out in rage, "Hear you this Triton of the minnows? Mark you / His absolute 'shall'?" (3.1.87–89). As when told that the people seek corn at their own price "whereof they say / The city is well stor'd" (1.1.188–89), Coriolanus responds entirely to the presumption. A plebeian tribune has the effrontery to command a patrician.

Sicinius's provocation, pointing to the issue of who rules in Rome, provides Coriolanus with the opening part of his speech's proof (3.1.89–148).

As in encomium, the proof—the main part of the speech—sets forth the arguments supporting the speaker's case.[11] As he did in the narrative, Coriolanus combines the honorable and the advantageous, and, as is especially suitable for a deliberative speech, he uses examples.[12] Examples are to inductions, Aristotle says, as enthymemes are to syllogisms.[13] They are rhetorical inductions, differing from inductions proper in that while an induction reasons from part to whole (and a syllogism reasons from whole to part), an example reasons from part to part.[14] It reasons that what happened in a familiar case is likely to happen in a similar case. Whereas induction proper proceeds from all the instances to a general conclusion, example proceeds from one or several well-known instances to a conclusion and then immediately applies the conclusion to the instance in question.[15] Examples, particularly historical examples, are fitting to deliberative rhetoric, for deliberative rhetoric concerns the future, and in most respects future events will resemble those of the past.[16]

Coriolanus begins with the example at hand. Addressing the nobles as "good but most unwise patricians," "grave but reckless senators" (3.1.91, 92), and repeating Sicinius's imperative "Shall!" (3.1.89), he asks why have they

> Given Hydra here to choose an officer,
> That with his peremptory "shall," being but
> The horn and noise o'th'monsters, wants not spirit
> To say he'll turn your current in a ditch
> And make your channel his?
>
> (3.1.92–96)

Just as he addresses the nobles with a pair of oxymoronic antitheses, Coriolanus poses his question as a pair of implicit oppositions between the people and their tribune, and between the nobles' power and the tribune's. While the people resemble Hydra, they have chosen "an officer," who, unlike the many-headed monster itself, issues "peremptory" orders. He has the decisiveness which they lack. And though he is "but / The horn and noise o'th'monsters," he "wants not spirit / To say" that he will divert the patricians' power and seize its authority for himself. A man who uses the people, for whom he pretends to speak and behind whom he hides, the tribune frankly declares, by his very manner of voicing commands, that he intends to take the nobles' power and use it for his own ends. He is, at once, open and duplicitous, whereas the senators are good but unwise, grave but reckless.

Having described combinations of contraries, Coriolanus, drawing the conclusion from his first example, denies the possibility of a mixed regime.

Using a mode of speech mirroring his thought, he first poses two pairs of necessary alternatives, stated as paradoxical antitheses and couched as four conditional propositions, each ending with an imperative:

> If he have power,
> Then vail your ignorance; if none, awake
> Your dangerous lenity. If you are learn'd,
> Be not as common fools; if you are not,
> Let them have cushions by you.

> (3.1.96–100)

Coriolanus, indignant that the nobles are acting like fools by needlessly rewarding fools, suggests that their claim to rule is founded on their wisdom. Precisely because the wise should rule the unwise, those who act like fools forfeit their claim to rule. Coriolanus then turns directly to the nature of a mixed regime. "You are plebeians / If they be senators," he warns (3.1.101–1). For Coriolanus, power sharing is impossible. If the tribunes have any power, they are in effect senators and the senators are plebeians. A mixed regime is not a mixture of aristocratic and democratic elements, but a democracy dominating and destroying an aristocracy: "[A]nd they are no less [than senators], / When, both your voices blended, the great'st taste / Most palates theirs" (3.1.101–3). Since a regime is defined by the sort of men who rule and what they honor most highly, "[w]here virtue is not honored above all, an aristocratic regime cannot exist securely" (Aristotle, *Politics*, 1273a40–b1). A mixed regime, however, must always make concessions to non-virtue. Because it must satisfy the people's thirst for freedom, respect, and material goods, it can never fully honor virtue. As the types of men who rule are mixed, so is what the city truly honors. Thus, in a mixed regime, noble and vulgar tastes are blended together. And since in any such mixture numbers count, the predominate taste smacks of the greater number. A mixture of patrician and plebeian is necessarily plebeian.

Turning to his second example, Coriolanus compares Rome to Greece. The Roman people, he says,

> choose their magistrate,
> And such a one as he, who puts his "shall,"
> His popular "shall," against a graver bench
> Than ever frown'd in Greece.

> (3.1.103–6)

The gravity of the Roman Senate, to which nothing in Greece compares, makes the democratic affront in Rome all the more debasing. "By Jove himself," Coriolanus swears by the tutelary god of Rome, "It makes the consuls base" (3.1.106–7).

The fundamental problem of a mixed regime, however, is not simply that the low dominates and degrades the high. In the end, a mixed regime is no regime at all. "[A]nd my soul aches / To know," Coriolanus continues,

> when two authorities are up,
> Neither supreme, how soon confusion
> May enter 'twixt the gap of both, and take
> The one by th'other.
>
> (3.1.107–11)

Because a regime is a city's manner of life as activity directed toward the end which it honors and for which it exists, when that end changes, so does the regime. A confusion of ends is a confusion of regimes. In a mixed regime, however, there are two authorities and therefore no authority—no authoritative end. The mixed regime's political division reflects a division not only of power but of ends—not only of who rules the city, but of what the city honors and the end for which it exists.

Coriolanus refers to his own soul twice. He called Aufidius "my soul's hate" (1.5.10), and now he tells how "my soul aches" to know of Rome's divided authority. The two references complement each other. Coriolanus's spirited soul demands external contention, on the one hand, and internal singleness, on the other—outward opposition and inward indivisibility.

When Cominius tries to end Coriolanus's speech by urging him to move on to the marketplace, Coriolanus, presenting his third example, returns to the issue of the corn dole, the issue which initially sparked his speech. Once again, he compares Rome to Greece:

> Whoever gave that counsel, to give forth
> The corn o'th'storehouse gratis, as 'twas us'd
> Sometime in Greece—
>
> (3.1.112–14)

While the affront of the "popular 'shall'" is greater in Rome because nothing in Greece possesses the gravity of the Senate, the excuse for granting the corn is weaker in Rome because in democratic Athens "the people had more absolute power" (3.1.115). Whereas the Athenian nobles were forced by their weakness to give the people corn, the Roman nobles have needlessly made themselves appear weak by doing the same. Necessity cannot excuse in Rome what it excuses in Athens.

Coriolanus explains why granting the corn in Rome was a grievous mistake. The people know that the corn was not a reward for their public service, he says, for they know that they never performed any good service. When conscripted, they would not serve, "[e]ven when the navel of the state was touch'd" (3.1.122), and when they did serve, "[t]heir mutinies and revolts, wherein they show'd / Most valour, spoke not for them" (3.1.125–26). By the former, Coriolanus is presumably referring to the plebeians' succession to the Sacred Mount;[17] by the latter, to their decrying the patricians when forced to fight.[18] The people thus know that the Senate rewarded rather than punished them for their poor service. Nor do they think that the Senate granted them corn because the patricians had been starving them, as they charged, for they know their accusation was untrue.[19] How then did they understand the grant of corn? "How shall this bosom multiplied digest / The senate's courtesy?" Coriolanus asks, underscoring the people's manyness while confounding their stomachs, hearts, and minds (3.1.130–31). Letting their deeds bespeak their silent thoughts, he quotes the people as thinking, "'We did request it, / We are the greater poll, and in true fear / They gave us our demands'" (3.1.132–34). The Senate granted the people's demands because they feared their numbers. And the likely result of this capitulation will be a mixture of dishonor and disadvantage to the Senate:

> Thus we debase
> The nature of our seats, and make the rabble
> Call our cares fears; which will in time
> Break ope the locks o'th'senate, and bring in
> The crows to peck the eagles.

> (3.1.134–38)

By debasing their position and making themselves appear afraid, the Senate will make the people more headstrong, more rebellious, and hungrier for political power.

Ignoring Menenius's real and Brutus's feigned attempts to stop him, Coriolanus, completing his proof, denies that a mixed regime can have a serious purpose. Swearing more forcefully than he ever does elsewhere, he invokes everything "both divine and human" (3.1.140) that can be sworn by—that is, Rome's gods and Senate—to confirm his indictment of the "double worship" (3.1.141) of the regime's divided authority. The defect of the double worship is itself twofold. First, the double worship implies equality where there is none. As a result, "one part does disdain with cause, the other / Insult without all reason" (3.1.142–43). Owing to their genuine inequality, the nobles, with good reason, disdain the people. But owing to their presumed equality, the people, beyond all reason, insolently object to being treated as unequals. Second, the double worship makes it necessary for wisdom to gain the consent of ignorance. And the need for "gentry, title, [and] wisdom" (3.1.143) to compromise with "general ignorance" (3.1.145), without whose "yea [or] no" (3.1.144) it cannot reach decisions, forces the regime to neglect "[r]eal necessities" and to yield, instead, to "unstable slightness" (3.1.146, 147). The need to compromise prevents the regime from having resolute or substantial actions. Thus, summing up (and quibbling on the word "purpose"), Coriolanus proclaims, "Purpose so barr'd, it follows / Nothing is done to purpose" (3.1.147–48). Sound policy thus thwarted, nothing serious is accomplished. A city without a single, noble end is a city without significant purpose.

Coriolanus concludes with a peroration (3.1.148–60). As in epideictic oratory, a peroration in deliberative speech stirs the listeners' passion, sums up, and amplifies.[20] "Therefore beseech you—," Coriolanus begins, appealing to the patricians' spirited pride by describing the patricians themselves,

> You that will be less fearful than discreet,
> That love the fundamental part of the state
> More than you doubt the change on't; that prefer
> A noble life before a long, and wish
> To jump a body with a dangerous physic
> That's sure of death without it—
>
> (3.1.148–54)

Coriolanus, speaking in intensifying comparisons and in a manner reminiscent of his successful attempt to shame the soldiers in the field (1.6.67–75), appeals to those who wish to be less timid than wise, who love the Senate more than fear changes to protect it, who prefer a noble life to a long life, and who are willing to risk a dangerous cure to save an otherwise incurable body. Amplifying, Coriolanus finally says what the senators should do, which until now he has only implied: "[A]t once pluck out / The multitudinous tongue" (3.1.154–55). The Senate should abolish the tribunate, because the people, enjoying the taste of power, will only want more, and that will be their (and Rome's) undoing ("let them not lick / The sweet which is their poison" [3.1.155–56]). Then, presenting the advantageous as the honorable, the prudent as the decorous, Coriolanus calls for the Senate to preserve or restore justice and integrity in the name of what is becoming. "Your dishonour / Mangles true judgement," he says, referring to the just order of the city;

> and bereaves the state
> Of that integrity which should becom't,
> Not having the power to do the good it would
> For th'ill which doth control't.

> (3.1.156–60)

Identifying the Senate with the Roman state and hence with Rome itself (as he does four times in the speech [3.1.117, 122, 150, 157]), Coriolanus calls for the same integrity from Rome that he claims for himself. Like himself, Rome should be only one thing. Aristocratic justice should rule; virtue alone should be rewarded. So long as anything but virtue governs, Rome lacks the power to do the good that it wishes to do.

"'Has said enough," Brutus declares (3.1.160). Brutus means that Coriolanus has gone too far, that he has said "[e]nough, with over-measure" (3.1.139). But, wittingly or not, he also indicates that Coriolanus has said enough to serve the tribunes' purpose. That purpose, however, has changed. Originally, the tribunes sought to have the people reverse their vote. Their goal was to deny Coriolanus the consulate. Now, Sicinius charges Coriolanus with speaking like a traitor and promises to bring him to trial: "'Has spoke like a traitor, and shall answer / As traitors do" (3.1.161–62). Coriolanus's election, which turned into his campaign to revoke the people's suffrage, has now turned into his trial for treason. In their first exercise of their power, the tribunes go beyond the right of veto (3.1.144) and usurp a plebeian prerogative of prosecuting a patrician on political charges. Early in the scene, Coriolanus suspected the tribunes of plotting to block his election in order to increase their power (3.1.37–40). But, like the tribunate itself, their newest power is the product of chance or accident. Ironically, Coriolanus's attempt to abolish their office has handed the tribunes their opportunity. In one sense, however, Coriolanus seems correct. Although he mistook the tribunes' attempt to defend their power (see 2.2.219–21) for their attempt to expand it, only a thin line separates the two. As with Rome itself (see, e.g., 1.1.222–50; 3.1.1–20), it is hard to distinguish between the tribunes' defense and their offense, their self-protection and their self-aggrandizement. Given the competitiveness and constant flux of Roman politics, one cannot keep what one has in Coriolanus's Rome without pushing for more.

Coriolanus, cursing Sicinius as vehemently as he can, execrates him with overpowering contempt: "Thou wretch, despite o'erwhelm thee!" (3.1.162). Coriolanus speaks as though the contempt itself should destroy Sicinius; the thought alone should produce the effect. Then, dropping his trope, he resumes and concludes his peroration. "In a rebellion, / When what's not meet, but what must be, was law, / Then they were chosen," he states (3.1.165–67). This is the first time Coriolanus has acknowledged that the establishment of the tribunate was not mere foolishness, but a concession to necessity. However, he no sooner distinguishes between "what's . . . meet" and "what must be"—between what is becoming and what is necessary—than he collapses the distinction. "In a better hour," he urges, playing on the word "meet," "Let what is meet be said it must be meet, / And throw their power i'th'dust" (3.1.167–69). What is becoming ("meet") is what must be done ("meet"). Necessity, rather than impede what is becoming, must require it. Integrity— the unity of pure principle and political action—must prevail.

Although he hates "promise breakers" (1.8.1–2), Coriolanus shows no concern about the Senate's breaking its word to the people. Unlike a promise, which, because it is freely given, involves one's honor, an agreement made under duress may be broken without dishonor. Just as courage requires that men fight not from the necessity to defend themselves but from the willingness to die, so, likewise, honor attaches not to agreements made by necessity but to ones made willingly. This may be the reason Coriolanus acknowledges, here for the first time, that instituting the tribunate was a concession to constraint.

With Brutus's cry of "Manifest Treason!" (3.1.170), Rome's ever-simmering civil strife boils over into an incipient street battle. This is the only such battle we see. A similar battle was averted at the start of the play. The tribunes, who, as Menenius said, "can do very little alone" (2.1.34), call upon the aediles[21] and "a rabble of Plebeians" (s.d. 3.1.178) for help. The nobles, however, are divided. Menenius, Cominius, and the First Senator seek peace, but Coriolanus and the Second Senator want to stand and fight ("Weapons, weapons, weapons!" [3.1.183]). Sicinius, speaking in the name of the people and with the authority of his office, demands Coriolanus's arrest and perhaps his punishment ("answer") "as a traitorous innovator, / A foe to th'public weal" (3.1.173–74). The tribunate, although only very recently established, is already defended as the old, while the defender of the old is attacked as an innovator. If the tribunes' earlier ambitions coincided with changing the regime, their present ambition coincides with maintaining it.[22] Having new interests they fear to lose, the tribunes defend the status quo against innovation, while masking their own innovations as the preservation of the old.

Sicinius will soon call the tribunes' prosecution of a patrician an "old prerogative" (3.3.17).

Sicinius, who was the first to accuse Coriolanus of being a traitor (3.1.161–62) and whom Plutarch calls "the cruelest and stoutest of the Tribunes" (Plutarch, *Coriolanus*, 18.4; North, 2:164), plainly outdoes his colleague in fanning the flames. Once he orders the aedile to call them, Sicinius speaks for the people expressly in his own name ("in whose name myself . . ." [3.1.172]), and Brutus does little more than second him. While Brutus continues to use only plural first-person pronouns (3.1.199, 206[twice], 207[twice], 209), Sicinius, beginning with his emphatic "in whose name myself," shifts entirely to singular first-person pronouns (3.1.172, 175, 190). He always implicitly distinguishes himself from his colleague and explicitly identifies himself with the people. Thus, proclaiming that he himself arrests Coriolanus in the people's name, Sicinius orders him to obey: "Obey I charge thee, / And follow to thine answer" (3.1.174–75). Where Coriolanus complained that the people, depending upon the tribunes, no longer obey the Senate (3.1.163–65), Sicinius, backed by the people, demands that Coriolanus obey him. And just as he commands Coriolanus, Sicinius, compounding the insolence, addresses him with familiar personal pronouns: ". . . in whose name myself / Attach thee . . . / . . . Obey I charge thee, / And follow to thine answer" (3.1.172–75). This is the only time any commoner addresses a noble in this fashion. When Menenius asks for more respect on both sides, Sicinius declares to the people and the aediles, "Here's he that would take from you all your power" (3.1.180). And when Menenius, alarmed by the growing prospect of battle ("Confusion's near" [3.1.188]), appeals to Coriolanus for patience and to "good Sicinius" (3.1.190) to speak to the people, Sicinius, omitting the surname "Coriolanus" that honors the deeds meriting the consulate,[23] only repeats his charge. "You are at point to lose your liberties," he warns; "Martius would have all from you, Martius / Whom late you have nam'd for consul" (3.1.192–94). Menenius is "out of breath" and "cannot speak" (3.1.187, 188) in more than one sense. No longer able to speak directly to the people, he must speak to them through the tribunes, and Sicinius, as Menenius says, seeks "to kindle, not to quench" (3.1.195) the political fire.

The First Senator warns that Sicinius's incitement is the way "[t]o unbuild the city and to lay all flat" (3.1.196). And Cominius, echoing him, warns that it is the way "to lay the city flat, / To bring the roof to the foundation, / And bury all which yet distinctly ranges" in a heap of ruins (3.1.202–4). To the patricians, Rome consists, at once, in its political order and its buildings. Hence, the city is reflected in its architectural structure, combining its hierarchical and physical forms.[24] Indeed, Volumnia went so far as to describe her fondest political wishes as "the buildings of [her] fancy" (2.1.198). Sicinius, however, only further inciting the crowd, denies that Rome is anything but the people: "What is the city but the people?" And the people answer, "True, / The people are the city" (3.1.197–98). To the people, Rome consists not of classes arranged in a definite order, but solely of the people themselves.

Ignoring the warnings, Sicinius passes sentence on Coriolanus: "This deserves death" (3.1.205). And when Brutus supports him, Sicinius orders the punishment carried out right away: "Therefore lay hold of him. / Bear him to th'rock Tarpeian, and from thence / Into destruction cast him" (3.1.210–12). Menenius, trying to coax Sicinius ("Be that you seem, truly your country's friend" [3.1.216]), urges him to "temp'rately proceed to what [he] would / Thus violently redress" (3.1.217–18). But Sicinius spurns his plea: "Sir, those cold ways, / That seem like prudent helps, are very poisonous / Where the disease is violent" (3.1.218–20). Just as Coriolanus proposed a extreme remedy to cure the sick and dying body politic ("To jump a body with a dangerous physic / That's sure of death without it" [3.1.153–54]), Sicinius, rejecting temperance, demands a violent remedy to cure the body politic's violent disease. Where Coriolanus sees the tribunate as the people's "poison" (3.1.156), Sicinius sees temperance in dealing with him as "very poisonous." The people's poison would destroy the Senate; Coriolanus's would destroy the tribunate.

When Coriolanus, sword drawn, beats back all of those trying to arrest him, forcing the tribunes, aediles, and people to leave, all the nobles, including the Second Senator, who had urged resorting to weapons (3.1.183), try to convince him to go home rather than to stand and fight. Others, they say, should try to settle things. Coriolanus, wanting to stay and fight, says that the nobles can win ("Stand fast. / We have as many friends as enemies" [3.1.229–30]). Unlike Menenius ("Shall it be put to that?") and the First Senator ("The gods forbid" [3.1.231]), he is not horrified by the prospect of civil war in Rome, if only because he does not regard the commoners as Romans. Sicinius and the people identified the city with the people. Coriolanus, in contrast, denies that they are any part of the city: "I would they were barbarians—as they are, / Though in Rome litter'd; not Romans—as they are not, / Though calv'd i'th'porch o'th'Capitol" (3.1.236–38). Not everyone born in Rome is a Roman. Like the word "man," "Roman" is a term of distinction. It refers to a certain type of human—a man with the sort of virtue the city claims to honor. The people are therefore no more Roman than the animals littered in Rome.[25] In Coriolanus's view, it is virtue, not birth, that determines who is a citizen.

Menenius repeatedly attempts to persuade Coriolanus to go home. Saying that all will be lost if he stays (3.1.228–29, 231), he tries to soften Sicinius's offense by spreading it to the patricians, in general. Coriolanus should leave the offense to others to cure, he says, "For 'tis a sore upon us / You cannot tent yourself" (3.1.233–34). By depersonalizing the affront, Menenius hopes to diminish Coriolanus's rage and persuade him to allow others to answer it. When Coriolanus, however, instead of leaving, denies that the people are Romans (and therefore, he implies, may be attacked without wrongdoing), Menenius, shifting grounds, praises his rage but, asking for his silence ("Be gone! / Put not your worthy rage into your tongue" [3.1.238–39]), assures him that another time will make up for the present: "One time will owe another" (3.1.240). Coriolanus will get his deserved satisfaction at some future time. Coriolanus, nevertheless, still does not go. Rather than show any willingness to wait, he replies that in a fair fight he could beat any large number ("forty" [3.1.241]) of the commoners. Menenius, apparently much at a loss, tries to dampen Coriolanus's thirst for immediate revenge by making fun of his own martial prowess, vowing, with self-depreciating humor, that he could take on "a brace o'th'best of them; yea, the two tribunes" (3.1.242).

What humor is to Menenius, prudence is to Cominius. Cominius, who a short while ago tried but failed to lead Coriolanus away (3.1.235), attempts to temper him by subordinating courage to prudence, as he had done with his own troops in battle (1.6.1–3). "But now 'tis odds beyond arithmetic," he admonishes Coriolanus; "And manhood is call'd foolery when it stands / Against a falling fabric" (3.1.243–45). Courage is not courage if it is completely divorced from self-interest. Braving death is irrational ("beyond arithmetic") and sheer folly if it wholly disregards one's own ordinary welfare. And while Menenius feared Coriolanus's rage ("Put not your worthy rage into your tongue"), Cominius fears the people's:

> Will you hence
> Before the tag return? Whose rage doth rend
> Like interrupted waters, and o'erbear
> What they are us'd to bear?
>
> (3.1.245–48)

Cominius likens the people's rage to turbulent waters which burst the banks that usually contain them. Enraged, the people will find courage and strength and will overwhelm ("o'erbear") the nobles whom they usually endure ("bear"). Far from defeating the plebeians, Coriolanus's continued presence will only strengthen them.

With Coriolanus now silent, Menenius, again telling him to leave, says that he will try to use his "old wit . . . / With those that have but little," adding that "this must be patch'd / With cloth of any colour" (3.1.249–51). The combined appeals finally succeed in convincing Coriolanus to leave with Cominius. Although it is not yet clear what Menenius has in mind, it is clear he thinks that, under the circumstances, Coriolanus's sense of his honor directly conflicts with Rome's good. The one rejects, the other requires, compromise.

3.

Between Coriolanus's exit with Cominius and the tribunes' return with the people, Menenius describes Coriolanus's spirited character. A combination of impatience and admiration, his words answer a patrician's reproach that "[t]his man hath marr'd his fortune" (3.1.252). What Cominius and he at least implicitly criticized just a moment ago, Menenius now seems to praise, even as he impatiently wishes to moderate it (see 3.1.260–61). "His nature is too noble for the world" (3.1.253). Although the world requires concessions to necessity, Coriolanus regards only the noble as good. In effect a moral idealist, he has no concern for prudence or calculation. Menenius particularly emphasizes the two sides of Coriolanus's speech—his refusal to flatter anyone for favors, not even "Neptune for his trident, / Or Jove for's power to thunder" (3.1.254–55), and his saying whatever he thinks: "His heart's his mouth: / What his breast forges, that his tongue must vent" (3.1.255–56). What makes Coriolanus independent of what even the gods might give also allows everyone to read what is in his heart. As we have seen, his pursuit of self-sufficiency leaves him largely transparent.[26] "And being angry, does forget that ever / He heard the name of death" (3.1.257–58). Coriolanus's anger knows no fear. Seeking victory or vengeance at all costs, it is indifferent to death. Menenius thus appears to say more than he intends. What he initially praises as a "nature . . . too noble for the world" is, he seems inadvertently to concede, a nature that acts not for the sake of the noble, but for the sake of punishing what opposes it. As Coriolanus himself seemed to admit (1.9.84), his courage is wrath. What Coriolanus wishes to be his self-sufficiency is, in truth, his desire to overcome that which is other than himself. The core of his self-affirmation is negation.

4.

The tribunes, entering "*with the rabble*" (s.d. 3.1.261), return not to negotiate, but to demand Coriolanus's arrest. Coriolanus confined the word "Roman" to warriors. Sicinius understands the implication of that limitation: "Where is this viper / That would depopulate the city and / Be every man himself?" (3.1.261–63). Coriolanus will not be satisfied until the only Roman citizens

are warriors like himself, which ultimately means that he alone would constitute the citizen body. The aristocratic principle in its absolute form would destroy the city that gives rise to it. Sicinius thus characterizes Coriolanus as a
viper. Vipers, according to an ancient tradition, gnaw through the bowels of
their mothers. They kill their mothers in being born.[27]

Despite or, more likely, because of Sicinius's angry demand, Menenius,
though having just cursed them and the people ("I would they were in Tiber!"
[3.1.260]), greets the tribunes with a greater degree of respect than he has ever
shown them before: "You worthy tribunes—" (3.1.263).[28] Sicinius, however,
ignores the overture and, repeating that Coriolanus is to be summarily thrown
from the Tarpeian rock, explains that Coriolanus has resisted the law and
therefore has lost the protection of the law. "[L]aw shall scorn him further trial
/ Than the severity of the public power, / Which he so sets at naught"
(3.1.266–68). Coriolanus is to be punished, without benefit of a trial, by the
power of the people, which he has spurned. While the process is to match the
crime, the punishment is to belie the affront. It will demonstrate the people's
power. The First Citizen, somehow expecting Coriolanus to learn from his
death to fear or respect those he scorns, unites the tribunes—now "[t]he noble tribunes"—and the people in a single body: "He shall well know / The noble tribunes are the people's mouths / And we their hands" (3.1.268–70). Two
parts of the same body, the tribunes and the people serve each other. While
the Citizen seems to think that the division of labor is clear—the tribunes are
the people's mouths, and the people are the tribunes' hands—what he actually describes is that the tribunes, in speaking for the people, tell them what
to do with their hands.

Menenius and Sicinius trade warnings, couched in legal terminology.
Menenius first warns, "Do not cry havoc where you should but hunt / With
modest warrant" (3.1.272–73). Sicinius does not have the proper authority
to kill indiscriminately. Sicinius then warns, in turn, "Sir, how comes't that
you / Have holp to make this rescue?" (3.1.273–74). "Rescue," as a term of
law, is the forcible freeing of a person from an arrest or legal custody.[29] Where
Sicinius is exceeding his legal authority, Menenius is aiding an escaped prisoner. Menenius, demanding to be heard, evidently intends to describe both
Coriolanus's "worthiness" and his "faults" (3.1.275, 276), using the former to
explain and extenuate the latter. However, perhaps testing the resistance, he
gets off to a troubled start by twice referring to Coriolanus as "the consul"
(3.1.275, 277), an identification which the tribunes and the people immediately and emphatically reject ("Consul! What consul?"; "He consul!"; "No,
no, no, no, no" [3.1.276, 277–78]). The crowd's rejection of the title is even
more thorough than it initially appears. Menenius's reference to "[t]he con-

sul Coriolanus" is the last time anyone ever refers to him as holding the title (cf. 3.2.135; 3.3.59; 4.6.35; 5.6.28).

When Menenius, addressing the people directly for the first time since the establishment of the tribunate, asks both them and the tribunes for the chance to speak, Sicinius tells him to speak briefly, "[f]or we are peremptory to dispatch / This viperous traitor" (3.1.283–84). But although he wants Menenius to be brief, Sicinius himself says too much. He explains that he has a political necessity for killing Coriolanus:

> To eject him hence
> Were but our danger, and to keep him here
> Our certain death. Therefore it is decreed
> He dies tonight.
>
> (3.1.284–87)

Neither Coriolanus's exile from Rome nor his remaining in the city is safe for the tribunes. Therefore, they have no choice but to kill him.

Menenius, as he tried to awe the people into pious submission at the start of the play (1.1.64–77), tries to shame the tribunes into sparing Coriolanus by linking gratitude to the gods:

> Now the good gods forbid
> That our renowned Rome, whose gratitude
> Towards her deserved children is enroll'd
> In Jove's own book, like an unnatural dam
> Should now eat up her own!
>
> (3.1.287–91)

If Sicinius sees Coriolanus as a son killing his mother (3.1.261–63), Menenius sees Rome as a mother killing her son. Ingratitude is not only monstrous (2.3.9–10); it is unnatural and impious. For Rome to kill her deserving son is an act against Jove as well as against nature. Sicinius, unimpressed and adopting Coriolanus's own frequent metaphor, replies that Coriolanus is "a disease that must be cut away" (3.1.292). Menenius tries to weaken Sicinius's metaphor by distinguishing between Coriolanus and the disease: "Oh, he's a limb that has but a disease: / Mortal, to cut it off; to cure it, easy" (3.1.293–94). Then, asking what Coriolanus has done to deserve death, Menenius recounts "the blood he hath lost . . . / . . . for his country" (3.1.296–98), which, he says, is more than he has left: "And what is left, to lose it by his country / Were to us all that do't and suffer it / A brand to th'end o'th'world" (3.1.299–301). For Coriolanus to lose his remaining blood at the hands of his country, after losing so much blood in fighting for it, would be to condemn all the Romans to endless infamy.

Like his attempt to awe the people, Menenius's attempt to shame the tribunes fails. To Sicinius, Menenius's words are completely beside the point ("clean kam" [3.1.301]). To Brutus, echoing him, they are "[m]erely awry" (3.1.302). Brutus adds that when Coriolanus loved his country, it honored him. And Sicinius, evidently encouraged by Menenius's tacit concession that Coriolanus is the cause of city's sore, extends his medical metaphor, stating the converse: "The service of the foot, / Being once gangren'd, is not then respected / For what before it was" (3.1.303–5). Rome honored Coriolanus when he served it and will kill him now that he no longer serves it. Past service secures no present consideration or gratitude.

When Brutus, attempting to end the discussion ("We'll hear no more" [3.1.305]), urges the crowd to go to Coriolanus's house and draw him out, "[l]est his infection, being of catching nature, / Spread further" (3.1.307–8), Menenius makes a new effort to stop or at least to slow the tribunes. Instead of trying to shame them, he now warns of the danger of civil war unless they proceed by law: "Proceed by process. / Lest parties, as he is belov'd, break out / And sack great Rome with Romans" (3.1.311–13). Sicinius thought that the tribunes' only safe course was to kill Coriolanus. Menenius points out that Coriolanus is not alone, that he has friends who would make war against his killers. Violence will lead to further violence, only this time against the tribunes.

With perhaps their first display of genuine indignation, the tribunes, avoiding the question of civil war, angrily blame Coriolanus for disobeying them: "Have we not had a taste of his obedience? / Our aediles smote? ourselves resisted? Come" (3.1.315–16). Just as the people took offense at Coriolanus's mocking them to their faces when he solicited their votes (2.3.156ff.), the tribunes take offense at his resisting their authority to their faces when they tried to arrest him. The indignity of witnessing the affront to themselves increases it. Menenius therefore apologizes for Coriolanus's behavior. Blaming the offense on his lifelong warlike breeding (". . . he has been bred i'th'wars / Since a could draw a sword"), he implicitly denies that Coriolanus intended to offend: ". . . and is ill-school'd / In bolted language; meal and bran together / He throws without distinction" (3.1.317–20). As the one unwitting citizen had said, "'[T]is his kind of speech" (2.3.159; also 1.1.40–41). Not done to dishonor the tribunes, the behavior is not an insult because it was not meant to be one. Without the intention there is no affront.

Menenius promises to bring Coriolanus to trial, even if that means his facing the chance of capital punishment: "Where he shall answer by a lawful

form— / In peace—to his utmost peril" (3.1.322–23). And after the First
Senator, flattering the tribunes as "[n]oble tribunes" (3.1.323), combines hu-
mane considerations with the tribunes' advantage, the tribunes accept the
offer, their sense of dignity restored and their self-interest protected—or, perhaps more accurately, their indignation replaced by fear. Sicinius even goes
so far as to deputize "[n]oble Menenius / . . . as the people's officer"
(3.1.326–27). Menenius and the Senator seem to have persuaded the tribunes of the need to "proceed by process." The "lawful form" may only mask
popular violence, but the appearance of the lawfulness of the punishment is
vital. The elimination of enemies or the purging of popular anger against individuals is more safely achieved through public justice than through private
violence. While private violence is unending, with each violent act provoking retaliation, criminal justice has settled steps and stops, namely indict-
ments, verdicts, and punishments. In the absence of legal process, the aggrieved are angry at the perceived injustice and fear for their lives and
property. They naturally seek allies to help defend themselves and to get revenge for the offense. As Menenius cautioned, the implacable partisanship
ultimately divides the city into not merely hostile but warring parties. And
the need for allies in the resulting civil war may force the weaker party to
seek the support of the city's enemies (see 4.3.31–33)[30]—as Coriolanus himself will do. And so this course, as the Senator remarks, "[w]ill prove too
bloody, and the end of it / Unknown to the beginning" (3.1.325–26).

While the tribunes see the advantage of the color of law for what
amounts to a lynching, we must wonder what Menenius is thinking. When
Sicinius, who wants the people not to go home but to meet in the marketplace, warns that, if Coriolanus fails to return there, the tribunes will proceed in their original way, Menenius, affirming that he will bring him, tells
the other senators, "He must come, / Or what is worst will follow"
(3.1.332–33). But how does he think the trial will end? Menenius may be
hoping that Coriolanus's willingness to be tried by the people will resolve
the dispute. His very willingness might appease them, for it would imply
that he accepts their authority over his life and death. As Livy writes, with
the prospect of Coriolanus standing trial, the people's "furious anger was
suppressed. For now every man saw that he was himself to be the judge and
lord of his enemy's life and death" (Livy, 2.35; Holland, 55). Or, as Plutarch
puts it, the moderate senators thought that "when the people should see
that they had authority of life and death in their hands, they would not be
so cruel and fierce, but gentle and civil" (Plutarch, *Coriolanus*, 19.3; North,
2:166). The gesture itself might acquit Coriolanus. On the other hand, it is
not clear that all the senators share Menenius's hope. When warning of civil

war, Menenius suggested that Coriolanus is "belov'd" by all the senators, but, in fact, one patrician seems already to have abandoned him ("This man has marr'd his fortune" [3.1.252]). In the view of some senators, Livy explains, the people were so hateful toward Coriolanus "that there was no other remedy, but one man must pay for it, to save and excuse the rest of the nobles" (Livy, 2.35; Holland, 55). By sacrificing Coriolanus, the nobles could deflect the popular fury away from themselves as a class by focusing it on one of their members, whose own achievements and ambition, in any case, may be a threat to all of them. The gods may forbid Rome's eating up her deserving children, but some nobles might think they can cut their losses and benefit themselves by eliminating a troublesome man of prowess and ambition.

Act Three, Scene Two

1–2.
Coriolanus is defiant. He would rather go to the most horrible death, and take Rome with him ("pull all about mine ears" [3.2.1]), than change his way with the people. Coriolanus, however, cannot understand why his mother, who shares his opinion of the people and by whose words he has always lived, disapproves. For the first time in his life, he cannot do what she wants and still be true to himself. "Why did you wish me milder?" he asks her. "Would you have me / False to my nature? Rather say I play / The man I am" (3.2.14–16). Coriolanus refuses to be false to his nature. He refuses to seem to be other than what he is. Yet, his assertion, though meant to be unequivocal, is tellingly ambiguous. "I play / The man I am" could mean that Coriolanus will play no role at all or that he will play the role of the man he is. Coriolanus, of course, intends the former. Yet, as events show, the man that he is requires him to play a role—to play the role that he plays no role. Volumnia immediately suggests a deception. Expressing her exasperation ("O sir, sir, sir" [3.2.16]—a term of address she uses elsewhere only to Brutus [4.2.37])—she likens power to a suit of clothing: "I would have had you put your power well on / Before you had worn it out" (3.2.17–18). Coriolanus should not have shown the people how he was disposed to them until they no longer had the power to reject him. He should have hidden his inclinations from them, until they had elected him consul. His error was his timing. Urged by her son simply to stop ("Let go" [3.2.18]), Volumnia, echoing his own words to her, attempts to correct him: "You might have been enough the man you are, / With striving less to be so" (3.2.19–20). Had Coriolanus striven less to be the man he is, he would have been enough the man he is.

"[E]nough" would have been enough. Where Coriolanus's standard or end is uncompromised virtue, Volumnia's is public honor.

Menenius, coming to fetch him, tries to make light of what Coriolanus has done and must now do: "Come, come, you have been too rough, something too rough. / You must return and mend it" (3.2.25–26). The First Senator, who, like Menenius, does not mention that Coriolanus faces trial, stresses that the consequence of his refusal would be civil war: "our good city" would "[c]leave in the midst, and perish" (3.2.27–28). Volumnia, however, silent about Rome's welfare, returns instead to Coriolanus's need to act to his own advantage. She has "a heart" as unyielding ("as little apt") as his, "[b]ut," she counsels, "yet a brain that leads my use of anger / To better vantage" (3.2.29–31). Coriolanus does not have to abandon his anger, but merely let his brain, not his heart, govern it so that it serves his interest. He can satisfy his anger, if he dissembles and delays. Menenius, as to be expected, approves ("Well said, noble woman" [3.2.31]) and, in effect apologizing to Coriolanus for his request, explains that, were it not for urgent needs of a convulsed Rome, he would put on his armor and fight to avoid having him stoop to the people. Unlike Volumnia, Menenius speaks of Rome ("the whole state" [3.2.34]), not only of Coriolanus, and avoids encouraging him to believe that he can have his revenge if he waits and is wily. At the same time, he tries to show his good will to Coriolanus by vowing his (conditional) willingness to fight. Just as in the previous scene he tried to check Coriolanus's desire for immediate revenge by (self-mockingly) boasting of his own ability to fight (3.1.241–42), he now tries to assuage his intransigence by speaking of his own willingness to fight. Courage, he tries to suggest, does not foreclose compromise.

When Coriolanus asks what he must do, Menenius answers as briefly as possible: "Return to th'tribunes" (3.2.36). And when Coriolanus impatiently asks, "Well, what then? what then?" (3.2.36), Menenius again replies in the fewest possible words, "Repent what you have spoke" (3.2.37). Coriolanus, however, cannot bring himself to repent to anyone, let alone to the people: "For them? I cannot do it to the gods, / Must I then do't to them?" (3.2.38–39). To repent is not only to accuse oneself to another, but to lower oneself before the other. One humbles oneself doubly in repenting.

Volumnia again reproaches Coriolanus. "You are too absolute," she replies, "Though therein you can never be too noble, / But when extremities speak" (3.2.39–41). By "too absolute," Volumnia means that Coriolanus is too uncompromising: treating virtue as unconditional, he makes no concessions to necessity and allows nothing but virtue to determine his deeds. Volumnia, however, contradicts herself. She says that a person can "never" be "too noble" in being "too absolute," but then she adds the critical exception: except when necessity makes itself felt. The exception cancels the rule; Volumnia's "but" cancels her "though." Rather than rising above necessity, nobility is limited by necessity. Nobility can never be absolute (cf. 3.1.168).

Volumnia wishes to persuade Coriolanus to win by deception what he wants to win by his sword. Fraud is to substitute for force, words for deeds. Volumnia attempts to support her suggestion by assimilating the deception to military action. If "[h]onour and policy" grow together in war "like unsever'd friends," as Coriolanus himself has said, she asks, what then in peace does "each of them by th'other lose / That they combine not there"? (3.2.42, 44–45) What is honorable in war is honorable also in peace. Coriolanus can reply with only inarticulate disparagement: "Tush, tush!" (3.2.45). Pressing her point, Volumnia becomes more explicit and states what she means by "policy." "Policy" means "to seem / The same you are not" (3.2.46–47). "If it be honour in your wars" to deceive "for your best ends," she asks,

> how is it less or worse
> That [policy] shall hold companionship in peace
> With honour, as in war, since that to both
> It stands in like request?

> (3.2.47–51)

Volumnia, tacitly answering her own question, assumes that there is no significant difference between war and peace, that opponents in the city are the same as enemies on the battlefield. What one may honorably do to an enemy in war, one may honorably do to an opponent in peace. Need nullifies the difference ("since that to both / It stands in like request"). Volumnia, ignoring why her son hates promise-breakers (1.8.1–2), overlooks the distinction between intentionally deceiving someone who does not trust you (an enemy in war) and intentionally deceiving someone to whom you have given at least your implicit word of honor (a fellow citizen in peace). The former may dishonor the deceived, but the latter dishonors the deceiver.

Volumnia neglects an opposite sort of difficulty, as well. Rome, we have seen, rests on political deception. Both the nobles and the tribunes deceive the commoners and try to deceive each other. Yet, unlike "great pretenses" in war, which come to light "when / They needs must show themselves" (1.2.20–21), deceptions in politics must remain veiled even after they have worked. Volumnia, however, seems to suppose, as she expressly said earlier, that, having concealed his intention from the people before the election,

Coriolanus could plainly reveal it once "they lack'd power to cross [him]" (3.2.23).[31] She disregards the need for secret victories in domestic politics. Or perhaps she does not so much disregard the need as make a concession to Coriolanus's spirit—her own concession to necessity. Always seeking complete and open victories, Coriolanus could never settle for a partial victory or conceal his true victory over the people. Just as he could not deceive the commoners when soliciting their votes without openly mocking them to their faces (2.3.94–102, 125ff.), he could not win their votes by deceiving them without eventually openly declaring his deception. Pride prevents him from prudently preserving the pretense.

When Coriolanus, still of few words, asks why she urges the similarity of deception and honor in peace and war, Volumnia, telling him that he must speak to the people, distinguishes sharply between what he says and what he means. He must speak to the people, she says, but not according to his own convictions ("by your own instruction" [3.2.53]), nor according to the "prompt[ings]" of his "heart" (3.2.54),

> But with such words that are but roted in
> Your tongue, though but bastards and syllables
> Of no allowance to your bosom's truth.

> (3.2.55–57)

Coriolanus was concerned that not saying to the people what he truly means would make him false to his nature. By being untrue to them, he would be untrue to himself. Volumnia turns his concern around. By lying to the people, Coriolanus would remain true to himself. Words that he does not mean, "[b]ut" are "but roted in / [His] tongue," are "but bastards and syllables." As Volumnia emphasizes with her triple "but," neither legitimate ("bastards") nor even really words ("syllables"), they are spoken merely by rote, and thus in no way acknowledged by his "bosom's truth," and so in no way detract from his honor. Because honor attaches only to words of honor (cf. 1.1.237–38; 1.8.1–2), Coriolanus's intention—his unspoken thought, not his spoken word—is all that counts. Thus, what is politically safe is also morally safe, precisely because it is a lie. So long as Coriolanus does not mean what he says, it is honorable for him to say whatever he must—whatever is expedient. His intention to deceive the people protects his honor and keeps him true to his nature.

Returning to her military analogy, Volumnia says that her suggestion would no more dishonor Coriolanus than his capturing a town with gentle words, which otherwise would cause him to risk fortune and lives. "I would dissemble with my nature," she states, "where / My fortunes and my friends at stake requir'd / I should do so in honour" (3.2.62–64). If her fortunes and friends were at risk, she would pretend to be different from her nature. As a matter of honor, she would be false to her enemies and her nature, in order to be true to her friends and fortunes. Suggesting that she is appealing to a higher kind of honor than being true to one's own nature ("I am in this / Your wife, your son, these senators, the nobles" [3.2.64–65]), Volumnia stresses that Coriolanus's insistence on "frown[ing]" rather than "spend[ing] a fawn" upon the people to win their favor threatens not only his destruction but the "ruin" of his family, class, and Rome itself (3.2.67, 69). However deceitful, policy that safeguards one's family, class, and country is, by definition, honorable. Honor and policy are "unsever'd friends" when one's family, friends, and country are at stake.

While praising Volumnia again ("Noble lady!" [3.2.69]), Menenius, as though encouraged, bids Coriolanus to go to the people and speak courteously, so that he might salve not only "what is dangerous present," but also "the loss / Of what is past" (3.2.71–72). By the latter, Menenius plainly means the consulship. By the former, he leaves uncertain whether he means civil war, Coriolanus's threatened life, or both.

Unlike when, campaigning for votes, he told the people that he would flatter them and then mockingly did so (2.3.94–96, 98–100), Coriolanus must now say what he knows is untrue but make it seem to be true. Volumnia therefore gives him a lesson in conciliatory rhetoric. Coriolanus should say to the people (much as Menenius already tried [3.1.317–20]) that he is their soldier who, bred in battles, lacks "the soft way" which, he does "confess, / Were fit for [him] to use, as they to claim," in his asking for their "good loves," but he will make himself truly ("forsooth") "hereafter theirs, so far / As [he] hast power and person" (3.2.82–86). Coriolanus, in other words, is to apologize, admit that the people were right and promise to do to the fullest extent of his ability whatever they wish in the future. Most of all, since what makes an affront an affront is that another should dare to affront one, he should deny his intention to offend them (see 1.1.40–41; 2.3.159).

Coriolanus is to humble himself not only by his words, however, but especially by his gestures.[32] Volumnia, demonstrating the gestures by her own actions (3.2.74, 78; cf. 1.3.32), emphasizes that Coriolanus is to go hat-in-hand, kneel on the ground, and bow his head to correct his proud heart. "Action is eloquence, and the eyes of th'ignorant / More learned than the ears" (3.2.76–77). As Coriolanus himself has suggested (2.3.94–102), while the people care most about intention, they are fooled by gestures, which they take to reflect the speaker's true heart. The people care most about what they cannot see and determine it by what they can see. Judging the inside by the outside, they make the most superficial part of oratory, and the part closest to playacting, the most powerful part and place it above speaking itself. It seems no accident that Volumnia, though a Roman matron, speaks with apparent coarseness ("bussing" [3.2.75] rather than "kissing"), uses a homey comparison ("Now humble as the ripest mulberry / That will not hold the handling" [3.2.79–80]), employs loose grammar, and confounds speech and deed. She mimics popular speech while demonstrating popular gestures.

After Menenius underscores how easy Coriolanus's tactical apology will be—the people will gladly give their pardons for a few trifling words requesting them—Volumnia, thinking that she is bringing the matter to an end, lets an important truth slip out: "Go, and be rul'd" (3.2.90). To win power in Rome, Coriolanus must be ruled.[33] Volumnia means that he should rule himself; his brain rather than his heart should rule his anger (3.2.29–31). But if Coriolanus must rule himself in this way, he must do so only because, in order to be elected in Rome, he must let himself be ruled by the people. Just as he must submit his anger to his brain and not to his heart, so, in the first place, he must submit his heart to the people's wishes. To rule the people, he must allow the people to rule him, as he himself has already protested to his mother (2.1.200–2). At least in a republic, ruling is inseparable from being ruled.[34]

4.

Cominius enters with the troubling news that "[a]ll's in anger" in the marketplace (3.2.95). Sicinius and Brutus have evidently been at work there (see 3.1.328–29). Cominius says that Coriolanus must "make strong party, or defend [him]self / By calmness or by absence" (3.2.94–95). Menenius, who assured the tribunes that he would bring Coriolanus to the marketplace, gives no consideration to his going with a strong party or remaining absent: "Only fair speech" (3.2.96). And when Cominius agrees that fair speech will serve "if [Coriolanus] / Can thereto frame his spirit" (3.2.96–97), Volumnia states flatly, "He must, and will" (3.2.97). Coriolanus, who has been uncharacteristically at a loss for words since his mother's initial admonishment (3.2.16–18),[35] has not spoken for nearly fifty lines. His last words were to ask Volumnia why she urged the similarity of deception and honor in war and peace (3.2.51). His silence may have misled her and Menenius, who may have taken it as compliance. Thus Volumnia, continuing, turns to Coriolanus and says, "Prithee now, say you will, and go about it" (3.2.97–98). She speaks with at least as much peremptoriness as prayer.

Volumnia instructed Coriolanus on what he must do and say—his gestures and his speech. Coriolanus, speaking again, responds to each, in turn. "Must

I go show them my unbarb'd sconce?" (3.2.99). To show his bare head to another is to show his deference or respect. "Must I / With my base tongue give to my noble heart / A lie that it must bear?" (3.2.100–1). Like Volumnia, Coriolanus distinguishes sharply between his heart and his tongue, but he inverts the two. As when he could not make his heart consent to take a bribe to pay his sword (1.9.36–38; also 1.9.28–29), he implicitly divides himself and speaks of himself as one thing and his heart as another. Must he ("I"), with his tongue ("my base tongue"), give to his heart ("my noble heart") a lie that it cannot bear? Coriolanus, while identifying himself with his tongue, uses a synecdoche to refer to himself by a part ("my noble heart"), which he separates and projects from himself, and personifies as if it were a separate being. As on the earlier occasion, he identifies himself with his soul's potentially ignoble party, while placing the virtuous party—his noble heart— outside himself. He maintains his heart's nobility by isolating it from the party that might succumb to his ignoble demand.

Unlike when he refused the reward, however, Coriolanus abruptly, if reluctantly, reverses himself. "Well, I will do't," he suddenly declares; "Yet were there but this single plot to lose, / This mould of Martius, they to dust should grind it / And throw't against the wind" (3.2.101–4).

Whereas his identifying himself with the potentially corrupt party was meant to indicate his soul's noble singleness, Coriolanus, seeing that he has no one else's support, recognizes that he is not single in another sense. He has ties to others, and so his actions are conditioned by their effects on others. This is the only time Coriolanus refers to himself by his patronym in Rome.

But even as he agrees, Coriolanus, reverting to the language of the theater, says that he will fail as an actor: "To th'market-place! / You have put me now to such a part which never / I shall discharge to th'life" (3.2.104–6). Coriolanus will never perform his part convincingly. His acting will never be lifelike. Cominius therefore promises to coach his performance: "Come, come, we'll prompt you" (3.2.106). With the help of others, Coriolanus will be able to convince the people that he is the man he is not. Volumnia, tacitly acknowledging her power over him, responds to his apparent acquiescence by promising her "sweet son" new praise:

> [A]s thou hast said
> My praises made thee first a soldier, so,
> To have my praise for this, perform a part
> Thou hast not done before.
>
> (3.2.107–10)

As he initially acted in battle to win his mother's praise (1.1.37–38), so he should now act his part to do the same.

Resigned to acting the part ("Well, I must do't" [3.2.110]), Coriolanus describes the performance as his emasculation and degradation. Where Volumnia talked of his performing a new part, he speaks of his acquiring a new spirit: "Away my disposition, and possess me / Some harlot's spirit!" (3.2.111–12). He, not simply his part, must change. Thus, transforming himself into his contrary, Coriolanus calls for his "throat of war" to be turned into the high, soft voices of "a eunuch" and "the virgin" who lulls babies to sleep (3.2.112, 114; cf. 1.4.56–61; 1.6.25–27). The manly is to become unmanned. Then, with two incongruous military metaphors, Coriolanus bids the smiles of knaves to encamp ("tent" [3.2.116]) in his cheeks and the tears of a schoolboy to occupy ("take up" [3.2.116]) his eyes. The hard is become soft. And, finally, Coriolanus asks for "[a] beggar's tongue" to move through his lips and "[his] arm'd knees," which have "bow'd but in [his] stirrup," to bend like a beggar's who has received an alms (3.2.117–20). The independent is to become dependent, the noble is to become base. Coriolanus is to become everything he despises, the loathsome opposite of his true self. Yet, Coriolanus distances himself from responsibility for the change. Instead of telling what he will do, he tells what will happen to him. He will be passive, as he underscores not only by calling upon some harlot's spirit to possess him, but by speaking in the optative (via the subjunctive[36]), expressing nothing more than wishes which have been forced upon him. Not he, but necessity, will act.

Coriolanus, however, suddenly reverses himself, again. He will not play the part, he says, "Lest I surcease to honour mine own truth, / And by my body's action teach my mind / A most inherent baseness" (3.2.121–23). Coriolanus cannot separate the performer from the performance. He must respect what he truly is ("honour mine own truth") in order to maintain what he truly is. A body's base actions—even mere gestures—teach the mind "[a] most inherent baseness." They corrupt the soul, making it inherently base. Coriolanus therefore cannot dissemble without destroying his virtue and dishonoring himself. He must be himself or else lose himself. Volumnia may wish to separate his mind and heart from his tongue and gestures, but, for Coriolanus, whose own surname, suitably, identifies the doer and the deed, what he says and does is inseparable from what or who he is. He is what he does.[37]

Volumnia, showing lost patience ("At thy choice then" [3.2.123]), attempts to shame her son. In defending his own honor, she says, he dishonors her, for it is more a dishonor for her to beg of him than for him to beg of the people. Then, calling for "all [to come] to ruin" (3.2.125), she declares or threatens that she—"[t]hy mother" (3.2.126)—would rather suffer his pride's fatal effects than live in fear of confronting his obstinacy, "for I mock at death / With as big a heart as thou" (3.2.127–28). His failure to yield will bring about her death. Finally, telling Coriolanus, again, to do as he wants ("Do as thou list" [3.2.128]), Volumnia distinguishes between the sources of his courage and of his pride: "Thy valiantness was mine, thou suck'st it from me, / But owe thy pride thyself" (3.2.129–30). While Coriolanus owes his noble courage to his mother, she disowns his stubborn pride. To the extent that he is valiant he is her son; to the extent that he is obstinate he is not hers. Volumnia speaks as if what she has nurtured in him has no connection to what he has become.

Coriolanus, yet again, reverses himself. Asking Volumnia to stop chiding him, he promises to go to the marketplace and trick ("mountebank" [3.2.132]) the people of their loves, cheat ("[c]log" [3.2.133]) them of their hearts, and come home consul, loved by all the trades in Rome, "[o]r never trust to what my tongue can do / I'th'way of flattery further" (3.2.136–37). He will do everything he can to flatter the people. Volumnia leaves without acknowledging his decision. "Do your will," she says curtly (3.2.137) and exits.

5.

Cominius, who warned of dangers in the marketplace, now urges Coriolanus to be ready to answer "mildly" (3.2.139). The tribunes, he says, are preparing stronger accusations than the original ones. Although this is the first that anyone has suggested to Coriolanus that he will be facing trial, he seems unsurprised and unperturbed. "The word is 'mildly,'" he repeats. "Pray you, let us go. / Let them accuse me by invention: I / Will answer in mine honour" (3.2.142–44). Menenius, of course, recognizes the tension between Coriolanus's answering mildly and his answering in his honor. "Ay, but mildly," he insists (3.2.144). And Coriolanus promises, "Well, mildly be it then. Mildly!" (3.2.145). Mildness is the hallmark of conciliatory rhetoric.[38]

Act Three, Scene Three

1.

Brutus and Sicinius, in the marketplace, are plotting their tactics. Brutus says that Sicinius should be ready to bring three charges against Coriolanus: that he seeks tyrannical power, that he hates the people, and that he kept the spoils of the war. The first charge, based on Coriolanus's call to remove the tribunate, is supported by his harsh, undisguised pride, which the people see as tantamount to the ambition for tyrannical power. If that charge fails ("If he evade us there, . . ." [3.3.2]), the second is to be substituted for the first. And if that fails, the third is to replace the second. The third charge seems entirely trumped up (cf. 1.1.41–42; 1.9.37–30, 2.2.124–29). The weakest of the three, it is also the one which is most likely to incense Coriolanus—in no small measure because it is fabricated. By provoking his fury, it will arouse the people's fear of him and prove him guilty in their eyes of the first charge, which is the one that really counts ("In this point charge him home . . ." [3.3.1]). Their fear, aroused by his wrath, will convict him of aiming at tyrannical power.

When an aedile enters, Brutus asks him whether Coriolanus will come—something that evidently cannot be taken for granted, notwithstanding Sicinius's threat (3.1.329–31)—and who is accompanying him. The tribunes are presumably relieved to hear that only "old Menenius, and those senators / That always favour'd him," (3.3.7–8) are with him. "[T]he young Nobility of Rome" (s.d. 4.1.1), who will accompany Coriolanus to Rome's gate after his banishment and may have been with him at the beginning of scene 2 (see s.d. 3.2.1), are not with him now (see also s.d. 3.3.30).

The tribunes are careful to have the voters "collected . . . by tribes" (3.3.11). As noted earlier, Roman elections are not decided by a simple majority. Rather, votes are cast in designated groups, with a majority of individual votes determining each group's vote and a majority of the groups deciding the election. There are, however, alternative ways to group voters—by centuries and by tribes. The one is aristocratic, the other democratic. Centuries are based on military rank, while tribes (from which the word "tribune" is derived) are based on residence. As a result, whereas assembly by centuries gives property owners predominance—a clear majority of 98 of the 193 centuries—assembly by tribe gives control to the poor.[39]

When the aedile reports that he has collected the voters by tribe, Sicinius instructs him that the people are to take their cue from him, Sicinius: "[W]hen they hear me say . . . / . . . death, . . . fine, or banishment, then let them / If I say fine, cry 'Fine,' if death, cry 'Death'" (3.3.13–16). There is no question of Coriolanus's guilt, only of his punishment. And as Sicinius is to claim to speak "[i]'th'right and strength o'th'commons," the people, echoing his call with their cries, are to "[i]nsist . . . on the old prerogative / And power i'th'truth o'th'cause" (3.3.14, 17–18). One might think that Sicinius means the "strength" that lies in the political "right" of the commoners and the "power" that lies in the "truth" of their cause. But when the aedile says that he will inform the people to listen for Sicinius's prompting, Brutus emphasizes, and Sicinius repeats, that once the people have begun to cry out, "Let them not cease, but with a din confus'd / Enforce the present execution / Of what we chance to sentence" (3.3.20–22). The people's "strength" or "power" lies not in their "right" or in the "truth" of their cause, but in their sheer numbers. Accordingly, afraid that the nobles will seek a delay when Coriolanus's punishment is announced, the tribunes want the punishment carried out immediately ("the present execution") so their strength does not slip away.

Alone again, the tribunes continue to discuss their tactics. The crucial step, Brutus says, is to get Coriolanus angry right away ("Put him to choler straight" [3.3.25]), for "he hath been us'd / Ever to conquer, and to have his worth / Of contradiction" (3.3.25–27). Coriolanus fully opposes what opposes him and measures himself against the opposition that he can overcome. Having his fill ("worth") of opposition, he knows his own merit ("worth") by what he can vanquish. Coriolanus can therefore be easily manipulated, Brutus suggests. Having no natural end beyond its own victory and thus lacking a specific object, his spirit—or its manifestation as anger—can be transferred from one object to another without his awareness, by the manipulation of those who cross him. Although spirit seeks to command, its negativity and reactivity hand control to others. Thus, once Coriolanus becomes angry ("Being once chaf'd"),

> he cannot
> Be rein'd again to temperance; then he speaks
> What's in his heart, and that is there which looks
> With us to break his neck.
>
> (3.3.27–30)

Unable to rule himself because of his anger, he can readily be ruled by those who arouse it. The tribunes need only give the cue and Coriolanus will say what is in his heart, and what is in his heart will break his neck.

2.

While Brutus urges putting Coriolanus to "choler," Menenius, entering with Coriolanus, urges him to speak "[c]almly" (3.3.31). With undisguised sarcasm, Coriolanus speaks of his own meekness—of how like a stable-keeper he will endure repeated insults for the most worthless coin—and then, with a mock prayer, of civil peace in Rome. "Th'honour'd gods / Keep Rome in safety," he derisively prays;

> and the chairs of justice
> Supplied with worthy men, plant love among's,
> Throng our large temples with the shows of peace
> And not our streets with war.

> (3.3.33–37)

Prevented from saying what he thinks, Coriolanus resorts to sarcasm. Sarcasm is his compromise with caution. Blaming under the guise of praising, it allows Coriolanus to say what he thinks without saying it, by using words that say exactly the opposite of what he means.[40] Not surprisingly, in mocking civil peace, Coriolanus speaks as though Rome's "safety" depends wholly upon love and peace among the citizens. Utterly silent about the danger of foreign enemies, he mentions the danger of war only in the city itself. Despite or perhaps because of his sarcasm, the First Senator and Menenius both solemnly ratify his words: "Amen, amen"; "A noble wish" (3.3.37–38). Coriolanus is performing his appointed part.

Coriolanus asks the tribunes whether he will be "charge'd no further than this present. / Must all determine here?" (3.3.42–43). Sicinius, although ready to bring new charges (3.2.138–41; 3.3.1–5, 77), says that the present will determine all if Coriolanus agrees to meet three conditions. He must submit himself to the people's votes, acknowledge the tribunes' authority and accept his lawful punishment for the charges proven against him. When Coriolanus, however reluctantly, agrees ("I am content" [3.3.47]), Menenius, seizing upon his agreement to smooth things over ("Lo, citizens, he says he is content" [3.3.48]), calls upon the citizens to consider his "warlike service" and to "think / Upon the wounds his body bears, which show / Like graves i'th'holy churchyard" (3.3.49–51; cf. 2.2.154–55), and then explains his "rougher accents" (3.3.55) as his speaking like a soldier. Menenius's attempt—the first time since the establishment of the tribunate when he speaks directly to the people while ignoring the tribunes (cf. 3.1.279)—has the opposite of his intended effect, as Cominius sees coming ("Well, well, no more" [3.3.57]). In response to Menenius's praise, Coriolanus, once again, belittles his wounds in a way that magnifies his martial virtue: "Scratches with briers, / Scars to move laughter only" (3.3.51–52). Then, in response to Menenius's explanation, Coriolanus, evidently offended by the need to justify his behavior to the people, angrily demands that they explain theirs. As though forgetting who is on trial, he becomes the accuser; the people, the defendant. "What is the matter," he demands, "That being pass'd for consul with full voice, / I am so dishonour'd that the very hour / You take it off again?" (3.3.58–61). Although he has never acknowledged their election as an honor, Coriolanus denounces the people's reversal as a dishonor. Earlier, he referred to the Senate's concessions to the plebeians as the patricians' dishonor (3.1.156). Never before has he mentioned his own.

Sicinius, ordering Coriolanus to "[a]nswer to us" (3.3.61), delivers a truncated forensic oration. Dispensing with the *exordium* (since he already has his listeners attention and good will), he begins with the narrative, setting forth his first charge:

> We charge you, that you have contriv'd to take
> From Rome all season'd office, and to wind
> Yourself into a power tyrannical;
> For which you are a traitor to the people.
>
> (3.3.63–66)

Just as he called the people's appropriated power to punish patricians their "old prerogative," Sicinius now calls his new office "all season'd," by which he seems to mean not only settled by time but aged to perfection.[41] And, as when accusing Coriolanus of being a "traitorous innovator," he tacitly identifies the people with the city (cf. 3.1.173, 197–98). A traitor to the people is a traitor to Rome. As though to underscore that the people and the city are one, this is the first time either tribune mentions Rome by name.

Sicinius's charge of treason has its designed effect. Incensed by the charge of betrayal ("How? Traitor?" [3.3.67]), Coriolanus vehemently curses the people and their tribunes: "The fires i'th'lowest hell fold in the people! / Call me their traitor! Thou injurious tribune!" (3.3.68–69). His promise forgotten ("Nay, temperately: Your promise!" [3.3.67]), Coriolanus, outraged at the false charge of his own falseness, responds with full fury, not caring that it might mean his death:

> Within thine eyes sat twenty thousand deaths,
> In thy hands clutch'd as many millions, in
> Thy lying tongue both numbers, I would say
> "Thou liest" unto thee, with a voice as free
> As I do pray the gods.
>
> (3.3.70–74)

No fear could keep him from openly accusing his lying accusers.

Sicinius, turning quickly to his speech's proof, gets more than he bargained for. Trying to offer evidence and to incite the people, he asks, "Mark you this, people?" (3.3.74). And the people, not waiting for their cue, cry,

"To th'rock, to th'rock with him" (3.3.75). Ironically, the people are not al-ways as easily led or controlled as the tribunes would like.

Calling for "[p]eace" (3.3.76) and saying that they need not bring fresh charges, Sicinius, continuing his evidence, reminds the people of Cori-olanus's offenses against them—what they have seen him do and heard him say: "Beating your officers, cursing yourselves, / Opposing laws with strokes, and here defying / Those whose great power must try him" (3.3.79–81). This defiance, Sicinius states, is a crime that "[d]eserves th'extremest death" (3.3.83). But Brutus, apparently remembering Menenius's warning, immedi-ately suggests that Coriolanus get something else, ostensibly in gratitude for his service to Rome ("But since he hath / Serv'd well for Rome—" [3.3.83–84]). Coriolanus, however, wants no forbearance or favor. He wants nothing that the people can give him. Nor does he fear losing anything that they might take from him. Expressly disregarding his promise to his mother (3.3.86–87), he declares that no matter how horrible the punishment the people pronounce, he would not "buy / Their mercy at the price of one fair word" or "check [his] courage for what they can give, / To have't with saying, 'Good morrow'" (3.3.90–93). Nothing will restrain Coriolanus, who, once more, considers candor as equivalent to courage. Under such circumstances, even the most common courtesy amounts to cowardice.

Sicinius, turning to his peroration and affecting the language of law, an-swers Coriolanus's outburst by recapitulating and amplifying his charge, fur-ther provoking the people. Coriolanus has, he says, "[a]s much as in him lies, from time to time," shown malice to the people, sought to take away their power, and even now "[g]iven hostile strokes, and that not [only] in the pres-ence / Of dreaded justice, but on the ministers / That doth distribute it" (3.3.94, 97–99). Coriolanus has attacked the dignity of the officers as well as of the office. Then, delivering the verdict, Sicinius, "in the name o'th'peo-ple, / And in the power of us the tribunes" (3.3.99–100), finds Coriolanus guilty and banishes him from Rome, "our city" (3.3.101), "never more / To enter our Rome gates" (3.3.103–4). While Sicinius speaks in the name of the people ("I'th'people's name, / I say it shall be so" [3.3.104–5]), the people, fol-lowing their initial instructions ("[W]hen they hear me say, 'It shall be so . . .'" [3.3.13]), repeat his words: "It shall be so, it shall be so! Let him away! / He's banish'd, and it shall be so!" (3.3.106–7). Tractableness replacing their recent unruliness, they will repeat such repetition thrice more (3.3.119, 136–38, 142). The people's ostensible mouthpiece literally puts words in their mouths. The people speak for him, while he pretends to speak for them. In his sarcastic prayer for public peace, Coriolanus asked the gods to keep Rome's "chairs of justice / Supplied with worthy men" (3.3.34–35). Sicinius, as though demonstrating Coriolanus's suppressed thought, claims that title for the tribunes themselves. The tribunes are the ministers who distribute dreaded justice in Rome. Sicinius, accordingly, speaks of "our Rome" and "our city." If the tribunes mention Rome for the first time when accusing Coriolanus, they speak of "our Rome" when announcing his punishment. This is the only time either tribune (or any plebeian) speaks this way. The commoners speak of "our Rome" only when banishing its hero.[42]

Menenius is silent. Ever since mistakenly praising and explaining him— in effect, apologizing for him (3.3.48–51, 52–57)—he has spoken only to Coriolanus, briefly twice, to remind him of his promise to his mother (3.3.67, 86). He will not say another word in the scene.

Cominius, however, sounding much like the flattering Menenius when he originally addressed the people ("Hear me, my masters, and my common friends!" [3.3.108; cf. 1.1.61; also 1.1.64, 126]), tries to intercede. Sicinius, however, wants no delay: "He's sentenc'd: no more hearing" (3.3.109). The punishment is final and to be carried out right away. Cominius, nevertheless, persists in trying to appeal directly to the people. As though delivering an ex- ordium to his own forensic oration, he prefaces what he has to say with a dec- laration of his good will not only to the judges, his "masters, and . . . com- mon friends," but to Rome itself. No other Roman states his love of Rome more completely than Cominius does here. While saying that he has been consul and can show Rome's enemies' marks upon his body, he declares that he loves his country's good "with a respect more tender, / More holy and pro- found" than his own life, his dear wife's honor or reputation ("estimate"), and their cherished children ("her womb's increase / And treasure of my loins" [3.3.112–15]). Cominius subordinates every private good of his to the good of Rome. His love for his country overrides his love of what is purely his own. Before he gets to deliver the main body of his speech, however, the tribunes cut him off. And when Brutus repeats the sentence of banishment, adding the imperative "It shall be so!", the people respond with their incantatory, imperative cry: "It shall be so, it shall be so!" (3.3.119). The "popular 'shall'" is, indeed, an "absolute 'shall,'" a "peremptory 'shall'" (3.1.89, 93, 105).

Banished from Rome by the tribunes and the people, Coriolanus banishes the people and the city. He begins his parting execration by combining two senses of "cry": "You common cry of curs!" (3.3.120). The people are, at once, a pack of dogs and the bark of dogs. They are, as Brutus had accused Cori- olanus of thinking, "of no more voice / Than dogs that are . . . [kept] for bark- ing" (2.3.213–14). Their political "voice" is nothing more than the cry of beasts. Moreover, that cry is "common," also, in two senses. It is base and sounded in unison. Nothing properly human distinguishes the people. Coriolanus, having lowered the people to a bestial, unisonant cry, describes them as literally and figuratively stinking. Just as they are reducible to their votes ("voices"), their votes are indistinguishable from their nauseating "stinking breaths" (2.1.234):

> [You] whose breath I hate
> As reek o'th'rotten fens, whose loves I prize
> As the dead carcasses of unburied men
> That do corrupt my air.
>
> (3.3.120–23)

Coriolanus, speaking in hyperbolic comparisons and stark antithesis, combines sensory and spirited, physical and moral, disgust. Just as he hates the people's "breath" as he hates the putrid vapor of rotting marshes, so he prizes their honors ("loves") as he prizes the stench of the most disgusting human mortal decay— "the dead carcasses of unburied men." As we saw earlier, his soul's revulsion at mortal decay, particularly human decay, underlies his moral revulsion at the people.

Disgusted by them, Coriolanus banishes his banishers: "I banish you!" (3.3.123). Hurling his banishers' words back upon them, he, in effect, "de-populate[s] the city and / Be[comes] every man himself" (3.1.262–63). A part of the city becomes the whole city. Coriolanus, then, pronounces a curse upon his banishers. The curse is equally an invocation and prediction of evil: the people, left to themselves, are consigned by their own nature to their own destruction. In punishing Coriolanus, they will punish themselves. "And here remain with your uncertainty!" Coriolanus begins; "Let every feeble rumour shake your hearts! / Your enemies, with nodding of their plumes, / Fan you into despair!" (3.3.124–27). But while every slight rumor will terrify them and every slight movement of their enemies will fill the people with despair, their fear of great warriors will lead them to banish all of their defenders until they are captured without a fight:

> Have the power still
> To banish your defenders, till at length
> Your ignorance—which finds not till it feels,
> Making but reservation of yourselves,
> Still your own foes—deliver you as most
> Abated captives to some nation
> That won you without blows!
>
> (3.3.127–33)

Lacking prudence as well as courage (cf. 1.1.169–71), the people have no foresight. Wholly taken up with the present, they recognize only immediate threats—only ones whose consequences they already feel. And incapable of judging what may be by what has been, they banish their defenders one by one, leaving unbanished only themselves, always their own worst enemy. In "[their] ignorance," they know neither their real friends nor their real foes, their real dangers nor their real needs.

"Despising / For you the city, thus I turn my back" (3.3.133–34). With a parting gesture of utter contempt, Coriolanus declares that he despises the city on account of the people. We must wonder, though, whether he says more than he intends. He intends to say that he despises not only the people but Rome as a whole, because of the people. If the people have power, the city cannot be noble. But, knowingly or otherwise, Coriolanus, at bottom, despises not only the people and Rome, but "the city," that is, political life, as such. What he imagines to be his conflict with the people and hence with Rome is, ultimately, his conflict with political life in any form. It is a conflict with everything which heroic virtue tries to rise above, but which, nevertheless, makes that virtue possible. It is Coriolanus's conflict with the very conditions of his virtue.

Accordingly, turning his back on the city, Coriolanus declares decisively but equivocally, "There is a world elsewhere" (3.3.135). Where in the world is that world? Coriolanus, who may already be thinking of going to Antium, will soon show that he means a city other than Rome. Notwithstanding his tenuous ties to Rome or to any city, to Coriolanus "a world elsewhere" is a city elsewhere. In order to satisfy Coriolanus, though, that city would have to be entirely unlike Rome, Antium, or any real city. It would have to honor heroic virtue, but without either fearing or envying it, thus rewarding its greatest heroes with the unsolicited honors they deserve, while sparing them the need to acknowledge that they desire the honors they disdain. More generally, it would have be a city in which virtue alone is rewarded, virtue rules non-virtue, necessity receives no concessions, and fortune has no role in human affairs. Governed by the aristocratic principle in its pure or absolute form, "elsewhere" would, in fact, be nowhere.

Coriolanus's enemies are exultant. "The people's enemy is gone, is gone!" a victorious aedile shouts (3.3.136). And the people, again repeating what they hear, throw up their caps and shout, "Our enemy is banish'd! He is gone! Hoo! hoo!" (3.3.137). Sicinius, however, wants more. He wants to mortify Coriolanus still further. The people are to "[g]o see him out at gates" (3.3.138) and with all contempt ("with all despite" [3.3.139]) give him his "deserv'd vexation" (3.3.140). Giving him what he gave them, they are to torment their tormentor. This is an indignity Coriolanus will not forget (see 4.5.78–79; also 4.6.130–37). Despite his aggressiveness, however, Sicinius is concerned for the tribunes: "Let a guard / Attend us through the city" (3.3.140–41). Banishing Coriolanus may be safer for the tribunes than killing him, but it nonetheless may not be safe. Coriolanus still has friends in the city, and, besides, he has not yet left. The people, once more echoing Sicinius, gladly agree to follow and hoot Coriolanus out of Rome: "Come, come, let's see him out at gates!" (3.3.142). On one point, however, they do not simply echo him. What Sicinius thinks he needs bodyguards to do, the people, as though corroborating Coriolanus's curse of them, trust to the gods: "The gods preserve our noble tribunes!" (3.3.143).

Notes

1. Cantor, 76.
2. Aristotle, *Nicomachean Ethics*, 1149a25–b3.
3. Quintilian, 3.8.6.
4. Cicero, *De partitione oratoria*, 28; *De inventione*, 1.20.
5. Cicero, *De inventione*, 1.20–25; Anonymous, 3.7.
6. Cicero, *De oratore*, 2.80; *De inventione*, 1.27.
7. Cicero, *De oratore*, 2.80, 326; *De inventione*, 1.28–29; *Topica*, 97.
8. Aristotle, *Rhetoric*, 1358b21–26, 1375b3–4, 1417b35–37; Cicero, *De oratore*, 2.334; *De inventione*, 2.156–69; Anonymous, 3.7; Quintilian, 3.8.22.
9. The pun is the first of many disease images in the scene. See, e.g., 3.1.77–79, 86–87, 152–56, 160, 177, 219–20, 233–34, 292–94, 304–5, 307–8. Although disease images are found throughout the play, they are particularly concentrated in 3.1.
10. Cicero, *De inventione*, 1.31–33.
11. Cicero, *De inventione*, 1.34.
12. Aristotle, *Rhetoric*, 1368a29–31.
13. Aristotle, *Rhetoric*, 1356b2–5; *Posterior Analytics*, 71a9–11.
14. Aristotle, *Prior Analytics*, 69a16–19.
15. Aristotle, *Rhetoric*, 1393a25–b8.
16. Aristotle, *Rhetoric*, 1394a7–8.
17. Livy, 2.32–33; Plutarch, *Coriolanus*, 6–7.1.
18. See Plutarch, *Coriolanus*, 16.3.
19. Shakespeare leaves uncertain when the corn was granted gratis (cf. 3.1.42, 113, 124 with 1.1.9–10) and whether the shortage of grain was caused by the patricians' hoarding, as the people charged (1.1.9–24, 78–85), or by a bad harvest, as Menenius tried to suggest (1.1.71–73).
20. Anonymous, 2.47, 3.9; Cicero, *De inventione*, 1.98; Quintilian, 6.1.
21. Aediles are plebeians who assist the tribunes. Their office was established at the same time as the tribunate. See Dionysius of Halicarnassus, 6.90.2.

22. Cantor, 61–62.

23. Lee Bliss, *Coriolanus*, New Cambridge Shakespeare (Cambridge: Cambridge University Press, 2000), 190.

24. See also 4.2.39–42; 4.6.83, 86–88; 5.1.14–17; and note 4.4.1; 4.5.5. For the Romans' attachment to the physical city, see, e.g., Varro, 5.143; Dionysius of Halicarnassus, 1.88; Livy, 1.6.3; 1.73; Ovid, *Fasti*, 4.819ff.; Plutarch, *Romulus*, 10. Plutarch writes that the Romans consider not only the Senate but the city's walls and land sacred and inviolable, so that men "may fight valiantly and die generously in defense of them." Plutarch, *Roman Questions*, 27; tr. Philemon Holland (1603), *The Philosophy Commonly Called the Morals* (London: J. Kirton, 1657), 859.

25. Cantor, 81.

26. Cf. Menenius's self-concealing claim about his own open-hearted transparency, 2.1.52–56.

27. Pliny, 10.82.

28. The closest to showing respect occurred earlier in the scene when, with the people and the aediles trying to seize Coriolanus, Menenius implored "good Sicinius" to speak to them (3.1.190). That was also the only time he ever calls either tribune by name.

29. *OED*, s.v. Rescue, n. 2a.

30. See Machiavelli, *Discourses*, 1.7.1–2, where he discusses Coriolanus; also Coby, 60.

31. Cantor, 87.

32. For the importance of gestures in public speaking, see Cicero, *De Oratore*, 3.233; Anonymous, 3.19, 26–27; Quintilian, 11.3.65ff.

33. Cantor, 87–88.

34. It is thus not flattery alone that prompts the tribunes, who are themselves called "Masters of the people" (2.2.51, 77), to call the people their "masters" (2.3.153; 3.2.228; 4.6.150). See also 1.1.61; 3.3.108; 4.6.154; 5.6.131, 133.

35. Since then, he has had just one speech as long as two lines (3.2.38–29) and six of half a line or less (3.2.18, 23, 35, 36, 45, 51).

36. Abbott, §365.

37. "Shakespeare is using at this moment the language of the Schools. It is the only time in his whole *oeuvre* that he uses the word *inherent*." D. J. Gordon, "Name and Fame: Shakespeare's *Coriolanus*," in *The Renaissance Imagination*, ed. Stephen Orgel (Berkeley: University of California Press, 1975), 214.

38. Cicero, *De oratore*, 2.211–12.

39. Plutarch, *Coriolanus*, 20.2. See also Cicero, *Republic*, 2.39; Livy, 1.43; Dionysius of Halicarnassus, 4.16ff.

40. Quintilian, 8.6.57.

41. See Furness, 380–81, and *OED*, s.v. Seasoned, a, 3b.

42. Although "Rome" is mentioned ninety times in the play and "Roman[s]" another twenty-three, the plebeians hardly ever mention either. Apart from the tribunes, who do so only three times each, including thrice in this scene (3.3.64, 84, 104;

4.6.36; 5.1.41, 46), a soldier mentions Rome once, when looting Corioles (1.5.1), all the people once, when, in ritual fashion, they echo the Herald's welcoming Coriolanus back to Rome (2.2.166), and an aedile once, when reporting war news (4.6.40). Cominius, however, puts the phrase "[o]ur Rome" in the mouths of the tribunes when they purportedly say the opposite of what they mean (1.9.9). While Brutus mentions the "[common]weal" once and "the state" twice (2.3.176, 179, 180) and Sicinius mentions "th'public weal" and "the commonwealth" once each (3.1.174; 4.6.14), the tribunes and the other commoners mention "country" nine times, but, with a single telling exception, never as their own country, but always as Coriolanus's or Menenius's (1.1.30, 37; 2.3.87, 105–6, 162, 234; 3.1.302; 3.3.118; 4.2.30; 5.1.36). The exception ("our countryman" [5.1.38]) will be part of Sicinius's desperate attempt to persuade Menenius to plead with Coriolanus to spare Rome. The tribunes also refer to the Roman noblewomen as "[o]ur veil'd dames" (2.1.213) and to Rome's water as "our best water" (2.3.240). Except perhaps for Sicinius, the commoners, having just acquired their first political office, do not seem to regard themselves, yet, fully as Romans.

ACT FOUR

~

Act Four, Scene One

Scene one reverses the first scene of act two. There, Coriolanus entered Rome in triumph (2.1.161ff); here, he is banished in shame. There, his family and friends were joyous, while the widows and mothers without sons in Corioles were in tears (2.1.158, 177–78); here, his family and friends are in tears (4.1.1, 22–23, 54). And, there, Roman crowds thronged to see him, as though he were a god (2.1.203–19, 260–66); here, only a handful of Romans say farewell, while "[t]he beast / With many heads butts [him] away" (4.1.1–2).

Apart from Menenius and Cominius, the older, more moderate nobles— "the most ancient senators and such as were given to favor the common people" (Plutarch, *Coriolanus*, 19.3; North, 2:165–66)—are absent, while "*the young Nobility of Rome*" (s.d. 4.1.1)—"the lustiest young gentlemen, whose minds were nobly bent, as those that came of noble race, . . . [and in whom Coriolanus] stirred up . . . a noble emulation of honor and valiantness" (Plutarch, *Coriolanus*, 15.5; North 2:160)—are present. Although he is present, Menenius remains silent, in tears, until nearly the end of the scene.

Coriolanus, appearing fully composed, tries to comfort his mother. Calling her to show her "ancient courage" (4.1.3), he reminds her of what she used to say to him of the circumstances which allow one to demonstrate nobility. Nobility offers distinction only because it is difficult. In order to prove one's nobility, one must face extreme difficulties, for while "common chances common men [can] bear" (4.1.5), "extremities [are] the trier of spirits" (4.1.4), and "fortune's blows, / When most struck home, being gentle wounded, craves / A noble cunning" (4.1.7–9). Coriolanus has spoken of constancy and contempt for fortune before. But, unlike now, he has always spoken of them in connection with warlike prowess, not stoic patience (cf. 1.1.237–38; 1.4.44).

Although he scorned the people for "sigh[ing] forth proverbs" (1.1.204) to voice their complaints, Coriolanus credits Volumnia's precepts for making his heart invincible: "You were us'd to load me, / With precepts that would make invincible / The heart that conn'd them" (4.1.9–11). Precepts resemble proverbs. Both offer general truths about human affairs, which listeners learn largely by heart. And, learned by repetition, they are often spoken in clusters. For example, when quoting both the people's proverbs in mockery and his mother's precepts in approval, Coriolanus recites several (four) different ones for a single thought (1.1.205–7; 4.1.4–9), as Aufidius will do when speaking for himself (4.7.54–55). And, in all the instances, the sayings are simple. Seemingly self-evident in themselves, they are statements or conclusions without arguments.[1] Variations on a repeated theme or story, such sayings derive their power from the directness of their effects on the passions or sensibilities of the Romans.[2] Despite their similarity, however, precepts and proverbs differ. As Coriolanus's contrasting judgments indicate, their difference reflects the difference between the city's two classes. While proverbs are commonplaces in more than one sense—common sayings of common men—and express in general terms homey truths that the listener already believes in his own case and enjoys hearing stated in general, precepts are intended to exhibit the speaker's wisdom and authority and prescribe a moral duty, as Coriolanus emphasizes here.[3] Proverbs gratify commoners; precepts guide nobles. Coriolanus, reared, like some other great Romans, not so much at his mother's breast as by her speech,[4] frequently echoes her words[5] and cites her sayings.[6] Her education of him was an education to courage via shame (cf. 3.3.108). Although courage itself may not be teachable through speech alone,[7] shame—the concealment of our presumed defectiveness—is. And as a spirited fear of disrepute in the opinion of someone we honor or revere, it can form a courageous heart by spurring us to surpass ourselves.[8] If homey platitudes can articulate the thought of the ignorant, spirited words can inspire noble action in the souls of the spirited.

When Volumnia calls for a curse upon all the crafts and trades of Rome, Coriolanus reassures her, "I shall be lov'd when I am lack'd" (4.1.15). Hated when he is present, he will be loved when he is absent. When at war, the people will want the same martial qualities they fear when at peace. Coriolanus, again referring to her accustomed words, exhorts Volumnia to resume her Herculean spirit:

> Resume that spirit when you were wont to say,
> If you had been the wife of Hercules,
> Six of his labours you'd have done, and sav'd
> Your husband so much sweat.

> (4.1.16–19)

Coriolanus does not remind Volumnia that one of those labors was Hercules's slaying the many-headed Hydra[9] or that Hercules's wife, Deianira, inadvertently caused his death.[10] Bidding his mother and wife farewell, Coriolanus vows, "I'll do well yet" (4.1.21), though he does not say what he intends to do. Menenius, like the women, is crying. Coriolanus asks Cominius to tell "these sad women" (4.1.25)—and, by implication, Menenius, as well—that "'[t]is fond to wail inevitable strokes, / As 'tis to laugh at 'em" (4.1.26–27). One should neither laugh at nor cry at what is unavoidable. Only what depends on oneself is worthy of laughter or tears (cf. 2.1.175–78). Once more addressing his mother and reminding her that his dangers have always been her delight, Coriolanus assures her again:

> Believ't not lightly, though I go alone,
> Like to a lonely dragon that his fen
> Makes fear'd and talk'd of more than seen, your son
> Will or exceed the common, or be caught
> With cautelous baits and practice.

> (4.1.29–33)

Loved when he is lacked, Coriolanus will be feared when he is unseen. The fear and the love go together. The people will fear Coriolanus, as they fear a never-seen dragon, because they do not see him. They will fear him as the unknown. And because they fear, they will also want him back to defend them. Their fear will prompt their love. Coriolanus urges Volumnia to take his assurance seriously: he will either show his nobility ("exceed the common") or get caught by trickery. He seems to think, as Aufidius had suggested (1.10.15–16), that he is invincible except against craft or deceit. It is hard to know what he has learned. Although he frames his assurance as a sharp antithesis ("or . . . or . . ."), a combination of nobility and trickery caused his banishment from Rome. And both await him in Antium.[11]

Just as he entered Corioles "alone" (1.4.51; 1.8.8; 2.1.161; 2.2.110; 5.6.116), Coriolanus leaves Rome "alone" (4.1.29). His solitary departure often reminds commentators of Aristotle's famous saying that a man without a city is either a beast or a god (Aristotle, *Politics*, 1253a3–4).[12] Man, as a rational animal, has a composite nature. His specific nature combines reason and life. A man, however, who is by nature and not simply by chance without a city is either more than or less than human—having either reason without life, like a god, or life without reason, like a beast. While Coriolanus has frequently been compared both to beasts and to gods,[13] his mention of Hercules only heightens the ambiguity, for Hercules, the most ferocious of heroes,[14] obscures the distinction between the two. Deified by his father, Zeus, for making civil life possible by his labors, Hercules wore the skin of the Nemean lion over his body and head.[15] He was a god or a demigod who appeared as a beast. Like Coriolanus, who seems to take him as his heroic model, he seems at once higher and lower than man. His Herculean labors make possible a way of life that he is not, by nature, fit to share.

Coriolanus says that Volumnia talked of what she would do as Hercules's wife. But Hercules was cityless, and half of his labors were performed at the far reaches of the habitable world or beyond, while for Volumnia there can be no life apart from Rome. To Volumnia, "our country" is "our dear nurse" (5.3.107, 110). To be banished from Rome—"[N]ever more / To enter our Rome gates"—is to be lost forever. Thus, speaking her final words to Coriolanus in Rome, Volumnia asks, "My first son, / Where wilt thou go? (4.1.33–34). By her "first son," she evidently means not only her first- or only-born, but the first or noblest of men. The phrase's ambiguity captures the tension between her son's maternal origin and the virtue she raised him to embody. Thinking that he has no plan, Volumnia desperately suggests that Coriolanus take Cominius with him for awhile to help him determine a course more than wildly exposing himself to whatever chance puts in his way. Cominius readily agrees, though for a different reason. While Volumnia seems concerned about Coriolanus's personal safety, Cominius is thinking of his political return. He offers to go with Coriolanus and help him find a place to live, so that in the future each can hear from the other. That way, he explains, if circumstances change in Rome and "the time thrust forth / A cause for [his] repeal" (4.1.40–41), Coriolanus's friends will know where to find him and not "lose advantage, which doth ever cool / I'th'absence of the needer" (4.1.43–44). Cominius apparently thinks that the Romans would recall Coriolanus if they were pressed by the danger of war, as Coriolanus himself seems to think (see 4.1.15).

Coriolanus, rejecting help, asks everyone—"my sweet wife, my dearest mother, and / My friends of noble touch" (4.1.48–49)—to bid him farewell "and smile" (4.1.50). Paradoxically, by suppressing everything but his consuming desire for revenge, his fury, unlike their sorrow, allows him to appear

free of pain and completely in control of his temper.[16] Although—or because—he is nothing but rage, he seems entirely equanimous. One last time,
Coriolanus gives a general assurance but does not tell what he has in mind:
"While I remain above the ground you shall / Hear from me still, and never
of me aught / But what is like me formerly" (4.1.51–53). But, in addition to
his apparent equanimity, he has already changed. Formerly, Coriolanus
would say whatever was in his heart, particularly when angry. His pride demanded his outspokenness. But, now, even though it stems from his offended
pride, his fury permits the dissembling that his pride previously prevented.
Coriolanus, "vengeance proud" (2.2.5–6), is interested only in getting revenge, and revenge will pay any price for its satisfaction.[17] If his pride prevented his dissimulation, his thirst for revenge prompts it.

When Menenius, finally speaking, praises Coriolanus's vow and declares
that if he were younger he would go with him, Coriolanus ends the scene
with the same word with which he began it: "Give me thy hand. / Come"
(4.1.57–58). Initially, the word was a mild rebuke ("Come, leave your tears"
[4.1.1]). Now, it is an imperative of motion. When Coriolanus returned to
Rome in triumph, he asked for Volumnia's and Virgilia's hands (2.1.192).
Now, leaving in shame and anger, he asks for theirs and Menenius's. He will
repeat this gesture with his mother the next time he sees his family.

Act Four, Scene Two

1.

Although victorious, the tribunes fear their own weakness, as they did at the
end of act 3. They know that the nobility who sided with Coriolanus "are
vex'd" (4.2.2). Afraid to lose what they have gained, they want the people to
go home, as they say three times in seven lines (4.2.1, 5, 7; cf. 2.2.158–60;
2.3.251–52; 3.1.328; 3.3.138–40). Having "shown [their] power," they must
now seem "humbler" (4.2.3, 4) than when they were showing it. The tribunes thus minimize their achievement, even as they boast of it. "Say their
great enemy is gone, and they / Stand in their ancient strength," Sicinius instructs an aedile (4.2.6–7). Notwithstanding their unprecedented action, the
tribunes present their victory as the restoration, not the expansion, of the
people's "ancient" power.

2.

While the tribunes try but are unable to avoid the "mad" (4.2.9) Volumnia,
Volumnia first sarcastically welcomes and curses them ("Oh, y'are well met:
the hoarded plague o'th'gods / Requite your love!" [4.2.11–12]) and then says

both one thing and the reverse ("If that I could for weeping, you should hear— / Nay, and you shall hear some" [4.2.13–14]). This is the only time either Volumnia or Virgilia speaks to the tribunes or to any plebeian. Throughout the exchange, Volumnia, filled with impotent rage, interrupts herself, quickly changes her mind and gives self-contradictory commands (4.2.11–12, 13–14, 22–23, 37–38, 41). At least in Sicinius's view (as he says framing the exchange), she is "mad" in both senses of the word. Enraged, she "wants her wits" (4.2.44).

When Volumnia commands the tribunes to stay, Sicinius contemptuously asks, "Are you mankind?" (4.2.16). Only a man commands men (cf. 3.1.87ff.). Notwithstanding her own Roman view of manliness (1.3.16–18), Volumnia understands the affront differently. She takes "mankind" to refer not only to men, but to human beings, in general: "Ay, fool; is that a shame? Note but this fool. / Was not a man my father?" (4.2.17–18). Volumnia's proof that she is human is that she had a father. To be human is to have a mixed nature—to be born of both a mother and a father. On two occasions, Volumnia calls someone a fool. She does so, here, when speaking of man's mixed origin and nature. And she did so when, comparing Hector and Hecuba, she described a man spilling blood from his head, while contemning the enemy that struck him, as looking lovelier than his mother suckling him (1.3.39–43). A man is human in his birth, but may be manly in his death. How one faces death distinguishes the manly from the human. As Volumnia seemed unwittingly to indicate when she called Coriolanus "[m]y first son" (4.1.33), in rising above the human, the manly warrior ultimately repudiates what he came from. In the end, his noble virtue denies his natural origin and mixed nature.

Unable to act, Volumnia can do little more than curse the tribunes with the wish that Coriolanus or the gods would act (4.2.11–12, 23–27, 44–48). Just as she explicitly contrasts Coriolanus's blows to the tribunes's words (4.2.19–21), she implicitly contrasts his acts to her own words. While she wishes the gods would requite the tribunes' hatred—"love," as she bitterly calls it (4.2.12)—with all their stored vengeance, she wishes Coriolanus were in Arabia, sword in hand, and Sicinius's descendants before him. "He'd make an end of thy posterity, / Bastards and all" (4.2.26–27). If Volumnia's humanity rests on her having a father, her revenge rests on her son's destroying his banisher's progeny.

Accused (with a mixture of sarcasm and direct blame) of having the cunning and ingratitude ("foxship" [4.2.18]) to banish Rome's defender, Sicinius, with utter brazenness, says he wishes that Coriolanus had "continued to his country / As he began" and had "not unknit himself / The noble knot he made" (4.2.30–32). The service that tied Coriolanus to Rome, tied Rome to

Coriolanus in gratitude; by unknitting the one, he unraveled the other. After Brutus echoes Sicinius's "I would he had" (4.2.32), Volumnia indignantly responds to the shameless sham ("'I would he had!' 'Twas you incens'd the rabble" [4.2.33]) and, then, with a pair of hyperbolic comparisons, to the gross presumption. In the first, she declares that the tribunes can "judge as fitly of [Coriolanus's] worth / As [she] can of those mysteries which heaven / Will not have earth to know" (4.2.34–36). Reminiscent of Menenius's original description of the Senate (1.1.64–71), she not only sets Coriolanus as high above the tribunes as the gods, but implicitly denies the possibility of the tribunes making the comparison that she invites between him and them. In the second, she declares that Coriolanus exceeds the tribunes and all his banishers as much as "the Capitol exceed[s] / The meanest house in Rome" (4.2.39–40). Reminiscent of the patricians' analogy of Rome's hierarchical structure to the city's architecture (3.1.196, 202–5), she attempts to make palpable to the tribunes what the first comparison denies they can know. The tribunes, in reply, have nothing but scorn for Volumnia. Leaving with Brutus and the aedile, Sicinius simply dismisses her, to her face, as crazy. "Why stay we to be baited / With one that wants her wits?" (4.2.43–44).

3.

When the tribunes depart, Volumnia makes explicit her futile rage. Able only to voice another sardonic wish ("Take my prayers with you" [4.2.44]), she wishes

> the gods had nothing else to do
> But to confirm my curses! Could I meet 'em
> But once a day, it would unclog my heart
> Of what lies heavy to't.

> (4.2.45–48)

Indignation desires a world in which the bad suffer and the good prosper. But unable to punish the bad or reward the good herself, Volumnia, as before, wishes the gods would do what she cannot. Able only to speak, she wishes the gods would act for her and set things right. Volumnia speaks of the gods more here than in any other scene (4.2.11, 35, 45, 53). Yet, despite her dispiriting frustration, she does not become indignant at their failure to act.

Now that the tribunes have left, Menenius, whose only words so far have been unsuccessful attempts to quiet Volumnia (4.2.12, 29), praises her for her angry words: "You have told them home, / And, by my troth, you have cause" (4.2.48–49). Menenius commends Volumnia for rebuking the tribunes thoroughly, but his praise, lauding her for words which the tribunes dismissed as mad and from which they walked away, only underscores her futility. Accordingly, when Menenius, who has not lost his appetite for food, asks whether she will sup with him, Volumnia replies, "Anger's my meat: I sup upon myself / And so shall starve with feeding" (4.2.50–51). Volumnia sups upon her anger and hence sups upon and starves herself. Anger seeks revenge. But when the revenge is thwarted, the anger, needing an object to punish but prevented from punishing its proper object and hence forced to transfer its vengeful desire to another object, turns upon the person who feels it, eating away at and finally consuming him. Thwarted anger is self-punishing and finally self-consuming.

Volumnia ends the scene urging Virgilia to stop her whimpering and lament, as she does, "[i]n anger, Juno-like" (4.2.53). Juno (Hera), the jealous, spirited wife of endlessly unfaithful Jove (Zeus) (see 5.3.46), is famous for her unrelenting wrath, her fierce anger and implacable heart (Virgil, *Aeneid*, 1.4; 5.781). It seems fitting in more than one respect that Volumnia would compare her anger to Juno's. For not only is Juno the mother of Mars (Hesiod, 923; Ovid, *Fasti*, 5.229–58), the god after whom Martius is named and whom he is said to resemble, but also Juno's anger against Jove, much like Volumnia's against the tribunes, is repeatedly frustrated and consequently turned upon other objects. In particular, Juno (Hera), unable to satisfy her anger against Zeus directly, delayed the birth of his son, Hercules, and thereby condemned Hercules to his twelve labors (Homer, *Iliad*, 19.96–133; Diodorus Siculus, 4.9, 14). Without her frustrated anger, Hercules would have had no labors to perform. The Herculean spirit to which Coriolanus called Volumnia (4.1.16–19) seems to be the consequence as well as the contrary of a female's implacable but impotent anger.

Volumnia refers to Juno twice. The references are paired. In her first words when Coriolanus returned from battle, Volumnia spoke of "the love of Juno" (2.1.100). And, now, in her last words in Rome, when he has been banished, she speaks of her "Juno-like" anger. First in love and then in anger, the mother of Mars frames Volumnia and Coriolanus, mother and son, together, in Rome.

Act Four, Scene Three

Scene three takes place on the road between Rome and Antium, the same road Coriolanus will soon take. Much earlier, Aufidius told of his having a spy in Rome (1.2.6–17). Now, we see a Roman who is spying for the Volscians meeting his Volscian contact: "I am a Roman; and my services are, as you are, against 'em" (4.3.4–5). The Roman's treason follows the charge of treason against Coriolanus and precedes his act of treason against Rome.

Although the pivot on which the two principal parts of *Coriolanus* turn, scene 3 seems in some sense superfluous. The only scene entirely in prose, it does not advance the plot in any ordinary way, and its only characters appear nowhere else and are never again mentioned. The scene thus appears to stand apart from the play as a whole.

A clue to Shakespeare's intention in the scene lies in his names for the two characters. Although he leaves many Roman and Volscian characters anonymous, and although the Folio's stage direction and headings refer simply to "*a Roman and a Volsce*" (s.d. 4.3.1), Shakespeare emphasizes right at the start of the scene the characters' names:

> *Rom.*: [Y]our name I think is Adrian.
> *Vol.*: Nicanor? No?
>
> (4.3.1–2, 6; also 4.3.30)

While the Volscian's name, Adrian, is Latin and refers to an inhabitant of a particular place in Italy (Adria, on the Adriatic coast),[18] the Roman's name, Nicanor, is Greek and means "victory without geographical boundary." Both in language and in meaning, the one name is local, the other cosmopolitan. While the former name implies the distinction between friend and foe, fellow citizen and foreign enemy, the latter name attenuates that fundamental political distinction.

More particularly, Nicanor's name alludes to the life and death of the Athenian general and statesman Phocion, who, "famous . . . for his justice and equity" (Plutarch, *Phocion*, 19.1; North, 5:89), died as a result of his trust in and accommodation with a Macedonian general named Nicanor. In contrast to Coriolanus, whose own education consists in arms, precepts, and praise (e.g., 1.3.55–57; 1.9.13–15; 3.1.317–18; 3.2.81; 4.1.3–11),[19] Phocion "was Plato's scholar and afterwards Xenocrates's scholar in the school of Academia" (Plutarch, *Phocion*, 4.1; North, 5:75). Philosophical in education, he was philosophical in manner or temperament, as well. While a man of austerity and integrity in his private life, he combined candor and kindness in dealing with the people. Like Coriolanus, Phocion "had never done nor said anything to flatter [the people] withal, but commonly had been against their desires" (Plutarch, *Phocion*, 8.2; North, 5:78). But, unlike him, he was "very courteous and gentle [by] nature" and "showed himself marvelous lowly and courteous to everybody" (Plutarch, *Phocion*, 4.1–2, 10.4; North, 5:75, 81). In fact, he was elected general by the people more often than any other Athenian—some forty-five times—even though he never sought the office or campaigned for it (Plutarch, *Phocion*, 8.1). In addition, and perhaps most characteristic, Phocion, "excelling all others in justice" (Aeschines, *On the False Embassy*, 184), disinterestedly defended his enemies against unjust charges in the political attacks waged in the Athenian law courts, while, by the same token, he refused to defend a family member who had been justly charged with a crime (Plutarch, *Phocion*, 10.4–5).

One might suppose that the kind and disinterested Phocion serves as a corrective example for the harsh and spirited Coriolanus. But just as Coriolanus's uncompromising spirit places him at odds with the good of Rome, Phocion's unspirited sense of justice placed him at odds with the good of Athens. Following Alexander the Great's death, Athens became split between one party, led by Phocian, which sought accommodation with Macedonia, and another party, led by Demosthenes, which yearned to restore Athenian democracy, independence, and dominance. With Athens thus deeply divided, the Macedonian garrison in the Piraeus, which Nicanor commanded, became a standing grievance with the people. When Phocion, pressed by the people to persuade the Macedonians to remove the garrison, had the chance but failed to arrest Nicanor, Phocion answered that he trusted the Macedonian and did not think he would harm the city. "[B]ut, if it should fall out otherwise," he added, "he had rather . . . [have] the wrong offered him than that he should offer any" (Plutarch, *Phocion*, 32.6; North, 5:102). Phocion's answer is a striking paraphrase of Socrates's well-known reply to Polus in the *Gorgias* that "if it were necessary either to do or to suffer injustice, I would choose to suffer rather than to do it" (Plato, *Gorgias*, 469c1–2). Even while he subordinated his private good to the public good within the city, Phocion failed to distinguish between the public and the private realm in dealing with the city's enemies. Out of his "Socratic" concern for transpolitical justice, he treated the city's good as he might treat his own. Thus Plutarch remarks,

> This appeared to be nobly spoken in respect of himself. But considering that he, being then General, did hazard the safety of his country, I cannot tell whether he did not break a greater faith which he ought to have had, to the safety of his countrymen.[20]

If Coriolanus, demanding the justice of revenge, makes too sharp a distinction between friend and foe, Phocion, seeking to avoid injustice, made too little of it. Although in opposite ways, both men place their concern for justice or virtue above their concern for their country. In both, virtue attenuates and finally vitiates patriotism.

Notwithstanding their contrasting conduct toward the people, both men also faced similar fates at their hands. Following Phocion's failure to arrest Nicanor, Polyperchon, who was regent for the infant Macedonian king, schemed to take control of Athens by promising to restore democracy and calling upon the Athenian people to exercise their political rights according to their original polity. "This was a wily and crafty fetch against Phocion. For Polyperchon . . . had no hope to obtain his purpose, unless he found means first to banish Phocion" (Plutarch, *Phocion*, 32.2; North, 5:101). Prompted by Polyperchon, a certain demagogue in the assembly "accused [Phocion] of treason" for failing to arrest Nicanor (Plutarch, *Phocion*, 33.3; North, 5:103). Phocian and his allies were put on trial before the people, ostensibly to determine their guilt or innocence, but in reality "not so much to have their causes heard . . . as to have them executed for condemned men" (Plutarch, *Phocion*, 34.1–2; North, 5:102). And with the people "cr[ying] out that such traitors should be stoned to death that favor the authority of a few and are enemies of the people," the defendants' friends were silenced, and the demagogue bringing the charge read his motion, "declaring how [the people] should be judged by voices whether the offenders had deserved death or not" (Plutarch, *Phocion*, 34.4, 5; North, 5:105). Some of the people demanded that Phocion be not only killed but also tortured ("[T]he wheel should be set up to break his joints upon it" [Plutarch, *Phocion*, 35.1; North, 5:105–6; cf. 3.2.1–2]). Condemned to death, "Phocion, looking as cheerful . . . as he was wont to do being general, . . . made many of [his friends] pity him in their hearts to consider his constancy and noble courage, [while] . . . many of his enemies . . . came as near unto him as they could to revile him" (Plutarch, *Phocion*, 36.1–2; North, 5:106). Phocion's gentleness no more protected him from the people's furious giddiness than Coriolanus's harshness protected him.

Aufidius will soon say that "our virtues / Lie in th'interpretation of the time" (4.7.49–50). The stories of both Coriolanus and Phocion seem to confirm his words. He who is loved for his virtue under one set of conditions becomes hated for the same virtue when conditions change. Coriolanus prides himself on the sufficiency of his virtue, the superiority of his virtue to fortune. Yet, in his case, as in Phocion's, fortune proves stronger than virtue.

> [W]hen [fortune] frowns upon any good and virtuous men, her force is so great that, where they deserve honor and favor, she violently heaps false and malicious accusations against them, which makes their virtue lame.[21]

Virtue and fortune may have joined forces in producing the mighty power of Rome, but not in protecting the life and honor of its hero. It thus seems no

surprise that Adrian stresses that his meeting Nicanor on the road is the outcome of fortune: "I am most fortunate, thus accidentally to encounter you"
(4.3.38).

When Nicanor reports that there "hath been" (4.3.13) insurrections in
Rome between the nobles and the people, Adrian seems greatly disappointed by the Roman's use of the present perfect tense: "Hath been! Is it
ended then?" (4.3.16). Adrian makes clear why he dislikes what he hears.
The Volscians, once more, want to take advantage of the strife in Rome,
thinking that the Romans are weak when "in the heat of their division"
(4.3.18–19). Nicanor explains (much as Menenius had warned
[3.1.309–13]) that the nobles take Coriolanus's banishment "so to heart"
(4.3.22) that they are ready to revoke all the people's power and abolish the
tribunate, and so civil war seems imminent. Adrian is, of course, stunned
and gladdened by the news that Coriolanus has been banished. "Coriolanus
banished? . . . You will be welcome with this intelligence, Nicanor"
(4.3.27–30). Besides removing Aufidius's "great opposer" (4.3.35) from battle, Coriolanus's banishment may cause the nobles to seek Volscian support
in an open civil war against the people. "I have heard it said," Nicanor remarks, "the fittest time to corrupt a man's wife is when she's fallen out with
her husband" (4.3.31–33). As we have seen with Coriolanus himself, spite
will do anything to be avenged.

Unlike those he describes, however, Nicanor is traitorous without showing any trace of anger. He is "joyful" (4.3.37) to hear that the Volscians have
a strong army mobilized, ready to attack the Romans. He even takes Adrian's
word of gladness out of his mouth. "You take my part from me, sir," the Volscian tells him. "I have the most cause to be glad of your [company]"
(4.3.51–52). Yet, Nicanor seems wholly removed from Rome's partisan strife,
blaming neither party (see 4.3.14–15), while describing Coriolanus as "worthy Coriolanus" (4.3.22–23). Tellingly, he always refers to the Romans and
the Roman parties in the third person, never in the first (4.3.4–5, 13–15,
21–25). As both the language and the meaning of his Greek name suggests,
his disloyalty may be a matter of cosmopolitan disinterest rather than of pas-
sionate political interest. In more than one sense, Nicanor seems hardly a
Roman. Indeed, although he initially identifies himself as "a Roman" (4.3.4),
he does not return to Rome after delivering his news, and Adrian ambiguously says that he will "accompany [Nicanor] home" to Antium (4.3.39).
Adrian's "home" may or may not be the same as Nicanor's. In the end,
Nicanor points past his Macedonian namesake from whom Phocion would
rather have suffered injustice than to whom he would do it, and, living up to
his name, points instead to Phocion himself.

Act Four, Scene Four

Coriolanus enters Antium "*in mean apparel, disguised and muffled*" (s.d. 4.4.1). Although he resisted wearing the gown of humility or disguising himself in any way in Rome, he not only wears mean apparel, but goes so far as to conceal his face in Antium. He is afraid that he will be recognized in the city to which he has caused so much suffering ("'Tis I that made thy widows" [4.4.2]) and be killed by "wives with spits, and boys with stones" (4.4.5). As when he returned to Rome in triumph (2.1.175–78), Coriolanus emphasizes the harm that he has done to Volscian women and families. Yet, this is the first time that he has shown any fear of being killed. His fear seems not so much for his life, however, as for his vengeance. The widows' and sons' revenge would prevent his own.

After learning that he is standing in front of Aufidius's house, Coriolanus reflects on friendship and enmity, and how each turns into the other. As in his initial soliloquy (2.3.111–23), he shows no self-reflection or attempt at self-understanding. Nowhere in the soliloquy does he appreciate the gravity of his decision to ally himself with Aufidius against Rome. Nor does he indicate even the slightest soul-searching in reaching his decision. On the contrary, although he has always prided himself on his constancy and scorned the people for their inconstancy, he now treats his own change as nothing more than an example of the way the world typically works: "O world, thy slippery turns!" (4.4.12). Far from being something he despises, the lack of constancy in the world now explains and excuses his own. Wholly out of his former character, Coriolanus never in the speech distinguishes himself from others. He is just one of many. In Rome, Coriolanus feared that he would come to resemble the part that he played, the humble costume that he wore (3.2.111–23). In Antium, he already has begun to.

Coriolanus begins by describing the closest of friends turning into the bitterest of enemies, in no time at all, over the most trivial matters. As he describes them, the friends are

> now fast sworn,
> Whose double bosoms seems to wear one heart,
> Whose hours, whose bed, whose meal and exercise
> Are still together, who twin, as 'twere, in love
> Unseparable.

> (4.4.12–16)

The friends are two who, in everything, are as though they were one. We might wonder whether Coriolanus has ever had such a friend. Later, he will say that he loved Menenius, who loved him above the measure of a father (5.2.87, 91; 5.3.12). And, earlier, when beseeching Cominius to let him fight Aufidius, he told of their vows of friendship, and later Cominius will speak of their old friendship (1.6.37–38; 5.1.10). But neither of the friendships seems to have the intimacy or the reciprocity that Coriolanus describes. Rather than closeness or mutuality, both friendships seem to rest on the friend's worship of him: "Lov'd me . . . / Nay, godded me indeed" (5.3.10–11). By the same token, the spirited Lartius, the only Roman nobleman Coriolanus clearly respects, has the highest regard for him, but neither of the men ever speaks of his friendship for the other. For Coriolanus, the more spirited the man, the more distant the friendship.[22] Coriolanus then describes how, "within this hour, / On the dissension of a doit, [the friends] break out / To bitterest enemies" (4.4.16–18). Just as he described the friends or their friendship in superlatives, Coriolanus describes the triviality of their dispute, the speed of their reversal and bitterness of their enmity in superlatives. Anger fickly, quickly, and completely destroys love.

Coriolanus next describes the contrary change—enemies becoming friends:

> [S]o fellest foes,
> Whose passions and whose plots have broke their sleep
> To take the one the other, by some chance,
> Some trick not worth an egg, shall grow dear friends
> And interjoin their issues.
>
> (4.4.18–22)

Coriolanus, continuing to speak in superlatives, believes the two changes are analogous. As friends become foes, "so" foes become friends. The changes, however, are not merely analogous, but identical. Anger causes both. Dissension forms as well as destroys friendship. Enemies become friends, not because they come to love each other or the same things, but because they have a common interest or a common enemy ("interjoin their issues"). A friend is simply an ally. Friendship is enmity in disguise. Friends are those who hate those we hate. "So with me," Coriolanus continues, "My birthplace hate I, and my love's upon / This enemy town" (4.4.22–24). Coriolanus loves Antium because both he and Antium hate Rome. For Coriolanus, enmity or hatred is primary, friendship or love is derivative.

Coriolanus concludes the soliloquy with a pair of antithetical conditionals: "[I]f he slay me / He does fair justice; if he give me way, / I'll do his country service" (4.4.24–26). Aufidius will be able to choose between justice and service, between killing Coriolanus and having Coriolanus serve him. Coriolanus is now silent about love. And, in contrast to what he will say, initially, to Aufidius's face, he does not speak of, or allude to, Aufidius's revenge upon—as distinguished from his conquest of—Rome. If Aufidius chooses revenge, the revenge would be upon Coriolanus, not Rome.

Act Four, Scene Five

1.

Coriolanus enters Aufidius's house, where servingmen, preparing a feast, treat him like a beggar and try to eject him, owing to the way he looks. As he had wished, he is unrecognized in Antium. But while the servingmen treat him poorly out of ignorance, Coriolanus thinks he deserves to be treated poorly because of, not despite, who he is. "I have deserv'd no better entertainment / In being Coriolanus," he says, mentioning his surname for only the first time (4.5.10–11). The Second Servingman, stressing sight, says that anyone who saw him would have thrown him out: "Has the porter his eyes in his head, that he gives entrance to such companions?" (4.5.12–14; also 4.5.21). The servingmen see Coriolanus, but do not see him for what or who he is. Consequently, Coriolanus gives a command ("Away!" [4.5.15]) and it is ignored or rebuffed by the Servingman as insolent: "Away? Get you away! . . . Are you so brave! I'll have you talked with anon" (4.5.16, 18–19). To be impressive, Coriolanus must be seen in action or else known by his name. Away from the battlefield, his greatness is not visible to a stranger. In the city—any city—he is dependent on his reputation or name. Without it, he seems "brave" only in the belittling sense of displaying bravado.

In his first words in exile, Coriolanus commented on the comeliness of Antium, "[a] goodly city" (4.4.1). And in his first words in Aufidius's house, he comments on the comeliness of the house, "[a] goodly house" (4.5.5). Like other noble Romans, Coriolanus closely associates a city with its distinctive buildings. But Coriolanus is now without a city. When the Second Servingman asks where he dwells, he answers, "Under the canopy . . . [i]'th'city of kites and crows" (4.5.39, 43). The only roof over his head is the sky (cf. 1.1.217–18; 3.1.202), and his only city is the one that he shares with scavenger birds (cf. 3.1.137–38). Yet, although—or because—he left Rome "alone / Like to a lonely dragon" (4.1.29–30), Coriolanus cannot leave Rome without going to another city. Just as he needed Roman soldiers to fight Aufidius, he needs Aufidius's soldiers to fight Rome. He cannot get his revenge alone.

Both his need to identify himself and his need to obtain soldiers illustrate that Coriolanus cannot take for granted away from Rome what he could largely take for granted in Rome. In Rome he could proudly disdain both the rewards and the conditions for his virtue because—or so long as—he enjoyed them. But away from Rome he does not possess them and must therefore be concerned with securing them.

A servingman says that Aufidius calls for "Cotus": "Where's Cotus? My master calls for him. Cotus!" (4.5.3–4). When Julius Caesar was about to fight a decisive battle against Vercingetorix, his most serious enemy in Gaul, Caesar's crucial allies, the Aedui, divided into two hostile parties over an election dispute. Cotus, who was (in Caesar's words) "born of an ancient house, a man of very great power and well allied,"[23] claimed to have been properly elected to the Aedui's highest office. His election, however, was bitterly disputed, not least of all because he had ignored or defied the city's traditional election custom. Caesar, seeing his allies on the verge of civil war, feared that the weaker party might ally itself with Vercingetorix in exchange for Vercingetorix's support at home. Here, Aufidius, in a situation directly parallel to Vercingetorix's, calls for another Cotus, as though hoping, as Nicanor suggested (4.3.31–33), that a disputed Roman election, in which the highest elective office was withdrawn from a noble warrior at the very moment when he seemed to have reached it, might cause the Roman nobles to leave their city and join forces with him in their attempt to defend themselves and regain their former power. In a moment Aufidius will get more than Nicanor suggested and than he himself appears to call for. Appropriately enough, the warrior's name, "Cotus," as a Greek common noun (*kotos*), means inveterate and implacable rancor.[24]

2.

Aufidius does not recognize Coriolanus. He needs to be told his name, for which he asks six times before Coriolanus reluctantly tells him (4.5.53, 54, 58, 60, 63, 65). Coriolanus, who does not want to have to give his name ("Why speak'st not? Speak, man: what's thy name?" [4.5.54]), wishes that his excellence, and hence the man he is, were recognizable by itself. Instead, however, he is known only by his name:

> If, Tullus,
> Not yet thou know'st me, and, seeing me, dost not
> Think me for the man I am, necessity
> Commands me name myself.

> (4.5.55–58)

This is the only time Coriolanus speaks of necessity commanding him in any-thing. "My name is Caius Martius," he announces,

> who hath done
> To thee particularly, and to all the Volsces,
> Great hurt and mischief: thereto witness may
> My surname, Coriolanus. The painful service,
> The extreme dangers, and the drops of blood
> Shed for my thankless country, are requited
> But with that surname.

(4.5.66–72)

Coriolanus's angry complaint contradicts much of what he has said before. Coriolanus originally said that he could not take a bribe to pay his sword (1.9.37–38). He wanted his actions to be independent of, or elevated above, any external reward. Now he bitterly complains that Rome paid him for his deeds with nothing more than his surname. Coriolanus originally disavowed his pain and danger, and claimed that his spilled blood was restorative to himself (e.g., 1.5.18–19; 1.9.27–28; 2.2.69–70, 72–73). Now he stresses the pain, dangers, and bloodshed that he endured. Coriolanus originally declared that he would abandon Rome just so that he could fight Aufidius in a private duel (1.1.232–34). Now he emphasizes that he fought for the sake of his country. Where his spirit originally caused him to claim unconditioned virtue, it now causes him to allege injustice. What he proudly claimed to be above, he now indignantly claims to have been deprived of or to have suf-fered. His spirit contradicts itself as it asserts itself.

Coriolanus, restoring the proper order of his personal and family names ("My name is Caius Martius"), says that he has lost those names. Referring to his surname, he declares, "Only that name remains" (4.5.74). One might suppose that Coriolanus has lost his birth name because he is preparing to at-tack his "birthplace" (4.4.33). But Coriolanus, who still calls Rome "my . . . country" (4.5.71, 92; 5.6.72), places full blame on the Romans. "The cruelty and envy of the people . . . / . . . hath devour'd the rest" (4.5.75–77). The people's banishment, not his intended revenge, has consumed his birth name. "Alone," he is only "Coriolanus." Separated from his birthplace, he is separated from his birth name. Ironically, the man who has wanted to sepa-rate his virtue from its conditions is now named entirely for his virtue and not at all for its conditions. The name that recognizes his action—"a good memory / And witness of the malice and displeasure / Which thou should'st bear me" (4.5.72–74)—has completely replaced the names that recognize his birth. Yet, Coriolanus sees the replacement as a loss, only increasing his deep sense of injustice. And he blames not only the people, but especially the nobles for what happened, angrily accusing them of abandoning him and allowing the plebeians to hoot him out of Rome: "Permitted by our dastard nobles, who / Have all forsook me . . . / And suffer'd me by th'voice of slaves to be / Whoop'd out of Rome" (4.5.76–79). No longer are any nobles "friends of noble touch" (4.1.49); "all" of them have cowardly betrayed him. The patricians as much as the plebeians are now his enemy.

Coriolanus finds himself forced to explain why he has come to Aufidius. "Now this extremity / Hath brought me to thy hearth," he begins,

> not out of hope
> (Mistake me not) to save my life: for if
> I had fear'd death, of all the men i'th'world
> I would have 'voided thee; but in mere spite
> To be full quit of those my banishers.

(4.5.80–85)

Coriolanus, expressly and emphatically disabusing Aufidius of a possible and even likely mistake, clearly recognizes that his situation is compromising and easy to misunderstand. Whereas, earlier, he proudly refused to lower himself, now he must stoop—or at least run the risk of looking as if he has. Although someone who would not compromise himself, in going to Aufidius he cannot avoid looking as though he has. Spite will even humble itself to gain satisfaction.

Despite his compromising circumstances, however, Coriolanus acts with an incongruous if characteristic haughtiness. Even when conceding that necessity commands him to name himself, he addresses Aufidius, in his first words to him, by his personal name, "Tullus" (4.5.55), as he did defiantly in battle (1.8.7; also 1.1.239). Nowhere in the scene, in fact, does he call Aufidius by his patronymic, while Aufidius, by contrast, greets him and always addresses him as "Martius," even adding the honorific "all-noble" and "[w]orthy" (4.5.102[twice], 107, 127).[25]

Why should Aufidius help Coriolanus get his revenge? What is Coriolanus's revenge to him? At the end of scene 4, Coriolanus said that Aufidius could get his revenge upon Coriolanus or else grant his request and Coriolanus would help him conquer Rome. The choice was between justice and service. Coriolanus said nothing about Aufidius's revenge upon Rome. Now, however, he combines rather than separates service and justice, and speaks of his serving Aufidius's revenge upon Rome:

> Then if thou hast
> A heart of wreak in thee, that wilt revenge
> Thine own particular wrongs, and stop those maims,
> Of shame seen through thy country, speed thee straight,
> And make my misery serve thy turn.

(4.5.85–89)

While necessity constrains Coriolanus to ask for help, pride forces him disguise his need. Even though he has come to ask for assistance, he presents his request as an offer of his own aid to Aufidius. Pride prevents him from asking for what his circumstances compel him to obtain. Spiritedly transforming his neediness into his sufficiency, Coriolanus disguises his asking as his giving, for, as we have seen, giving is a mark of a superior, asking of an inferior (cf. 1.4.1–7; 1.9.77–88). Service, in this context, signifies superiority.

Pride similarly forces Coriolanus to transform Aufidius's motives and speak as though they were as noble—indeed, the same—as his own. Lest expediency compromise his virtue, his alliance with Aufidius must be a matter of honor, not of policy, for both. Coriolanus therefore suggests that both Aufidius and he would get their revenge upon Rome. Coriolanus would pay back his ungrateful banishers, and Aufidius would get revenge for his own humiliations and the shameful injuries to his country. The two claims to revenge, however, are contradictory. Coriolanus's revenge is warranted only if he is Rome's great hero and Rome has been ungrateful to him, as Coriolanus claimed in the first twenty lines of the speech. But Aufidius's revenge upon Rome is warranted only if Coriolanus is not Rome's great hero, but rather Rome itself is responsible for the devastation and humiliation throughout his country, as Coriolanus has subsequently suggested. Revenge upon Rome cannot be justifiable for both. If it is for Aufidius, it is not for Coriolanus. And if it is for Coriolanus, only revenge upon Coriolanus himself and not upon Rome is justifiable for Aufidius.

Coriolanus seems aware of his dilemma. Although continuing as if he were simply concluding from what he just said, he speaks ambiguously of the "use" and "benefits" to Aufidius of his "revengeful services": "[S]o use it / That my revengeful services may prove / As benefits to thee" (4.5.89–91). By "my revengeful services," Coriolanus could mean his serving either Aufidius's revenge or his advantage, while serving his own revenge. What would be "revengeful" for Coriolanus might be "revengeful" for Aufidius, too, or merely "use[ful]" or "benefi[cal]" to him. The men may share a common cause or only a common interest.

Coriolanus thus tacitly shifts grounds. Initially, he challenged Aufidius's manly heart by saying that "if" Aufidius has "[a] heart of wreak" in him, he would revenge his own private wrongs and his country's dishonoring injuries. Whether he joins Coriolanus against Rome would be a test of his vengeful heart. Now, appealing again to his manly shame, Coriolanus poses the contrary condition with another conditional "if." This time, however, while, once more, proudly boasting of his injuries to Aufidius and the Volscians, he is silent about Aufidius's revenge upon Rome. "But if so be / Thou dar'st not this, and that to prove more fortunes / Th'art tir'd" (4.5.93–95), he says, then he is also too weary to live and is content to let Aufidius cut his throat. Coriolanus, however, does not leave it at this manly challenge. Emphasizing their mutual malice, he adds that Aufidius would be a fool to let him live without serving him;

> Since I have ever follow'd thee with hate,
> Drawn tuns of blood out of thy country's breast,
> And cannot live but to thy shame, unless
> It be to do thee service.
>
> (4.5.99–102)

As before, Coriolanus masks his need as an offer of aid and presents himself as serving Aufidius's revenge. But rather than speaking of his revenge upon Rome, he suggests that Aufidius would get his revenge upon Coriolanus himself. And rather than suggesting that serving implies superiority, he suggests that it implies subordination. Trying to resolve the tension between their contrary claims to "fair justice" (4.4.25), Coriolanus suggests that both men can have their revenge—Coriolanus upon Rome and Aufidius upon Coriolanus. Aufidius can have his revenge upon Coriolanus by having Coriolanus serve him in conquering Rome. While Coriolanus's revenge would be Rome's destruction, Aufidius's would be Coriolanus's service or subordination to him—revenge which, it is important to note, however humbling, nevertheless clearly acknowledges Coriolanus as the Volscians' great vanquisher.[26]

Coriolanus, seeming to take no thought beyond the satisfaction of his anger, says nothing about what is to happen after Rome is crushed.[27] Yet, given what he has already said, we must suppose that these "fellest foes" can "grow dear friends / And interjoin their issues" (4.4.18, 21–22) only because—and only so long as—Rome remains their common enemy.

Aufidius, calling out his name ("O Martius, Martius!" [4.5.103]), declares that Coriolanus's every word has "weeded from [his] heart / A root of ancient envy" (4.5.103–4). One might think that Coriolanus's humbling situation—to say nothing of his proclaimed misery—has mitigated Aufidius's deep-rooted malice: to be at mercy is to be defeated, as Aufidius himself has said (1.10.3–7). However, Aufidius speaks as though Coriolanus is still a more-than-human hero. With a series of hyperbolic comparisons, he, first, affirms that he believes what "all-noble Martius" (4.5.107) has said no less than he would believe "Jupiter / . . . speak[ing] divine things / And say[ing] 'Tis true'" (4.5.103, 105–6). Next, embracing him, he describes Coriolanus's body as having splintered his strong lance a hundred times and scarred the moon with the splinters. Then, still embracing him, he describes Coriolanus's body as "[t]he anvil of my sword" and proclaims, "[I] do contest / As hotly and as nobly with thy love / As ever in ambitious strength I did / Contend against thy valour" (4.5.111–14). And, finally, with a double comparison, he compares his present joy to that when he welcomed his bride into his house. "[N]ever man / Sigh'd truer breath" than he to his bride; "but that I see thee here, / Thou noble thing, more dances my rapt heart / Than when I first my wedded mistress saw / Bestride my threshold" (4.5.115–19). Coriolanus's words are as truthful as Jupiter's, his body as resilient as an anvil, and his presence as enrapturing as Aufidius's sight of his bride on his wedding day. Aufidius does not say what has caused him to "contest" Coriolanus in love as he used to in war. He does not explain what has turned his malice ("envy") into love. After their last fight, Aufidius vowed that he would violate the "hospitable canon" (1.10.26) in order to kill Coriolanus. Now, Coriolanus having arrived at his door, he invokes Jupiter, the god of hospitality, in welcoming him. That his extravagant greeting is carefully if quickly crafted for effect seems indicated not only by its hyperbole and its contrast with his earlier, deadly vow, but also by the fact that Aufidius nowhere else mentions his own heart or his love, or invokes the gods in his own name. On the contrary, he speaks of hearts elsewhere only when vowing to violate the code of hospitality by "[washing his] fierce hand in [Coriolanus's] heart" (1.10.27) and when taunting Coriolanus that "men of heart" looked at each other in amazement when he shed tears before his mother (5.6.99). And he mentions a god only when rebuking Coriolanus for apostrophizing Mars: "Name not the god, thou boy of tears" (5.6.101; also 5.6.118).[28]

Addressing Coriolanus as "thou Mars" (4.5.119), Aufidius discloses that the Volscians have been preparing for war against Rome. Instead of saying that he sought to take advantage of Rome's internal strife (cf. 4.3.16–19), he says that his "purpose" (4.5.120) was to fight Coriolanus, once more, so that he could either defeat him or die in the attempt. Indeed, Aufidius not only appears to exaggerate the number of times Coriolanus has beaten him ("[t]welve several times" [4.5.123; cf. 1.10.7–8]), but describes how Coriolanus beats him nightly in his dreams. Coriolanus, not Rome, is his great enemy. Nevertheless, Aufidius says that had the Volscians "no other quarrel else to Rome, but that / Thou art thence banish'd," he would enroll every man between the ages of twelve and seventy, and sack and destroy "ungrateful Rome" (4.5.128–29, 131). Coriolanus's cause is Aufidius's cause. Presenting his opportunism as disinterested indignation, Aufidius, undeterred by the contradiction that Coriolanus tried to finesse, vows to pursue revenge upon his unbeatable vanquisher's ungrateful city.

Aufidius reveals that he had been planning to attack the Roman territories, but not Rome itself. With Coriolanus thanking the gods for the chance to fight ("You bless me, gods!" [4.5.136]), Aufidius, addressing him as "most absolute sir" (4.5.137), offers him "one-half of [his] commission" (4.5.139) if Coriolanus will have "[t]he leading of [his] own revenges" (4.5.138). And deferring to his knowledge of "[his] country's" (4.5.141) strengths and weaknesses, he allows Coriolanus to decide whether they should alter his original plan and attack Rome right away. Despite everything, in Aufidius's view, as in Coriolanus's, Rome is still "[Coriolanus's] country." Urging him to come in so that he can commend him to the Volscian senators—"those that shall / Say yea to thy desires" (4.5.145–46)—Aufidius, taking his hand as a gesture of friendship (also 4.5.133) and welcoming him as strongly as he can, declares that Coriolanus is "more a friend than e'er an enemy" (4.5.147). Aufidius will soon come to regret his decision to split his command. The effects of the joint command will show themselves right away. Coriolanus will not be as easy to govern—his preeminence not as easy to manage—as Aufidius expects. Coriolanus's service to Aufidius will quickly become his subversion of Aufidius.

3.

Recognition reverses the servingmen's remembrance. The same servingman who stressed Coriolanus's poor appearance (4.5.12–14) and would "have beaten him like a dog, but for disturbing the lords within" (4.5.52–53) now claims that his "mind" warned him that Coriolanus's "clothes made a false report of him" and that he "knew by his face that there was something in him" (4.5.151, 152–53, 157–58). And the same servingman who thought Coriolanus was as "strange [a fellow] as ever [he] looked on" (4.5.21) and did what he could to throw him out (4.5.7–9, 21–23) now finds it difficult to describe his face adequately and claims to have "thought there was more in him than

I could think" (4.5.161–62). The servingmen's discovery of who Coriolanus is revises not only their opinions of him, but their memories of what they had thought. It brings the past into line with the present. "Here's a strange alteration!" in more than one sense (4.5.149). The servingmen see their correction as their corroboration.

The servingmen also revise their opinion of Aufidius. The First and Second Servingman, comparing Coriolanus and Aufidius, are initially cautious, concealing their judgments in a confusion of reversals and pronouns with ambiguous antecedents. Aufidius, for example, could be "[w]orth six" of Coriolanus, or Coriolanus "[w]orth six" of him (4.5.169). But when the Third Servingman returns from the next room, having seen the Volscian senators treat Coriolanus "as if he were son and heir to Mars" (4.5.196–97), and, announcing that he would rather be a condemned man than a Roman, states that Coriolanus "was wont to thwack our general" (4.5.182–83), the other servingmen not only become outspoken, but embellish. The Second Servingman, now suggesting that they can speak openly ("Come, we are fellows and friends" [4.5.187]), reports that he has heard Aufidius himself say that Coriolanus was too hard for him. The First Servingman, agreeing, describes Coriolanus as "scotch[ing] him and notch[ing] him like a carbonado . . . before Corioles" (4.5.191–92). And the Second Servingman, going him one better, says that if Coriolanus "had been cannibally given, he might have broiled and eaten him too" (4.5.193–94). In the revised view of the two servingmen, Coriolanus reduced Aufidius to little more than food. Much as they assimilate the past to the present, the servingmen, whose secondhand knowledge of the recent battle is at least partly incorrect ("before Corioles"), understand war in light of their own domestic work. Even as they change their heroes, what is most immediate or familiar to them shapes their thought.

The Third Servingman details the Volscian senators' gestures of honor for Coriolanus and the consequent effect on Aufidius's standing. Coriolanus, as though "son and heir to Mars," was seated in the place of honor at the head of the table; no senator asked him a question without first removing his hat; and Aufidius himself showed his pious adoration with his hand and eye. "But the bottom of the news is," the Servingman concludes, "our general is cut i'th'middle, and but one half of what he was yesterday; for the other has half, by the entreaty and grant of the whole table" (4.5.202–5). Aufidius, he says, has only half of the authority that he previously had. The joint command has already diminished his authority. But what the Servingman calls Aufidius's half of his former authority is actually even less. In the invidious comparison that the joint command makes inevitable, Aufidius has already been completely eclipsed, as the servingmen themselves indicate by celebrating at length and with delight what Coriolanus will do against Rome, while never mentioning Aufidius again. "[O]ur general is cut i'th'middle, and but one half of what he was yesterday" is their last mention of him. From this moment on, common Volscian soldiers will recognize only Coriolanus as "our general" (5.2.5, 9, 14, 29, 36, 48, 53, 54, 100, 108). Only a coconspirator will call Aufidius by that title (5.6.10).

The Third Servingman has no doubt that Coriolanus will conquer Rome, as Coriolanus has said he will. What Coriolanus promised, though, is not quite what the Servingman expects. While Coriolanus said that he will mow down and clear away everything before him (4.5.205–8), the Servingman speaks not so much of his prowess or actions, but of his effect on his friends in Rome. The sight of "his crest up again, and the man in blood" (4.5.216–17; cf. 3.3.126–27) will cause the Roman nobles to overcome their fearful restraint and turn against his partisan enemies. What Coriolanus sees as the victory of his sword, the Servingman sees as the work of a fifth column. He expects the sight of Coriolanus to arouse and encourage his friends in Rome, much as just happened in Antium.

Impatient for the battle to begin ("Tomorrow, today, presently" [4.5.221]), the servingmen speak of their much greater taste for war than for peace. War is lively, peace is dull. "[W]ar . . . exceeds peace as far as day does night" (4.5.228–29). Where peace is "a very apoplexy, lethargy; mulled, deaf, sleepy, [and] insensible" (4.5.231), war is "sprightly, waking, audible, and full of vent" (4.5.229–30). But even if war is full of more passion, peace has a strong passion of its own. Peace, by weakening sexual fidelity and restraint, is "a getter of more bastard children than war's a destroyer of men" (4.5.231–32). Both war and peace damage the family, though in opposite ways. "[A]s wars, in some sort, may be said to be a ravisher, so it cannot be denied but peace is a great maker of cuckolds" (4.5.233–35). War, however, is more conducive to civil peace, the servingmen say. Peace "makes men hate one another . . . because they then less need one another" than when at war (4.5.236–38). The servingmen, inspired by Coriolanus to expect an easy victory, voice a sanguine view of war. At the same time, they unwittingly point to the way in which foreign wars serve to moderate and strengthen Rome. Although the servingmen scorn peace for unleashing the pursuit of purely private pleasures ("increase tailors, and breed balladmakers"; "a great maker of cuckolds" [4.5.227, 235]), they themselves see war as serving private ends. As the upcoming war is "feast" to be enjoyed "ere [the fighters] can wipe their lips" (4.5.223–24), so "[t]he wars for my money," the Third Servingman declares, "hop[ing] to see Romans as cheap as Volscians" (4.5.238–39). A sign of Coriolanus's effect on the morale of his troops, the servingmen speak only of their hope of gain and not at all of their fear of loss.

Act Four, Scene Six

1.

The scene returns to the marketplace in Rome, where the tribunes are congratulating themselves on the city's civil peace. In Sicinius's view, the tribunes—or perhaps Rome ("we" [4.6.1])—have nothing to fear since no one has heard anything of Coriolanus. By banishing him, they have rendered him powerless ("tame" [4.6.2]). Moreover, the people are quiet and orderly, and this embarrasses his allies, for it shows that Coriolanus rather than the people or the tribunes was responsible for the city's civil strife. The tribunes overlook not only that their own power rests on "[d]issentious numbers pest'ring streets" (4.6.7), but that they had worked hard to produce the "wild hurry" (4.6.4) which they now take credit for ending. Sicinius seems to accuse Coriolanus's friends of wishing to suffer rather than be proved wrong in their prediction of trouble. The friends, he says, "[b]lush that the world goes well" and would rather behold what "they themselves did suffer by . . . / . . . than see / Our tradesmen singing in their shops and going / About their functions friendly" (4.6.5, 8–9). Spirit may certainly lead someone to take perverse pleasure in seeing his prophecy of doom fulfilled. The love of one's own may often conflict with the love of one's own life. But no less common is the spirited tendency to take moral credit, even to oneself, for achieving just the opposite of what one had intended and actually accomplished: "We stood to't in good time," says Brutus (4.6.10), deceiving Sicinius and himself about their own actions.

Sicinius, seeing Menenius approach, remarks that he has "grown most kind / Of late" (4.6.11–12), and Menenius quickly proves him correct. When Sicinius taunts him that Coriolanus—"[y]our Coriolanus," he calls him (4.6.13)—is not missed by anyone but his friends and that "the commonwealth doth stand, / And so would do, were he more angry at it" (4.6.14–15), Menenius readily concedes the point ("All's well" [4.6.16]), adding only that things might have been "much better" if Coriolanus "could have temporiz'd" (4.6.16, 17). He says nothing even to hint that the tribunes were at all to blame for the strife.

Several citizens enter and pray in gratitude for the tribunes: "The gods preserve you both!" (4.6.20); "Ourselves, our wives, and children, on our knees / Are bound to pray for you both" (4.6.22–23); "Now the gods keep you!" (4.6.25). The people's prayers and perhaps Menenius's acquiescence prompt the tribunes to extend their self-deception. "We wish'd Coriolanus / Had lov'd you as we did," Brutus tells the people (4.6.24–25). And when the people leave, the tribunes mingle their self-congratulations for Rome's decorum ("This is a happier and more comely time / Than when those fellows ran about the streets / Crying confusion" [4.6.27–29]) with their self-corroboration of Coriolanus's former danger ("Caius Martius was / . . . ambitious past all thinking . . . . / And affecting one sole throne, / Without assistance" [4.6.29–33]). Menenius, with his only word of protest, can say nothing more than, "I think not so" (4.6.33).

2.

Brutus, however, no sooner self-complacently states that "Rome / Sits safe and still without [Coriolanus]" (4.6.36–37) than an aedile comes to tell that a slave whom they have jailed reports that the Volscians have invaded Roman territory with two separate armies and are destroying everything in their path. Menenius suddenly finds reason to speak. The aediles may have thought the slave's report incredible, but Menenius does not. "'Tis Aufidius," he surmises, implicitly correcting and accusing the tribunes,

> Who, hearing of our Martius' banishment,
> Thrusts forth his horns again into the world,
> Which were inshell'd when Martius stood for Rome,
> And durst not once peep out.
>
> (4.6.42–46)

Menenius, exaggerating the Volscians' fear of Coriolanus, speaks as though Aufidius never took up arms against Rome when Coriolanus was there to defend it (cf. 1.1.222ff.). More than that, he speaks as though the "strange insurrections" in Rome (4.3.13), centering on the hostility between Coriolanus and the people, did not invite Aufidius's attack (cf. 4.3.16–19; 4.5.119–20, 135–36). Brutus, for his part, thinks the slave should not only be jailed; the "rumourer" should also be "whipp'd" (4.6.48). While Menenius claims that the Volscians "durst not once" to attack Rome when Coriolanus was there, Brutus is certain that "[i]t cannot be / The Volsces dare break with us" (4.6.48–49). If the tribunes speak of "our city" or "our Rome" only when expelling its hero (3.3.101, 104), they refer to Rome as "we" or "us" when congratulating themselves on its well-being. Menenius, partly correcting his own exaggeration, answers Brutus's "cannot be" by saying that he could cite three counterexamples in his lifetime. The tribunes, however, remain certain: "[T]his cannot be"; it is "[n]ot possible" (4.6.57). In fact, the more they hear, the more they refuse to believe. When a messenger reports that the nobles are rushing to the Senate with frightened looks, Sicinius defends the tribunes' error by insisting that the report is just more of the slave's rumors: "'Tis this slave— / Go whip him 'fore the people's eyes—his raising, / Nothing but his report" (4.6.60–62). Sicinius seems to think that the people will believe what they see with their own eyes, that if they see the slave punished they will believe that what he says is false, and that if they believe it so it will be so. Public punishment of the slave will put the lie to his report. Spirit not only demands punishment for wrongdoing, but easily believes that punishment is proof of wrongdoing. The punishment it insists upon confirms the blame that it wants to believe.

The Messenger, saying that the slave's report has been confirmed, delivers the more frightening report, as yet unconfirmed but spoken by many, that Coriolanus has joined with Aufidius—he leads an army against Rome and vows revenge wide enough to include everyone, from the youngest to the oldest. This time, Menenius and the tribunes concur. Both think the report is "unlikely" (4.6.69, 72), though for different reasons. Menenius thinks it is unlikely because of the extreme hatred between Coriolanus and Aufidius ("He and Aufidius can no more atone / Than violent'st contrariety" [4.6.73–75]). But the tribunes think it is the nobles' "trick" (4.6.71) to repeal Coriolanus's banishment: "Rais'd only that the weaker sort may wish / Good Martius home again" (4.6.70–71). Right after Coriolanus's banishment, Brutus seemed to fear that Coriolanus's friends would take back what the tribunes had gained (4.2.1–7). But now, no longer fearing the tribunes' own weakness, he describes Coriolanus's friends as "the weaker sort." Success has thoroughly gone to his head.

3.

After a second messenger confirms the most fearful news, Cominius enters and, viewing the situation as hopeless, immediately blames the tribunes: "O, you have made good work" (4.6.81). Not only will their daughters and wives be raped, their city and temples burned to the ground and their political powers destroyed. The tribunes have caused it themselves ("[y]ou have holp . . ." [4.6.83]) and will be forced to witness it themselves ("see [it] . . . to your noses" [4.6.84]). While punishment usually follows blame, Cominius seems to try to punish the tribunes by the way in which he blames them. Telling them of their forthcoming punishment is his punishment of them.

With Menenius still incredulous despite the confirmation ("If Martius should be join'd wi'th'Volscians—" [4.6.89]), Cominius describes Coriolanus as an avenging deity. "If!" he rebuts Menenius's hypothetical "if,"

> He is their god. He leads them like a thing
> Made by some other deity than nature,
> That shapes men better.

(4.6.90–93)

And just as some supernatural power seems to have made him more than human, Coriolanus makes his troops better than themselves by inspiring their absolute confidence in themselves:

> [A]nd they follow him
> Against us brats, with no less confidence
> Than boys pursuing summer butterflies,
> Or butchers killing flies.

(4.6.93–96)

Raised above themselves, Coriolanus's troops reduce the Romans to insects pursued by boys for the challenge or killed by butchers as pests. Coriolanus makes all the difference. There is no way to stop him.

Menenius, now convinced that Coriolanus has joined Aufidius, tries, like Cominius, to punish the tribunes by blaming them for their folly. Reversing the tribunes' self-congratulatory description of the city (4.6.8–9), he combines disgust for what the people are with disgust for what the tribunes have done ("You, and your apron-men; you that stood so much / Upon the voice of occupation and / The breath of garlic-eaters!" [4.6.97–99]). Menenius accuses the tribunes of destroying Rome in seeking to advance themselves on behalf of an utterly worthless cause. Like Cominius, he blames the tribunes for everything. And after Cominius warns or threatens, "He'll shake your Rome about your ears" (4.6.100), Menenius, seizing upon Cominius's words, offers a heroic comparison: "As Hercules / Did shake down mellow fruit" (4.6.100–1). As Hercules could steal the golden apples, although they were guarded by a dragon with a hundred heads,[29] Coriolanus will be able to take Rome, guarded by "the beast / With many heads" (4.1.1–2). Victory will come easily to the great warrior. Remarkably, Cominius and Menenius never criticize Coriolanus for joining Rome's enemy and attacking his country. In their eagerness to blame the tribunes, they excuse Coriolanus. When Brutus, now reduced to few words,[30] asks, "But is this true, sir?" (4.6.102), Cominius, telling of his sweep through Roman territories, denies that Coriolanus is to blame: "Who is't can blame him?" (4.6.106).

Menenius says that "[w]e are all undone / Unless the noble man have mercy" (4.6.108–9). Until now, he and Cominius have limited the expected destruction virtually to the tribunes alone.[31] The question then becomes, Who can ask for mercy? Cominius says that the tribunes cannot do it for shame, and the people do not deserve Coriolanus's mercy at all. And as for his best friends, if they were to ask Coriolanus for mercy they would be acting like his enemies, who deserve his hate. By overlooking the wrongs that he has suffered, they would deserve to be treated like those who had wronged him. Menenius strongly agrees ("'Tis true!" [4.6.115]), declaring that if Coriolanus were to set fire to his house, he would "have not the face" (4.6.117) to ask him to stop. Shame would prevent him. Menenius and Cominius, once again, blame the tribunes. Four times previously they blamed them for having "made good [or "fair"] work" (4.6.81, 89, 96, 101; also 4.6.147). Now, Menenius goes on to say, with further biting sarcasm (underscored by a chiasmus), "You have made fair hands, / You and your crafts! You have crafted fair!" (4.6.118–19). The tribunes have made a fine mess of things ("fair hands," "crafted fair"), by means of tradesmen and trickery ("your crafts"). Cominius, dropping the antanaclasic wordplay, states simply, "You have brought / A trembling upon Rome, such as was never / S'incapable of help" (4.6.119–21): Rome has never been so helpless. When the tribunes, for the first time, deny their responsibility ("Say not we brought it" [4.6.121]), Menenius tries to refute them: "How? Was't we? We lov'd him" (4.5.122). The substitute for blaming oneself is blaming another, especially when the other's blame exonerates oneself. Menenius, however, then makes a concession: "[B]ut, like beasts / And cowardly nobles, [we] gave way unto your clusters, / Who did hoot him out o'th'city" (4.6.123–24). This the nobles' first admission of any responsibility: the nobles, fearful of the people's numbers, cowardly acquiesced to their action, as Coriolanus has charged (4.5.76–77; cf. 3.1.131–34). Cominius, concluding that desperation is Rome's only defense against Coriolanus, emphasizes the ironic reversal of the people's action: as they hooted Coriolanus out of the city, "[t]hey'll roar him in again" (4.6.125). As he was banished with the people's jeers, he will return with their wails. Menenius similarly stresses the people's grimly ironic self-punishment. As the people cast their "stinking greasy caps" (4.6.132) when they hooted him out, so,

> [n]ow he's coming,
> And not a hair upon a soldier's head
> Which will not prove a whip. As many coxcombs
> As you threw caps up will he tumble down,
> And pay you for your voices.
>
> (4.6.133–37)

The punishment fitting the offense, Coriolanus will requite the commoners for their celebratory caps by paying them back with whippings and the caps of fools. But, having again singled out the people and the tribunes for blame and punishment, Menenius suddenly expands those who deserve both. "'Tis no matter, / If [Coriolanus] could burn us all into one coal, / We have deserv'd it" (4.6.137–19). All Romans deserve to be burned into a single cinder. Coriolanus's vengeance against all Romans, nobles and commoners equally, is warranted. All are guilty. Coriolanus is perfectly justified in coming with a foreign army to destroy Rome.

The citizens, "hear[ing] fearful news" (4.6.140), attempt to acquit themselves. Three of them claim that when they banished Coriolanus they "said 'twas pity," as did "very many of us" (4.6.141, 144). Moreover, their will or intention was good. The citizens did what they did "for the best," they say, and "though we willingly consented to his banishment, yet it was against our will" (4.6.144, 145–46). They willingly did what was against their will to do. Forgiving themselves, they take their regret as evidence that they did not will what they willingly did.

When Menenius and Cominius leave for the Capitol, the tribunes recover their voice. Urging the people to go home and not be dismayed, Sicinius says, "These are a side that would be glad to have / This true which they so seem to fear" (4.6.151–52). The nobles, wanting Coriolanus's return, are only feigning fear. The people, however, do not seem convinced. The First Citizen no longer claims that they did what they did for the best. Entreating "[t]he gods [to] be good to us" (4.6.154), he now blames himself and the other people: "I ever said we were i'th'wrong when we banished him" (4.6.155–56). And the Second Citizen adds, "So did we all" (4.6.157). If a moment ago they seemed to think that their good will toward Coriolanus when banishing him amounted their protection, the citizens now seem to think that admitting their guilt will protect them. While placing their desperate hope in the power of justice, they seem unsure whether being innocent then or self-accusatory now will save them.

4.

After the others leave, the tribunes briefly discuss the news. Contrary to what Sicinius has just said, both men admit that they do not like it. Brutus, however, as though unwittingly parodying himself, shows his concern by solemnly declaring, "Would half my wealth / Would buy this for a lie!" (4.6.160–61). It is hard to be sure that Brutus is more attached to his money than to his life. But just as Sicinius began the scene by suggesting that the nobles place the love of one's own in conflict with the love of one's own life (4.6.4–9), Brutus ends it by demonstrating that he does the same.

Act Four, Scene Seven

Aufidius's servingman described how the Volscian senators and servants alike began nearly to worship Coriolanus as soon as he joined the senators for their meal. Even Aufidius regarded him with reverence (4.5.175ff.). Now, Aufidius, his standing lowered among the Volscians, jealously asks his lieutenant, "Do they still fly to th'Roman?" (4.7.1). The lieutenant, characterizing Coriolanus as having bewitched Aufidius's soldiers, describes how they, too, virtually worship him. "Your soldiers use him as the grace 'fore meat, / . . . and their thanks at end," and make him "[t]heir talk at [the] table" (4.7.3–4). And so Aufidius is eclipsed in the current campaign ("darken'd in this action" [4.7.5]), even—or perhaps especially—among his own men.

Aufidius, unable to act against him now without injuring the attack against Rome, tells, with an emphatic, doubled comparative, how Coriolanus bears himself "more proudlier / Even to my person" (4.7.8–9) than he had expected when welcoming him. Aufidius, however, seems prepared to excuse Coriolanus. "Yet his nature / In that's no changeling, and I must excuse / What cannot be amended" (4.7.10–12). What cannot be otherwise should not be blamed (cf. 1.1.40–41). Aufidius will, nevertheless, soon seek to take advantage of what he now says he must pardon.

The lieutenant wishes that Aufidius had not offered Coriolanus joint command, but had either commanded the action himself or given it solely to Coriolanus. As Cominius, who had himself been overshadowed by Coriolanus, has reported, "Tullus Aufidius, / The second name of men, obeys his points / As if he were his officer" (4.6.125–27). Coriolanus commands, and Aufidius obeys.

Aufidius assures the lieutenant that "[w]hen [Coriolanus] shall come to his account, he knows not / What I can urge against him" (4.7.18–19). Despite what Coriolanus and the commoners think and what appears to be the case—that Coriolanus bears all things fairly, shows concern for the welfare of the Volscian state, fights savagely and alone ("dragon-like" [4.7.23]), and wins as soon as he draws his sword—"yet he hath left undone / That which shall break his neck or hazard mine," Aufidius says, "Whene'er we come to our account" (4.7.24–26). It is hard to be sure what Aufidius is referring to. According to Plutarch, when Coriolanus and his army came within five miles of Rome, the Romans sent a delegation to offer him the right to return to his country and to implore him to stop the war against them. Coriolanus answered by demanding the return of the land conquered from the Volscians in the recent war and the passage of a decree granting them the same civic rights as the Romans had recently given the Latins. Coriolanus then gave the Romans thirty days to consider the terms and withdrew his troops from Roman territory.

> This was the first matter wherewith the Volsces (that most envied Martius's glory and authority) did charge Martius with. Among those, Tullus was chief, who though he had received no private injury or displeasure of Martius, yet the common fault and imperfection of man's nature wrought him, and it grieved him to see his own reputation blemished through Martius's great fame and honor, and so himself to be less esteemed of the Volsces than he was before.[32]

Shakespeare stresses Coriolanus's victories against the Romans (4.6.76–80, 103–6; 4.7.23–24, 28; 5.3.1–2), but never mentions the thirty-day truce. After Coriolanus spares Rome, a Volscian Lord will speak of the "faults he made before the last" (5.6.64), but he will not specify them. And although we shall soon hear of Cominius's delegation to him, there will be no hint that Coriolanus offered anything like a thirty-day truce to deliberate his terms.[33] Shakespeare's silence seems to underscore that what is political in Aufidius's proposed charge is purely pretextual and what is purely personal is real, as Plutarch suggests. Just as Coriolanus's alliance with Aufidius against Rome is nothing more than a private concern,[34] Aufidius's design against him is a merely private matter.

The lieutenant asks whether Aufidius thinks that Coriolanus will capture Rome. The answer is important to Aufidius's design, for Coriolanus's success may outweigh his omissions. The Volscians have, after all, already forgiven him for killing many of their family members (4.4.1–6; 5.6.50–54). Their greed may stifle their rage.

Aufidius has no doubt that Coriolanus will capture Rome, even without a fight. The young nobility are his, the senators and patricians love him too, the tribunes cannot fight, and the people will repeal their banishment as hastily as they expelled him. "I think he'll be to Rome / As is the osprey to the fish, who takes it / By sovereignty of nature" (4.7.33–35). Just as (as Pliny explains) the osprey—literally, "bone breaker"—"when she spies a fish in the sea, down she comes with a power, plunges into the water, and breaking the force thereof with her breast, quickly catches up the fish and is gone,"[35] Coriolanus will conquer Rome quickly and easily by his natural superiority. How then will his—and Aufidius's—chances stand? Aufidius believes that the same things that brought Coriolanus down in Rome will do so in Antium. Coriolanus, he says, was a noble servant to the Romans, but was unable to "[c]arry his honours even" (4.7.37). As Sicinius noted (2.1.222–24), Coriolanus cannot move from honor in war to honor in peace without losing his balance. Aufidius offers three possible reasons for Coriolanus's failure. His analysis contains his most theoretical thoughts and the lengthiest description of Coriolanus's character by anyone in the play. It is also curiously inconclusive and puzzling.

The first possible reason is the pride resulting from an unbroken string of success ("out of daily fortune"), which "ever taints / The happy man" (4.7.38–39). The second is Coriolanus's "defect of judgment" (4.7.39) in failing to make the most of the opportunities that were his. The third is his one-sided

> nature,
> Not to be other than one thing, not moving
> From th'casque to th'cushion, but commanding peace
> Even with the same austerity and garb
> As he controll'd the war.
>
> (4.7.41–45)

One might suppose that the three reasons are consistent and belong together—that Coriolanus's failure stemmed from a combination of his pride, disdain of prudence and single-sidedness, all of which are of a piece. Aufidius, however, explicitly separates them, as he implicitly did with his three disjunctive, parallel clauses beginning with "whether": "Whether 'twas pride," "whether defect of judgement," "or whether nature" (4.7.37, 39, 41). "[B]ut one of these—," he explains,

> As he hath spices of them all, not all,
> For I dare so far free him—made him fear'd,
> So hated, and so banish'd.
>
> (4.7.45–48)

Aufidius offers a double qualification. Coriolanus has all three defects, but only a trace ("spice") of each. And only one of them, "not all," was the cause. The first qualification reduces a whole to separate parts; the second, elevates one of those parts to being the whole cause.[36] And although claiming to know that Coriolanus has some part of each of the three defects but that only one was the cause of his banishment, Aufidius, strangely, does not indicate which it was.

Instead, he says that the unnamed defect made Coriolanus "fear'd, / So hated, and so banish'd." The people's fear led to their hatred, which led to his banishment. Fear is often a powerful cause of hatred. As noted earlier, men hate what they fear, because they fear it. The two passions differ, however, in that while fear compels us to act (or not to act), hatred permits us to choose whether or not to act. Unlike fear, whose compulsion is immediate, hatred gives us some distance from its object, allowing us to act at the time of our own choosing. And while it thus contains an element of the voluntary, hatred also has a different end from fear. Whereas fear, which is aroused most basically by threats to our life, seeks safety, hatred, which is excited most especially by insults to our dignity, seeks revenge. As Aufidius's servingmen had emphasized, fear belongs to the compulsion of war; hatred, to the freedom of peace (4.5.236–38).[37] At once less constraining and less constrained, hatred is both freer and fiercer—and therefore more dangerous—than fear.

"[B]ut he has a merit / To choke it in the utt'rance" (4.7.48–49), Aufidius continues. While the safety of peace allows people to hate proud valor, the fears of war make them aware of their need for it. War's urgent needs thus quell criticism of Coriolanus's defect. Indeed, Coriolanus's merit and defect are one and the same. Generalizing, as he does perhaps nowhere else,[38] Aufidius explains, "So our virtues / Lie in th'interpretation of the time" (4.7.49–50). What during war the people see as a virtue, during peace they see as a vice. They are afraid in peace of the martial qualities they want in war. What changes is not the hero's virtue, but, on the contrary, while his virtue remains unchanged, the people's circumstances and hence their judgments change. Their judgments change with their external circumstances, as Coriolanus said of them in his opening tirade (1.1.169–73). Therefore, unless the hero adapts himself to the new conditions, what elevates him in war will bring him down in peace.

Moreover, not only the virtues themselves, but their praise undoes the hero: "And power, unto itself most commendable, / Hath not a tomb so evident as a chair / T'extol what it hath done" (4.7.51–53). The praise attracts envy, and envy, like fear, causes hatred. Where indignation demands a world in which the good are rewarded and the bad punished, envy, in contrast, is pained by the rewards bestowed upon the good.[39] Aufidius, breaking into rhyme, voices four synecdochic precepts to illustrate his general thought: "One fire drives out one fire; one nail, one nail; / Rights by rights falter, strengths by strengths do fail" (4.7.54–55). Things are destroyed not by their opposites, but by their similars working against them. Coriolanus will be destroyed by his own virtue. His victory contains his defeat. Thus Aufidius concludes, "When, Caius, Rome is thine, / Thou art poor'st of all: then shortly art thou mine" (4.7.56–57). This is the only time Aufidius addresses Coriolanus by his personal name, and he does it in his absence and in the prospect of Coriolanus's triumph becoming his downfall. Aufidius, who speaks here with an odd mixture of superiority and inferiority, must wait for a better time to defeat Coriolanus. He cannot destroy him until after the war, but then, he thinks, Coriolanus will lose by winning.

Aufidius's analysis of Coriolanus's character mimics what it describes. Its curious double qualification first resolves a whole into separate parts and then makes one of those parts the whole. Only one of the three possible causes was the cause, and it was the whole cause. Like Coriolanus himself, Aufidius's analysis is unable to reconcile whole and part. It sees the whole as a part and the part as the whole, and it therefore sees neither the whole nor the part. Aufidius's analysis thus presents a fitting foil for the play's final act. For while Aufidius's analysis demonstrates as well as describes the characteristic tendency of Coriolanus's spirited soul, act 5 will turn on Coriolanus's recognition of the impossibility of his "[n]ot [being] other than one thing." Aufidius says that Coriolanus is "no changeling." Yet, we shall see that, forced to recognize his own double nature, Coriolanus will indeed change. He not only will abandon his revenge against Rome, but will become in Antium what he scorned to be in Rome.

Notes

1. Anonymous, 4.24.
2. Seneca, *Letters*, 94.28.
3. Aristotle, *Rhetoric*, 1395b1–18; Quintilian, 8.5.7–8.
4. See Cicero, *Brutus*, 211; Quintilian, 1.1.6.
5. Cf., e.g., 1.3.10–18, 33–34, 4.1.5; 4.2.23–27 with 1.4.30ff.; 4.1.28, 32; 5.6.127–29.
6. E.g., 3.2.8–13; 4.1.16–19.
7. Aristotle, *Nicomachean Ethics*, 1103a14–1104b3.
8. Aristotle, *Nicomachean Ethics*, 1103a11–25, 1116a16–29, 1179a35–b12.
9. Cf. 2.3.16ff.; 3.1.65, 92, 130, 155; 4.1.1–2; see Hesiod, *Theogony*, 313–18; Apollodorus, *The Library*, 2.5.2; Diodorus Siculus, 4.11.5.
10. Apollodorus, 2.7.7; Diodorus Siculus, 4.38–39; Ovid, *Metamorphoses*, 9.134–272.
11. Wilson, 212.
12. F. N. Lees, "*Coriolanus*, Aristotle, and Bacon," *Review of English Studies* 1 (1950), 114–25; Charney, 187; Allan Bloom, *Shakespeare's Politics* (New York: Basic Books, 1961), 85–86; G. R. Hibbard, *Coriolanus* (New York: Penguin Books, 1967), 32; Leigh Holt, *From Man to Dragon* (Salzburg: Institut für Engliche Sprache und Literatur, 1976), 27; Cantor, 101–2.

13. To beasts, e.g., 1.127; 1.9.12; 2.1.10–11; 3.1.284; 4.7.23, 34; 5.4.12–14; to gods, e.g., 2.1.217–19; 3.1.80–81; 4.4.24–25; 4.5.119, 196–97; 4.6.91–93; 5.3.11.

14. See, e.g., Apollonius Rhodius, *The Argonautica*, 4.1436–40.

15. Diodorus Siculus, 4.11.3–4, 4.38–39. 4.21.4.

16. Plutarch, *Coriolanus*, 21.1–2.

17. Heraclitus, frag. 85; Aristotle, *Politics*, 1315a30–31; Plutarch, *Coriolanus*, 22.2.

18. Aufidius's name, the play's only other Volscian name, also refers to a location in Italy, the principal river of Apulia; see Pliny, 3.102; Horace, *Satires*, 1.1.58; *Carminum*, 3.30.10.

19. For Coriolanus's "lack of education," see Plutarch, *Coriolanus*, 1.3; North, 2:144.

20. Plutarch, *Phocion*, 32.6; North, 5:102.

21. Plutarch, *Phocion*, 1.3; North, 5:72.

22. Blits, *Ancient Republic*, 3–20.

23. Caesar, *The Gallic War*, 7.32; *The Eight Books of Julius Caesar conveying his Martial Exploits in the Realm of Gallia* . . . , trans. Arthur Golding (London: William Seres, 1565), fol. 197.

24. E.g., Homer, *Iliad*, 1.80–83; 13.517, 16.449; *Odyssey*, 11.102–3; 13.341–43; Aeschylus, *Suppliant Women*, 385–86, 615–18; *Eumenides*, 499–501, 840; Pindar, *Pythian Odes*, 8.10–11.

25. The only time Aufidius refers to Coriolanus as "Caius" will be in his absence, in a moment of imagined triumph (4.7.56).

26. "[S]ervice" frames as well as suffuses Coriolanus's offer. It is his last word before entering Aufidius's house (4.4.26) and his last word in his offer to him (4.5.102). It is also the obvious theme of the pantry scene. In addition to "servingman" and "servant" appearing nineteen times in Folio stage headings and seven times in Folio stage directions in the pantry scene's fifty-two lines, "serve," "service," and "servant" appear nine of the play's thirty-seven times in the approximately one hundred lines between Coriolanus's final word before entering Aufidius's house and his final word to Aufidius (4.4.26; 4.5.1, 46, 47, 48, 69, 89, 90, 102).

27. For anger's disregarding the future, see Aristotle, *Rhetoric*, 1385b29–31.

28. Instead, he swears "[b]y th'elements" (1.10.10).

29. Apollodorus, 2.5.11; Apollonius Rhodius, 4.1396–1484.

30. Neither tribune has said anything since the Second Messenger delivered his news, right after the tribunes were sure the earlier reports were the nobles' trick (4.6.69–71). Except for one half line, when Brutus asks whether the news can be true (4.6.102), and another half line when they deny their responsibility together (4.6.121), neither will say another word until after everyone else has left (4.6.158–61), seventy-five lines after the Second Messenger's entrance.

31. Except for Cominius once referring to "us brats" (4.6.94), he and Menenius have spoken of "your own daughters," "your pates," "your wives," "your noses" "[y]our temples," "[y]our franchises," "your Rome," "your ears," and "[y]our enemies" (4.6.82, 83, 84[twice], 86, 87, 100[twice], 107).

32. Plutarch, *Coriolanus*, 31.2; North, 2:178.

33. 5.3.12–15 would appear to imply that there was no thirty-day respite.

34. H. C. Beeching, in Furness, 420.

35. Pliny, 10.3; tr. Philomen Holland (1601), *The Historie of the World* (London: Adam Islip, 1634), 272.

36. As commentators often point out, Aufidius seems to mingle his two qualifications; see, e.g., B. H. Kembell-Cook, *Coriolanus*, The New Clarendon Shakespeare (London, 1954), 208.

37. Machiavelli, *The Prince*, 17, 19. Also cf., e.g., 1.1.175–76, 182; 1.8.6–9; 2.2.11–15; 2.3.217–18 with 1.4.23, 37–38; 3.1.75–76, 132–34; 4.5.81–83.

38. For his only other possible generalization, see 1.10.6–7.

39. Aristotle, *Nicomachean Ethics*, 1108b3-5; Cicero, *De oratore*, 2.210.

ACT FIVE

~

Act Five, Scene One

Rome is desperate. Cominius said that none of Coriolanus's friends could ask him for mercy without appearing to resemble his enemies (4.6.112–15). But Cominius himself has gone to entreat him. Coriolanus, however, heard him only scornfully ("he coy'd / To hear Cominius speak" [5.1.6–7]) and listened only reluctantly ("He would not seem to know [him]" [5.1.8]). Nevertheless, Coriolanus did hear Cominius and answered him. "Yet one time he did call me by my name" (5.1.9). Just as Coriolanus had appealed to their old friend-ship and the blood they shed together when beseeching Cominius to let him fight Aufidius in the field (1.6.55–59), Cominius, beseeching Coriolanus, "urg'd our old acquaintance, and the drops / That we have bled together" (5.1.10–11). This time, however, the ties of old friendship and spilled blood failed.

> "Coriolanus"
> He would not answer to; forbad all names:
> He was a kind of nothing, titleless,
> Till he had forg'd himself a name o'th'fire
> Of burning Rome.
>
> (5.1.11–15)

Coriolanus's name is his identity. Without his name, Coriolanus is a nobody, a non-being, " a kind of nothing." He is identified not only by his name, but

193

with it. As his name is derived from his defeated enemy, his defeated enemy constitutes his identity. Not only doer and deed, but victor and vanquished, are one. Coriolanus's identity thus amounts to a double negative: his destruction of his enemy transforms his own nothingness into who or what he is ("forg'd himself a name o'th'fire / Of burning Rome"). He is the enemy which he has most recently defeated. As his anger and enemies shift, so consequently does his identity. Although Coriolanus seeks "[n]ot to be other than one thing," his identity is no more constant than the object of his anger. Cominius says that Coriolanus spoke of forging himself a new name in the fire of burning Rome. That name would be "Romanus." Fittingly, the destroyer of Rome would be Romanus—in Latin, "a Roman" or "of, or belonging to, Rome." To the extent to which Rome epitomizes spiritedness and spiritedness owes its content to what it opposes and defeats, the fulfillment of Rome and the destruction of Rome become one and the same. The fulfillment of spiritedness implies the destruction of what gives it its particular content and identity. Whereas Romulus, Rome's founder, gave his name to Rome, Coriolanus, Rome's destroyer, would take his new name from Rome. Rather than the rising city being named after him, he would be named after the razed city.

Menenius at first refuses to attempt to persuade Coriolanus to relent. Previously, agreeing with Cominius that Coriolanus's friends cannot plead with him without acting like his enemies, he said that even if Coriolanus were about to burn down his house he would not have the face to ask him to stop (4.6.115–18). Now, he says something quite different. It is not his shame but his broken heart that prevents him. "No, I'll not go," he firmly declares;

> you hear what he hath said
> Which was sometime his general, who lov'd him
> In a most dear particular. He call'd me father:
> But what o'that? . . .
> . . . Nay, if he coy'd
> To hear Cominius speak, I'll keep at home.
>
> (5.1.1–4, 6–8)

Menenius, who stresses private goods throughout much of the scene (5.1.1–4, 28–32, 42–45, 47–58) and mentions Rome only to blame the tribunes (5.1.15–17), would rather not try than be personally pained by Coriolanus's rebuff.

After Menenius, with a bitter pun, blames the tribunes for having worked for Rome's ruin ("wrack'd for Rome" [5.1.16]), Cominius reports that he re-

minded Coriolanus how royal it is to pardon when least expected, but Coriolanus replied that the request for pardon was both barefaced and threadbare
("bare" [5.1.20]). Although Rome has offered him no pardon, it asks him to
pardon Rome. Perhaps because the retort heaps blame upon the people,
Menenius approves it: "Very well. / Could he say less?" (5.1.21–22). As before, his anger at the tribunes gets the better of his concern for himself (see
4.6.129–39). But when Cominius tells that he tried to awaken Coriolanus's
regard for his "private friends" (5.1.24) and Coriolanus answered that he
could not spare Rome for the sake of "one poor grain or two" among the "noi-
some musty chaff" (5.1.26, 27), Menenius, no longer approving, is again
deeply hurt and despondent:

> For one poor grain or two?
> I am one of those; his mother, wife, his child,
> And this brave fellow too: we are the grains,
> You are the musty chaff, and you are smelt
> Above the moon. We must be burnt for you.
>
> (5.1.28–32)

Coriolanus's wrath ignores the distinction between his enemies and his family and friends. In seeking satisfaction, it will indiscriminately punish the innocent along with the guilty, those he loves along with those he hates.

Despite his initial refusal, however, the tribunes quickly convince Menenius to try to persuade Coriolanus. Sicinius first admonishes him that if he
refuses to help, he must stop upbraiding the tribunes for what they have
done. Menenius must act if he is to continue to blame. Sicinius then sweet-
ens his rebuke with warm praise and conciliation. "Be sure," he assures
Menenius, that if he were to be "[his] country's pleader, [his] good tongue"
might stop "our countryman" better than any army "we" could levy at the
moment (5.1.35, 36, 38). Sicinius combines his flattery of Menenius with his
conciliation of Coriolanus, who is suddenly "our countryman"—something
the tribunes nowhere else call him—and with his associating the tribunes
with the nobles as fellow Romans—something neither tribune has done before. Menenius, however, still refuses ("No, I'll not meddle" [5.1.38]). And
when Brutus urges him to try to do what he can for Rome, Menenius repeats
that he fears being returned unheard, like Cominius, "a discontented friend,
grief-shot / With [Coriolanus's] unkindness" (5.1.44–45). But when Sicinius
reminds him that his "good will / Must have that thanks from Rome after the
measure / As you intended well" (5.1.45–47), Menenius immediately
changes his mind: "I'll undertake't. / I think he'll hear me" (5.1.46–47).

Menenius will earn Rome's thanks just for trying. His good will alone will count. Rome, although destroyed, will thank Menenius in proportion to his good intention. No matter how much he fears that Rome confronts its utter doom, Menenius seems to take for granted that it will somehow survive its own destruction. His fear and hope are not so much opposed as confusedly combined. While fear leads to desperation, desperation, in turn, gives rise to hope and even to confidence ("I think he'll hear me"), though a confidence that still leaves him dispirited ("Yet to bite his lip / And hum at good Cominius, much unhearts me" [5.1.48–49]).

Menenius, desperate for hope, attributes Cominius's failure to Coriolanus's hunger rather than to his rage. "He was not taken well; he had not din'd" (5.1.50), he says, before explaining (to himself) what he claims is true of humans in general. With six indefinite first-person plural pronouns ("our," "we") in as many lines, and no reference to Coriolanus in particular, he argues that the stomach rules the heart: unfilled veins make our blood cold and our souls ungiving and unforgiving, while when we have stuffed these pipes with wine and food we have suppler souls (5.1.51–56). Rendered over-credulous by his fear, Menenius seems to fall for one of his own pretty tales. More exactly, turning to what is most familiar to him, he judges Coriolanus by himself. He considers that what is true of himself—"a humorous patrician . . . that loves a cup of hot wine, with not a drop of allaying Tiber in't" (2.1.46–48)—is equally true of a vengeful warrior. Menenius thus announces that he will watch Coriolanus and wait until he has eaten and then make his plea. Brutus, no less desperate, is completely confident that he will succeed. "You know the very road into his kindness, / And cannot lose your way" (5.1.59–60).

After Menenius departs on his mission, Cominius says there is no chance that Coriolanus will hear him. "I tell you, he does sit in gold, his eye / Red as 'twould burn Rome; and his injury / The gaoler to his pity" (5.1.63–65). Vengeful Coriolanus combines the outer trappings of majesty, an eye that transfers the fire of his rage into the destruction of its object, and the sense of his wrongs that locks the door on his pity. Brutus had rebuked him for speaking as though he were a punishing god (3.1.79–81). Now, no longer merely resembling the god of war (2.1.216–19; 4.5.119, 196–97), Coriolanus has come to act like a god of pitiless vengeance. His sense of Rome's wronging him represses in him any sense of his wronging Rome. Wrath overwhelms his pity (cf. 1.9.84). Transmuting the subjunctive into the indicative ("as 'twould burn Rome"), he will become what his eye resembles.

In his initial account of their hapless meeting, Cominius emphasized what Coriolanus and he had said to each other: "[H]e did call me" (5.1.9); "I urg'd"

(5.1.10); "He would not answer" (5.1.12); "[F]orbad all names" (5.12); "I minded him . . ." (5.1.18); "He replied . . ." (5.1.19); "I offer'd . . ." (5.1.23); "His answer to me was . . ." (5.1.24); "He said . . ." (5.1.26). Almost every sentence began by referring to an act of speech. Now, describing the meeting further, Cominius emphasizes its speechless character: "I kneel'd before him: / 'Twas very faintly he said 'Rise,' dismiss'd me / Thus, with his speechless hand" (5.1.65–67). Speechless gestures nearly entirely replace spoken words. While the recent Roman consul humbles himself by kneeling, the man who once served under him dismisses him imperiously with his "speechless hand." While public speech goes together with the freedom and equality of republicanism, such mute gestures denote the vast disproportion between the human and the divine.

Coriolanus, nevertheless, could not leave things at dumb gestures. Given Cominius's stark description of his peremptory "speechless hand," one might think that Coriolanus refused to offer any terms of settlement, whatever. What he refused, however, was not offering terms, but discussing or negotiating them. His terms were final: "What he would do, / He sent in writing after me: what he would not, / Bound with an oath to yield to his conditions" (5.1.67–69). Coriolanus stated the concessions he would grant and those he would not, and he required an oath of unconditional acceptance of the terms. The Romans must accept all of the Volscians' conditions or else face war. Shakespeare never tells us the terms. In a way, they do not matter. Later, we shall hear that Rome "did refuse" them (5.3.14). And, here, Cominius implies as much: "So that all hope is vain, / Unless his noble mother and his wife / . . . solicit him / For mercy to his country," which, he adds, he has heard they intend to do (5.1.70–73). Shakespeare's silence seems show that the Romans do not so much refuse the Volscians' specific terms as refuse to make concessions through fear or at the dictation of an enemy. As Plutarch explains, the Romans, "no men that would ever yield for fear," told Coriolanus that if he thought

> the Volscians had ground to demand reasonable articles and conditions, all that they would reasonably ask should be granted unto, by the Romans, who of themselves would willingly yield to reason, conditionally, that they did lay down their arms.[1]

Cominius may humble himself and supplicate Coriolanus, but, despite their desperate situation, the Romans would sooner suffer their own destruction than yield through fear or at an enemy's command. Thus, their only hope is to persuade Coriolanus to lay down his arms and withdraw from the gates of

Rome. "Therefore, let's hence," Cominius concludes, "[a]nd with our fair entreaties haste [the women] on" (5.1.73–74).

Act Five, Scene Two

1.

Menenius tries to see Coriolanus, but the Volscian sentinels stop him, declaring that "our general / Will no more hear from [Rome]" (5.2.5–6). Since Coriolanus's terms leave nothing for discussion, Menenius, who initially calls himself "an officer of state" (5.2.3), quickly shifts and presents himself, instead, as Coriolanus's personal friend. It is not as a Roman officer, but as "your general['s] . . . friend" (5.2.9, 10), that he has come. Addressing the guards as "[g]ood my friends" (5.2.8), as he had the rebellious commoners in the play's opening scene (1.1.61, 64, 126; also 1.1.129, 140) and as Cominius had in the trial scene (3.3.108), Menenius says that if they have heard their general talk of "his friends" (5.2.10) in Rome, it is virtually certain that "[m]y name hath touch'd your ears: it is Menenius" (5.2.11). But contrary to what Menenius seems to expect or at least to hope, the First Watch tells him to go back. Quibbling contemptuously on the word "passable," the guard says that he may not pass, because "the virtue of [his] name / Is not here passable" (5.2.12–13): he may not go though, because the power of his name is not sufficient to be acceptable here.[2] Menenius, rebuffed again, shifts once more and tries to combine his claim to Coriolanus's friendship with what he has said rather than with what he is called. The guards' general, he insists, is not only his dear friend ("my lover" [5.2.14]), but "chief" of his "friends" (5.2.17, 18), and Menenius has been "[t]he book of his good acts whence men have read / His fame unparallel'd, haply amplified" (5.2.15–16). Not his own name, but his amplification of Coriolanus's fame, should gain him entrance here.

Menenius's boast that he has perhaps exaggerated Coriolanus's deeds works both for and against him. It shows his good will; he wants Coriolanus to enjoy singular fame. But it also detracts from Coriolanus's fame by implying that not all it is fully deserved. What shows Menenius's benevolence derogates from Coriolanus's merit. To be entirely loyal to a friend, Menenius suggests, means not to be entirely loyal to the truth. Menenius, to be sure, claims that he stays within the truth. He has always testified to the merit of ("verified" [5.2.17]) his friends, he says, with the most ample praise that truth ("verity" [5.2.18]) could allow without slipping into error. Amplification may avoid exaggeration. But Menenius no sooner says that he stays within the truth than he repeats, without his earlier qualification ("haply"), that he has at times exceeded it:

Nay, sometimes,
Like to a bowl upon a subtle ground,
I have tumbled past the throw, and in his praise
Have almost stamp'd the leasing.

(5.2.19–22)

Menenius has sometimes overshot the mark and almost made the lies pass for truth. "Therefore, fellow," he concludes, "I must have leave to pass" (5.2.22–23). Menenius, however, fails, again. The First Watch, spurning his attempt to win credit for his friendship by confessing his lying, says that he would not let Menenius through even if he "had told as many lies in [Coriolanus's] behalf as [he has] uttered words in [his] own," not even if, as he states with a bawdy pun, "it were as virtuous to lie as to live chastely" (5.2.24–25, 26–27).

Seeing his effort faltering but again insistent upon the force of his name, Menenius replaces his personal friendship with his partisan activity in support of Coriolanus in Rome: "Prithee, fellow, remember my name is Menenius, always factionary on the party of your general" (5.2.29). The Second Watch, however, is derisively dismissive. While apparently continuing the First Watch's pun, he says, notwithstanding that Menenius has been Coriolanus's "liar, as you say you have, I am one that, telling true under him, must say you cannot pass" (5.2.30–32). Where Menenius appealed by trying to separate loyalty from truth, the sentinels reject his appeal by keeping them together. To be loyal to Coriolanus means not to magnify his deeds but to be true to his orders. Ironically, whereas truth means verity or accuracy to Menenius, to the Volscian sentinels the word carries the older, more traditional Roman sense of faithful or steadfast. It means conformable to duty, not conformable to fact. It is a trial of the soul rather than a grasping of the mind.[3]

When Menenius asks whether Coriolanus has eaten, saying that he "would not speak with him till after dinner" (5.2.33–34), the First Watch responds incredulously, "You are a Roman, are you?" (5.2.35). Menenius seems oblivious to the utterly unspirited, un-Roman impression that he is making on soldiers who already expect to see Rome burned to the ground (5.2.7, 44–46). And when Menenius answers, "I am as thy general is" (5.2.36), the Watch replies, "Then you should hate Rome, as he does" (5.2.37). Coriolanus's cause should be every Roman's cause. The Watch then voices his indignation at Rome. Echoing both Coriolanus's curse upon Rome (3.3.127–33) and Cominius's accusation of the tribunes (4.6.82–84), he asks reproachfully,

Can you, when you have pushed out your gates the very defender of them, and, in a violent popular ignorance, given your enemy your shield, think to front

his revenges with the easy groans of old women, the virginal palms of your
daughters, or with the palsied intercession of such a decayed dotant as you
seem to be? Can you think to blow out the intended fire your city is ready to
flame in, with such weak breath as this?

(5.2.38–46)

The guard asks whether the Romans think that their effeminate efforts and
weak words can avoid the destruction that they have foolishly brought upon
themselves. "No," he answers himself, "you are deceived" (5.2.46). Go back
to Rome, he tells Menenius, "and prepare for your execution. You are condemned; our general has sworn you out of reprieve and pardon" (5.2.47–49).
To the Watch, Rome deserves punishment not simply for banishing its defender but for subsequently compounding its folly by thinking that it can
save itself with such effete, effeminate, enfeebled efforts.

The guard's condemnation, "our general has sworn you out of reprieve and
pardon," points to Coriolanus's ambiguous and precarious situation among
the Volscians. Coriolanus has "sworn" not to pardon the Romans. A sign of
the basic distrust at least some of the Volscians have for him, the oath makes
the gods sureties for his constancy toward the Romans. The Romans may desperately fear Coriolanus's implacable vengeful wrath, but not all the Volscians trust it. Also, in addition to the guards referring to Coriolanus, from the
start, as "our general" (5.2.5, 48; also 5.2.108), the First Watch, correcting
Menenius, ends the exchange by explicitly distinguishing "my general"
(Coriolanus) from "my captain" (Aufidius) (5.2.50–54). Coriolanus is the
leader of the army; Aufidius, of a company.

2.

When Coriolanus enters, Menenius, having been personally insulted as well
as rebuffed, attempts to turn tables on the First Watch. Addressing him as
"you companion," a term of contempt (5.2.59; see 4.5.13–14), Menenius
tries to show the sentinel that he is worthy of respect and that a petty, im-
pertinent officer such as the Watch cannot keep him from "[his] son Coriolanus" (5.2.62). No doubt encouraged by Cominius's report that Coriolanus
"call'd [him] father" (5.1.3), Menenius is not only confident that Coriolanus
will respond, but certain that a nominal family tie is the same as a natural
family tie. A surrogate father is a father. Menenius therefore assuredly calls
on the sentry to watch how he will be received. Just as the sentry told Menenius to go back to Rome and prepare for execution, Menenius tells him that
he should "[b]ehold" Coriolanus's reception "and swound for what's to come

upon thee" (5.2.65, 66). Anger looks with pleasure to punishment. The punishment, moreover, is twofold—of the body and the soul. Anger enjoys the sight not just of the physical punishment itself, but, as both Menenius and Cominius demonstrated with the tribunes, of the guilty party's seeing or imagining it coming. In beholding Coriolanus's reception, the sentinel will see his own impending punishment—either death by "hanging, or . . . some death more long in spectatorship and crueler in suffering" (5.2.63–65; cf. 4.6.82–84).

Menenius, turning to Coriolanus, calls upon the gods to preside continually over his well-being and to "love thee no worse than thy old father Menenius does" (5.2.68–69). A father's love, he seems to think, is the greatest love (cf. 5.3.10). Menenius then appeals to Coriolanus directly as his son: "O my son, my son, thou art preparing fire for us: look thee, here's water to quench it" (5.2.69–71). If a father's love is the greatest love, a father's tears are the greatest tears, particularly when brought on to prevent or extinguish a son's most grievous act. Menenius explains that he was reluctant to come, but was assured that only he could move Coriolanus to pardon Rome. He wisely omits revealing that it was the tribunes, not the nobles, who urged him and that it was Coriolanus's reception of Cominius that had made him loath to try. Finally, Menenius calls upon the gods to "assuage [Coriolanus's] wrath, and turn the dregs of it upon this varlet here" (5.2.75–76). He seems to hope that, by arousing Coriolanus's anger against the guard, he can deflect it from Rome, while satisfying his own desire to see the guard punished.

Menenius is, of course, as crushed as he is surprised by Coriolanus's brutally abrupt dismissal: "Away!" (5.2.78). Yet, despite his curt command, Coriolanus attempts to explain himself. He first denies that he has a family, at all: "Wife, mother, child, I know not" (5.2.80). Free from the natural ties of generation, he is free from the natural obligations and affections of family. But, at the same time, Coriolanus is no longer his own man. "My affairs / Are servanted to others," he says, turning the adjective "servant," fittingly, into a passive verb.[4] To get his revenge, he has had to make his affairs subservient to others. Thus, as he states explicitly, "Though I owe / My revenge properly, my remission lies / In Volscian breasts" (5.2.81–83). The right to revenge belongs to him, but the power to forgive belongs to the Volscians.

It is by no means certain, however, that Coriolanus would change his mind if he could. "That we have been familiar," he continues, "Ingrate forgetfulness shall poison rather / Than pity note how much" (5.2.83–85). Menenius has presented himself as Coriolanus's close friend and appealed as his father. But we get angrier with our friends and family than with others, for we expect them to treat us well, not badly.[5] Thus, his friends having deserted him, Coriolanus finds their past friendship a cause of greater present anger, not of pity. "Therefore be gone," he tells Menenius; "Mine ears against your suits are stronger than / Your gates against my force" (5.2.85–87; cf. 1.4.24–25). But, despite having just turned Menenius's expressions of love against him, Coriolanus, shifting to the familiar pronoun, softens his rebuff by offering Menenius a letter, owing to his love: "Yet, for I lov'd thee, / Take this along; I writ it for thy sake, / And would have sent it" (5.2.87–89). Coriolanus, nonetheless, regards himself as unwavering: "This man, Aufidius, / Was my belov'd in Rome: yet thou behold'st" (5.2.90–91). Coriolanus sees, and thinks others see, only his dismissive refusals. He views his ambivalence as constancy. Not surprisingly, Aufidius dryly answers, "You keep a constant temper" (5.2.92). These are Aufidius's only words in the scene.

3.

The guards get their revenge. As Menenius relished their imagined doom, they mock with impudent sarcasm his boastful (or hopeful) claims of the power of his name ("'Tis' a spell, you see, of much power" [5.2.94]) and his threats or warnings of the consequences of their stopping him: "Do you hear how we are shent for keeping your greatness back?"; "What cause do you think I have to swound?" (5.2.96–99). Menenius, however, replies with a mixture of despondency and defiance. He declares that he no longer cares for the world or for Coriolanus ("I neither care for th'world nor your general" [5.2.100]) and suggests that he wants to kill himself ("He that hath a will to die by himself, fears it not from another: let your general do his worst" [5.2.102–4]). He has the courage of someone who cares not to live. Yet, he remains disparagingly dismissive of the guards ("For such things as you, I can scarce think there's any, y'are so slight" [5.2.101–2]) and curses them with the fate of living their miserable lives to an old age ("For you, be that you are, long; and your misery increase with your age!" [5.2.104–5]). Death would be a blessing to him; life, a curse to them. Menenius, leaving to return to Rome, expressly hurls Coriolanus's command back against the guards: "I say to you, as I was said to, Away!" (5.2.105–6). What he means as spirited defiance marks nothing so much as his dispirited defeat.

The Second Watch, taking Coriolanus's conduct as confirming his constancy, ends the scene by acclaiming him: "The worthy fellow is our general: he's the rock, the oak not to be wind-shaken" (5.2.108–9). Coriolanus, constant in the face of his friends' personal pleas, cannot be moved by anything around him.

Act Five, Scene Three

1.

Where scene 2 ends with the sentinel commending his unwavering constancy when confronted by his friends' petitions, scene 3 begins with Coriolanus making much of how openly he has conducted himself in the matter: "You must report to th'Volscian lords how plainly / I have borne this business" (5.3.3–4). Coriolanus has dealt with the Romans in public, not in private. Integrity demands full publicity. Although his Roman friends appealed on the basis of their private ties, Coriolanus permitted no privacy, no secrecy. Just as he was not moved by his private interests, he allowed nothing to be hidden from public view. Aufidius, concealing his own thoughts, confirms Coriolanus's. "Only their ends / You have respected," he replies;

> stopp'd your ears against
> The general suit of Rome: never admitted
> A private whisper, no, not with such friends
> That thought them sure of you.
>
> (5.3.4–8)

Aufidius will not say another word until after Coriolanus has yielded to his mother.

Coriolanus, as before, fails to appreciate his own ambivalence, even while describing it. He says that Menenius "[l]ov'd me above the measure of a father, / Nay, godded me indeed" (5.3.10–11; cf. 5.2.68–69); yet, the personal affection between them counted for nothing. Although Menenius was the Romans' last hope ("Their latest refuge / Was to send him" [5.3.11–12]), Coriolanus sent him back to Rome with a "crack'd heart" (5.3.9). As we have seen, however, he did not send him back entirely empty-handed. Although Coriolanus "show'd sourly to him" (5.3.13), "for [Menenius's] old love" [5.3.12]), he says, he gave him a letter which "once more offer'd / The first conditions" (5.3.13–14). The offer, though, was hollow, for the Romans "did refuse [the conditions] / And cannot now accept [them]" (5.3.14–15). Merely a personal gesture, it was meant "to grace [Menenius] only / That thought he could do more" (5.3.15–16). Coriolanus does not explain how such a vacant gesture could gratify ("grace") Menenius. Nor does he consider whether the renewed offer might split the Romans into warring parties or cause one party to desert the city. He overlooks all but the personal, and he reduces the personal to good will. Coriolanus, then, finally acknowledges that his gesture amounted to his yielding to private affection, if just slightly: "A very little / I have yielded to" (5.3.16–17). If, as he seems to mean, the gesture was a token of his heart, his description of Menenius's broken heart—"This last old man, / Whom with a crack'd heart I have sent to Rome" (5.3.8–9)—could, syntactically, describe his own.[6] Its ambiguity mirrors his ambivalence. But, having yielded a very little, Coriolanus says he will do so no more. Hereafter, he vows, he will not listen to fresh embassies from the Roman state nor suits from private friends. Coriolanus no sooner says this, however, than he hears a shout and sees his family coming toward him. "Shall I be tempted to infringe my vow / In the same time 'tis made?" he asks himself in self-reproach.[7] "I will not," he declares (5.3.20–21). He will be so constant as not even to be tempted to break the vow.

Coriolanus describes his family approaching: "My wife comes foremost; then the honour'd mould / Wherein this trunk was fram'd; and in her hand / The grandchild to her blood" (5.3.22–24). His mother is central in more than one sense. While Coriolanus describes his wife only by her position within the group, he describes his son, who is holding Volumnia's hand, as "[t]he grandchild to her blood," and Volumnia herself as "the honour'd mould / Wherein this trunk was fram'd." The three generations of "blood" are Volumnia, Coriolanus, and young Martius. Virgilia, though necessary to carry on the line, is outside the "stock [Coriolanus] springs of" (2.3.235; cf. 5.3.125–27). She is neither his origin nor his offspring.

Coriolanus is deeply moved and tries to quell the effect. "But out, affection! / All bond and privilege of nature break!" (5.3.24–25). To keep his vow and remain constant, Coriolanus must break his ties of natural affection and duty. He must defy his love of, and obligation to, his family for the sake of maintaining his constancy. Virtue pulls him one way; birth, another. The two principal aspects of his soul pull apart. Coriolanus seems to realize, however, that he is incapable of constancy under the conditions. "Let it be virtuous to be obstinate," he proclaims, with an imperative that is really an optative, a command that is really a wish (5.3.26). Recognizing that he cannot be constant, he wishes to turn obduracy into a virtue. Hard-heartedness is to replace firm-heartedness. A man who has always prided himself on his singleness, Coriolanus finally realizes that he cannot separate himself from a natural part of himself. He cannot surpass his nature without suppressing his nature. Recognizing what has been true of him from the start, he finally sees that his battle is not so much between him and an external enemy as within his own soul.

Coriolanus describes the looks and gestures of his family members. He describes his wife's comely beauty ("that curtsy, . . . those doves' eyes" [5.3.27]), which he says " can make gods forsworn" (5.3.28). Next, he describes his mother's bowing to him as an inversion or perversion of authority and piety:

"My mother bows, / As if Olympus to a molehill should / In supplication nod" (5.3.29–31). The low should bow to the high: the son should supplicate his mother, not the mother her son. Then, Coriolanus describes his young son's pleading look "which / Great nature cries, 'Deny not'" (5.3.32–33). The love of comely beauty, the sense of pious shame, and the love of one's own all melt him. Recognizing that he is not a monolith ("the rock" [5.2.108–9]), but is instead made of the same mortal substance as others, he confesses, "I melt, and am not / Of stronger earth than others" (5.3.28–29).

Coriolanus, however, seeks to overcome his human nature. "Let the Volsces / Plough Rome and harrow Italy," he defiantly declares;

> I'll never
> Be such a gosling to obey instinct, but stand
> As if a man were author of himself
> And knew no other kin.
>
> (5.3.33–37)

Coriolanus's claim to self-sufficiency issues in his wish for self-generation. To be autonomous is to be autogenous. The separation of virtue from its conditions ultimately presupposes the separation of virtue from birth. Coriolanus can cut himself off from natural affection—can disobey instinct—only by knowing no kin, only by having procreated himself. To be his own origin and end, he must repudiate his maternal source and deny his soul's double nature. He must be ungenerated and ungenerative. Coriolanus tacitly concedes the impossibility of his wish. Earlier, before they appeared, he claimed not to "know" his wife, mother, and child (5.2.80). Now, in their presence, he will stand "as if . . . [he] knew no other kin." His wish to defy his natural instinct and be "author of himself" is not only unnatural; it is based on an untruth. It takes the subjunctive ("[a]s if") for the indicative, a wish for a fact. Coriolanus cannot be what he wishes to be without pretending to be what he is not.

Virgilia addresses Coriolanus as "[m]y lord and husband" (5.3.37). These are her first words directly to him. Virgilia speaks as though nothing has changed between them. Coriolanus, trying to deny her claim on him,[8] corrects her: "These eyes are not the same I wore in Rome" (5.3.38). He now sees things, including his wife, differently. Virgilia, dressed like the others in tattered garments and looking haggard (5.3.94–96), purposely misunderstands him and answers as though it is not Coriolanus's eyes but what they see that has changed: "The sorrow that delivers us thus chang'd / Makes you think so" (5.3.39–40). Coriolanus's family appear different to

him, not because of any inward change in him caused by his wrath, but because of an outward change in them brought on by their sorrow.

While Virgilia implicitly distinguishes between him and what he sees,
Coriolanus explicitly distinguishes between himself and what others see of
him. Earlier, he refused to seem other than what he is: "Would you have me
/ False to my nature? Rather say I play / The man I am" (3.2.14–16). Being
true to his nature, he thought or wished to think, meant playing no role at
all. It meant simply being the man he is. But now, once again using the language of the theater, he admits that he must play a role, although he has
forgotten his lines: "Like a dull actor now / I have forgot my part and I am
out, / Even to a full disgrace" (5.3.40–42). To be the man he wishes to be,
Coriolanus must play the part of that man. He must mask his nature to appear true to his nature. Absolute integrity demands playacting.

Coriolanus asks Virgilia for what he himself refuses to give. She should
forgive his refusal to forgive. "Forgive my tyranny," he says, "but do not say,
/ For that 'Forgive our Romans'" (5.3.43–44). Coriolanus acknowledges
that his pitiless revenge is in need of forgiveness. But even as he tacitly
concedes that his action is wrongful, he denies that its wrongfulness is any
reason for him to forgo it.

Having addressed her as his wife ("Best of my flesh" [5.3.42]), Coriolanus
and Virgilia kiss. Delivering his most erotic speech, Coriolanus compares the
pleasure of his wife's kiss to the pleasure of his revenge: "O, a kiss / Long as
my exile, sweet as my revenge!" (5.3.44–45). Earlier, enraptured by the an-
ticipation of fighting Aufidius, Coriolanus likened his joy to that of his wooing and wedding his wife (1.6.29–32). The marital was his simile for the martial. Now, even when kissing his wife after what he calls a long exile, he
subordinates love to revenge. Nothing, it seems, is sweeter to him than revenge. Then, swearing by Juno, the jealous goddess of marriage, Coriolanus
affirms his faithfulness to Virgilia: "Now by the jealous queen of heaven, that
kiss / I carried from thee, dear; and my true lip / Hath virgin'd it e'er since"
(5.3.46–48). Coriolanus's verb—one that Shakespeare coins here and uses
nowhere else—is striking. If revenge is Coriolanus's standard for sweetness,
virginity is his standard for fidelity. Coriolanus's most erotic moment is not
only austere and even severe, but largely unerotic. His passion and pleasure
belong to revenge. These are Coriolanus's final words to his wife.

As though suddenly catching himself, Coriolanus turns to his mother,
ashamed of having neglected her: "You gods! I pray, / And the most noble
mother of the world / Leave unsaluted" (5.48–50). Throughout the play,
kneeling is a gesture of supplication, reverence, or repentance.[9] Here, Coriolanus kneels in reverent salutation to his mother. Performing his pious duty,

he kneels as deeply as he can to show a duty deeper than that of ordinary sons: "Sink, my knee, i'th'earth: / Of thy deep duty more impression show / Than that of common sons" (5.3.50–52). Coriolanus, competing in filial piety with other sons, confounds the literal and the figurative. Because the ritual itself constitutes the duty, his depth of pious duty to his mother can be shown by taking the literal—how deep an impression in the earth he makes—as the figurative—how deep his reverence is. The outward expression of the duty is identical to the inward substance of the duty.

Volumnia, however, turns the gesture back against Coriolanus. Bidding him to rise ("Oh, stand up bless'd!" [5.3.52]), she kneels before him, ironically suggesting, against all propriety ("unproperly" [5.3.54]), that the "duty . . . all this while" of the child bowing before the parent has been "mistaken" (5.3.55). If she must beg her son, then parents should owe their children their reverence (cf. 3.2.123–25). Recognizing Volumnia's cutting irony and further shamed by her gesture ("What's this? / Your knees to me?" [5.3.56–57]), Coriolanus, her "corrected son" (5.3.57), cannot imagine a greater confusion in the world. If Volumnia may beg her son, then petty pebbles on the beach should strike against the stars, and wild winds should throw tall trees against the sun, elevating the low to the high, the earthly to the heavenly, and making any or every impossibility possible: "Murd'ring impossibility, to make / What cannot be, slight work!" (5.3.61–62). Other Romans can imagine no destruction greater than that of Rome itself (e.g., 3.1.196, 202–5). By contrast, Coriolanus, no longer—or perhaps never really—a Roman, imagines Volumnia's kneeling as tantamount to the overthrow of the cosmic order.

Volumnia seems greatly encouraged by Coriolanus's expression of shame and homage. With a note of triumphant joy, she exclaims, "Thou are my warrior: / I hope to frame thee" (5.3.62–63).[10] She evidently expects to shape him to the purpose for which she came.[11] Volumnia then asks whether Coriolanus knows Valeria. Valeria, who had visited Volumnia and Virgilia while Coriolanus was at war (1.3.48ff.) and was with them when he returned from battle (2.1.95ff.), has accompanied them, again. At first glance, her presence seems strange. Although Plutarch reports that Valeria was responsible for the delegation of women going to Coriolanus (Plutarch, *Coriolanus*, 33), Shakespeare suggests nothing of the sort and has her remain entirely silent throughout the scene. When asked whether he knows her, Coriolanus describes Valeria with hyperbolic praise of her chastity:

> The noble sister of Publicola,
> The moon of Rome, chaste as the icicle

> That's curdied by the frost from purist snow
> And hangs on Dian's temple! Dear Valeria!

(5.3.64–67)

As noted much earlier, Coriolanus's praise does not seem to agree with what we have seen of Valeria. While Coriolanus praises her stark austerity, Valeria has shown herself to be warm and whimsical, to have a taste for cheerful, even frivolous pleasure, to enjoy easy gossip, and to be irreverent about marital fidelity. Where he praises her chastity for resembling the purest of all frozen things, she jests about Homer's account of Penelope. Coriolanus's praise may, however explain Valeria's presence. As previously suggested, Coriolanus sees Valeria not as she is, but as he wishes her to be—indeed, as he wishes everything noble, especially himself, to be. His praise marks his spirit's simplification—its exaggeration and distortion of what it sees, its tendency to ignore all but one part and see that part as the whole. Coriolanus's antierotic view of Valeria indicates precisely what Volumnia's entreaty must overcome.

Volumnia turns, next, to young Martius. She describes the boy as an "epitome" (5.3.68)—literally, a small edition or abridgment—of Coriolanus, whom the fullness of time will, like an orator, expand and develop into a full copy (". . . by th'interpretation of full time / May show like all yourself" [5.3.69–70]). Coriolanus has a different wish for the boy. He does not wish him to be a copy of himself. Calling upon "[t]he god of soldiers, / With the consent of supreme Jove," Coriolanus asks Mars to imbue his son's "thoughts with nobleness," so that he will prove "[t]o shame unvulnerable" and stand firm and stand out in the wars, like a prominent landmark, "saving those that eye [him]" (5.3.70–75). While the son's nobility, like his father's, is to be seen by others, his glory, unlike his father's, is to come not from fighting alone, but from fighting along with his fellow citizens. His nobility is that of a citizen, not of a hero. Coriolanus thus invokes not just Mars, the god of war, but the consent of Jove, the tutelary god of Rome. What the father wants for his son thus contradicts what he wants for himself. Indeed, what he wants for himself—to be "author of himself"—ultimately denies the need for having a father. Coriolanus may praise the boy when he kneels to him in reverence ("That's my brave boy!" [5.3.76]), but his aspiration for self-sufficiency and his sense of filial reverence directly oppose each other. These are Coriolanus's only words to his son.

Coriolanus, attempting to stop Volumnia and the others from asking ("I beseech you, peace!" [5.3.78]), tells them that he has sworn ("forsworn" [5.3.80]) not to grant what they seek, and so they should not consider his refusals as "denials" (5.3.81). One can deny only what one is free to give. Coriolanus then specifies what the petitioners should not say or desire. First, he tells what not to ask for: "Do not bid me / Dismiss my soldiers, or capitulate / Again with Rome's mechanics" (5.3.81–83). Next, he states what not to say of him for refusing: "Tell me not / Wherein I seem unnatural" (5.3.83–84). Then, he says what not to want or try to do to change his mind: "Desire not / T'allay my rages and revenges with / Your colder reasons" (5.3.84–86). With a combination of casuistry and command, Coriolanus evidently seeks to avoid having explicitly to refuse his mother. Nevertheless, he permits Volumnia to shame him into hearing her. Stopping him ("O, no more, no more!" [5.3.86]), Volumnia, pointedly disregarding his evasive understanding of a denial, expressly states that she asks for nothing except what Coriolanus has already denied her: "[W]e have nothing else to ask but that / Which you deny already" (5.3.88–89). And, then, she not only asks for it, but places the blame on his stubbornness if he fails to grant it: "Yet we will ask, / That if you fail in our request, the blame / May hang upon your hardness: therefore hear us" (5.3.89–91). Shamed by his mother into listening, Coriolanus stresses the public setting of his hearing Roman pleas: "Aufidius, and you Volsces, mark; for we'll / Hear nought from Rome in private. Your request?" (5.3.92–93). As he underscores by his confident imperative "mark," Coriolanus expects to show himself publicly, still again, unyielding to private pleas from Rome (cf. 5.2.90–91; 5.3.2–4).

Volumnia's long entreaty has five parts or stages. In the first (5.3.94–125), Volumnia appeals for pity for those Coriolanus loves. Throughout it, she catalogs the reversals and contradictions of his family's piteous situation. While the sight of his family, with their rags and emaciated bodies, would show Coriolanus what life they have led since his exile, still worse, their sight of him makes his mother and wife "more unfortunate than all living women" (5.3.97). For the sight that should make their "eyes flow with joy, hearts dance with comforts," forces them, instead, to

> weep, and shake with fear and sorrow,
> Making the mother, wife and child to see
> The son, the husband and the father, tearing
> His country's bowels out.

> (5.3.99, 100–3)

Coriolanus's enmity to Rome is most fatal ("most capital" [5.3.104]) to his own family ("to poor we" [5.3.103]), Volumnia explains, for they, unlike other Romans, cannot pray to the gods. "Alas! How can we for our country pray, / Whereto we are bound, together with thy victory, / Whereto we are bound?" (5.3.107–9). Their prayers, like their duties, conflict. Coriolanus's family can not pray without praying against their own prayers.[12] Likewise, his family must lose either "[t]he country, our dear nurse, or else thy person, / Our comfort in the country" (5.3.110–11). And whichever side should win, the victory would be "an evident calamity" (5.3.112) for them, for Coriolanus would either be led in chains through the streets as "a foreign recreant" (5.3.114) or "[t]riumphantly tread on thy country's ruin, / And bear the palm for having bravely shed / Thy wife and children's blood" (5.3.116–18). Either way, victory would be their defeat.

For Volumnia, as for Romans in general, there is no life apart from Rome. Everything Volumnia holds dear, including her son, is founded on Rome. Volumnia therefore has no hesitation in choosing her country over her son. Addressing him as "son" for the first time in the scene (5.3.118) and declaring that she will not await the outcome of the war, she warns that if she cannot persuade Coriolanus to show "a noble grace to both parts" rather than "seek the end of one,"

> thou shalt no sooner
> March to assault thy country than to tread—
> Trust to't, thou shalt not—on thy mother's womb
> That brought thee to this world.
>
> (5.3.121–25)

Coriolanus cannot "tread" on his mother country without "tread[ing]" on his mother's womb. His twin sources are inseparable. As he implied in wishing to be "author of himself," Coriolanus cannot attack the country of his birth without destroying his own natural origin. It is important to note that Volumnia's mention of Coriolanus's showing "a noble grace" to both parties is her first hint—but only a hint—of a face-saving political solution. Because she will suggest the solution after she has made her private pleas in public, it will come too late.

Modeling the first stage of her entreaty on the rules of classical rhetoric for appeals to pity, Volumnia begins by displaying the suppliants' unkempt clothes and haggard faces, amplifying their suffering by not only telling of it, but bringing it before Coriolanus's eyes.[13] Then, throughout her lament, she uses many of the so-called rhetorical commonplaces or topics (*loci*) for arousing pity. Claiming that their life since Coriolanus's exile leaves them "more unfortunate than all living women" and that his enmity toward Rome is "most capital" to them (5.3.97, 104), she contrasts, first, what she and Virgilia should enjoy—and once enjoyed—with their present misery (e.g., 5.3.98–111) and, then, their present misery with their even worse future (5.3.111–25). Enumerating and explaining the consequences that will befall them if they fail to persuade him, Volumnia deplores each separate phase of their misfortune: the fear and sorrow of the mother, wife, and child seeing their son, husband, and father attacking his native country (5.3.98–103), their inconsolable inability to pray for either Rome's or Coriolanus's victory (5.3.104–11), the calamitous prospect of either Coriolanus's being led in chains as a traitorous deserter through the streets of Rome or else his coming in triumph over his country's ruin and his family's blood (5.3.111–18), and the death of his mother that his attack would bring (5.3.118–25). At the same time, Volumnia declares that even though her cause is hopeless, her heart will be brave.[14] In addition, besides speaking in piteous superlative hyperbole (5.3.97, 103–6), Volumnia amplifies her plea by repeating words and phrases in succeeding or parallel clauses (e.g., 5.3.106–9),[15] describing her misery concisely and vividly (e.g., 5.3.113–18),[16] and personifying the country Coriolanus would attack, making it the Romans' living nurse (5.3.103, 110), which she, furthermore, makes nearly indistinguishable from herself or her womb (5.3.110, 124–25).[17] And, from start to finish, she describes with balanced antitheses a series of doleful dilemmas (e.g., 5.3.106–18).[18]

Virgilia seconds Volumnia's warning. Just as Coriolanus would tread on his mother's womb that "brought [him] to this world" (5.3.125), so too, she says with defiance, he would have to tread on his wife's womb, "[t]hat brought [him] forth this boy to keep [his] name / Living to time" (5.3.126–27). Whereas Coriolanus thinks of keeping his name alive through his deeds, Virgilia speaks of keeping his name alive through his offspring. For him, fame brings immortality; for her, procreation. For Coriolanus, immortality is achieved through death; for Virgilia, through generation. Virgilia's surprisingly defiant speech contains her final words to her husband.

Young Martius similarly challenges his father. Combining a recognition of his present inability with a resolve to act in the future, he shows himself to be his father's son. "A shall not tread on me," the boy defiantly declares. "I'll run away till I am bigger, but then I'll fight" (5.3.127–28). If the fatherless Coriolanus would kill his mother, young Martius, in return, would kill his father. He, too, would repudiate his source (cf. 1.3.66–67). These are the boy's only words.

Coriolanus tries to leave for fear of softening. "Not of a woman's tenderness to be," he says, lapsing into rhyme,[19] "Requires nor child nor woman's face to see" (5.3.129–30). The sight of softness would soften him. Coriolanus therefore starts to leave: "I have sat too long" (5.3.131). But

Volumnia orders him to stay ("Nay, go not from us thus" [5.3.131]) and makes a new appeal. Whereas the first stage of her entreaty appealed to his pity for his family, the second (5.3.132–48) appeals to his sense of, or concern for, his honor.

Returning to what she seemed to mean by his showing "a noble grace to both parts," Volumnia denies that Coriolanus would poison his honor by granting the suitors' plea. If granting their request tended "[t]o save the Romans" and "destroy / The Volsces, . . . you might condemn us / As poisonous of your honour" (5.3.133–35). But there is no need to choose between the two parties. "No, our suit / Is that you reconcile them" (5.3.135–36). The Volscians could show their magnanimity in sparing the Romans, and the Romans their gratitude in having been spared, and Coriolanus could be acclaimed by all as the peacemaker:

> [W]hile the Volsces
> May say, "This mercy we have show'd," the Romans,
> "This we receiv'd"; and each in either side
> Give the all-hail to thee, and cry, "Be bless'd
> For making up this peace!"
>
> (5.3.136–40)

Volumnia, having imperceptibly shifted from honor in the sense of integrity to honor in the sense of reputation, does not explain why the Volscians would be satisfied with anything less than victory or why they would accept Coriolanus's abandoning their cause. She speaks as though their satisfaction in what they and the Romans could say about them would outweigh their giving up their conquest of Rome. Moreover, she speaks as though Coriolanus would be satisfied with receiving acclaim for something other than his invincible virtue. She seems to think—or at least to say—that, both for the Volscians and for him, acclaim for making peace outweighs victory and conquest in war.

As though recognizing the weakness of her case, Volumnia reminds Coriolanus of what he knows. "Thou know'st, great son," she says, juxtaposing an uncertainty and a certainty, "The end of war's uncertain, but this certain": even if Coriolanus wins the war, he will gain only

> such a name
> Whose repetition will be dogg'd with curses,
> Whose chronicle thus writ: "The man was noble,
> But with his last attempt he wip'd it out,

Destroy'd his country, and his name remains
To th'insuing age abhorr'd."

(5.3.143–48)

Quoting what would be said of him in lasting infamy, Volumnia argues that
if Coriolanus fights, he must lose his noble name. He cannot fight against his
country and win. Victory as much as defeat can bring him nothing but ig-
nominy.

Volumnia bases the second stage of her entreaty on the rules of classical
deliberative rhetoric. While recognizing that the authority of the speaker
carries the greatest weight (esp. 5.3.140–48),[20] she connects the advantageous and the honorable, showing the latter as the former,[21] compares what
is to be gained and what is to be lost, what is certain and what is uncertain
(5.3.132–48),[22] shows that her proposed course of action is both possible and
desirable, foresees and forestalls objections (5.3.132–40),[23] supports her proof
by citing a maxim and referring to the customary course of events
(5.3.141),[24] and, in contrast to her lament, employs simple language, simple
syntax and words in common use, which are appropriate to what she mentions.[25] She also demonstrates both the fame and the infamy that Coriolanus
would acquire by quoting what present Romans and Volscians and future
chroniclers would say.[26] But like her lament, her deliberative appeal fails. It
meets only silence.

Coriolanus's silence seems to anger and unnerve Volumnia, provoking the
third stage of her plea (5.3.148–68), which accuses him of filial ingratitude.
Urging him to speak to her and, again, calling him "son" (5.3.148), she says
that he has always aspired to "imitate the graces of the gods" (5.3.150), but
the gods temper their thunder with mercy. Although their thunder tears "the
wide cheek o'th'air," their bolt "but rive[s] an oak" (5.3.151, 153). The gods
thunder loudly, but are merciful to the weak and direct their lightning merely
at a tree (cf. 3.1.79–81). Coriolanus, however, still does not reply. Volumnia,
understanding his unbroken silence as an outward sign of his implacable
anger (cf. 3.1.51–60), asks whether he thinks it honorable for a noble man
always to remember wrongs, calls upon Virgilia and young Martius to try to
move him to speak by speaking to him, and, finally, accuses Coriolanus of ingratitude toward her. Turning away from political considerations, she appeals
to his sense of filial piety and tries to convict him in his own eyes of ingratitude. Although no man in the world is more obliged ("bound" [5.4.159]) to
his mother, she says, Coriolanus not only lets her "prate" (5.3.159) in public
humiliation ("[l]ike one i'th'stocks" [5.3.160]), but he has also never shown

her any consideration. "Thou hast never in thy life," she charges, "Show'd thy dear mother any courtesy, / When she, poor hen," wanting "no second brood," clucked him to the wars and safely home, laden with honors (5.3.160–64). His mother has given him everything, and given up everything for him, but he has given her nothing in return. Despite the flagrant false-hood, Coriolanus remains silent. Having failed to arouse him with her out-rageous charge, Volumnia now partly switches ground. Instead of speaking of her son's wholly unpaid, unsurpassed debt to her, she speaks of the duty that any son owes his mother. Coriolanus may call her request unjust and send her back to Rome, she says; but if it is not unjust, then he is not truthful or honorable ("not honest" [5.3.166]), and the gods will punish ("plague" [5.3.166]) him for denying her "the duty which / To a mother's part belongs" (5.3.167–68). Volumnia is asking only for the filial duty that any mother de-serves.

Volumnia's attempt to convict Coriolanus in his own eyes applies classi-cal forensic rhetoric's prescriptions for accusations. Volumnia establishes not what was done—for that is not in dispute—but the character of the matter: Coriolanus violated his filial duty.[27] And she uses the manner of his life to confirm the charge.[28] While resting her case on the duties of kinship, espe-cially between child and parent,[29] she not only uses embellishment, includ-ing simile and metaphor, to enrich and adorn her argument,[30] but, anticipat-ing her son's reply, couches her rejoinder in the form of criss-cross consequences: Coriolanus can punish his mother justly or the gods will pun-ish him justly.[31] This is, in fact, the only time Volumnia mentions the words "honest," "just," or "unjust," and one of only two times when she mentions "duty." The other occurred in the first stage of her appeal when she spoke, similarly, of the "duty . . . / Between the child and parent" (5.3.55–56).

When Coriolanus, instead of speaking, turns away, Volumnia, beginning her entreaty's fourth stage (5.3.168–77), urges the women to "shame him with [their] knees" (5.3.169). What she calls for is what she did when she initially spoke and first mentioned filial duty (5.3.52–56). "Action is eloquence" (3.2.76). Volumnia does to Coriolanus what she urged him to do to the peo-ple. Indeed, throughout the scene, the suitors' visible looks and gestures—Virgilia's "curtsy" (5.3.27), Volumnia's "bow[ing]" and "kneel[ing] (5.3.29, 53), the suitors' poor dress (5.3.39–40, 93–95), young Martius's "aspect" (5.3.32), Virgilia's "kiss" (5.3.44), young Martius's kneeling and supplicating with raised hands (5.4.75, 175), and, now, all the suitors' kneeling—have moved Coriolanus, as he himself has acknowledged (5.3.22–37, 56–62). Vo-lumnia, assuming, however, that Coriolanus's turning away is meant to deny her rather than to hide his rising distress, implicitly converts the meaning of his name: "To his surname Coriolanus longs more pride / Than pity to our prayers" (5.3.170–71). Too proud to pity his family's prayers, "the conqueror of Corioles" has become "man of Corioles."[32] As we noted when he returned to Rome in triumph, this is the only time Volumnia calls her son by his surname. Not only has he become what he has conquered. The deed-achieved name marks the unbridgeable separation between him and his mother. In the play's first mention of Volumnia, a citizen paired Coriolanus's pride and his wish to please his mother as the twin motives of his action (1.1.38–39). As was implicit before but is explicit now, the pair have pulled apart; each implies the destruction of the other. Bidding the suitors to make an end and announcing that they will return to Rome and die among the Romans, Volumnia speaks as though she has given up all hope. But, suddenly refusing to cease her effort, she tries to move Coriolanus with young Martius's silent but compelling gestures of kneeling and supplication:

> Nay, behold's,
> This boy that cannot tell what he would have,
> But kneels, and holds up hands for fellowship,
> Does reason our petition with more strength
> Than thou hast to deny't.
>
> (5.3.173–77)

The boy's speechless, pleading gestures should have more strength than Coriolanus has to deny the plea. But this attempt, too, fails. Like all of Volumnia's previous attempts, it leads only to Coriolanus's continued stubborn, silent resistance.

Volumnia's attempt to shame Coriolanus follows classical rhetoric's guidelines for censure. Volumnia tries to shame Coriolanus, both by word and by gesture (5.3.169–77), blames his character for his fault (5.3.170–71), calls a vice what he considers his virtue (5.3.170–71), uses strong comparisons (5.3.170–71, 176–77), paradoxically inverts an antithesis (5.3.176–77), corrects herself for emphasis (5.3.173), combines a threatened misfortune with an appeal for pity (172–77), and abandons all hope (5.3.172–73).[33]

In her entreaty's last stage (5.3.177–82), unable to break his silence, let alone to persuade him, Volumnia, again calling upon her party to leave, finally disowns Coriolanus. No longer referring to the suitors as his "mother, wife, and child" (5.3.101), she describes Coriolanus as the son, husband, and father of Volscians: "This fellow had a Volscian to his mother; / His wife is in Corioles, and his child / Like him by chance" (5.3.178–80). Unmoved by their piteous pleas, Coriolanus is no longer a member of their family. Indeed, he never was. In denying his family's cries, he denies that he was ever born of Volumnia, ever married Valeria, or ever begot young Martius. His silence bespeaks a stranger. Significantly but not surprisingly, Volumnia, in disowning Coriolanus, places him in another city and family. While he wishes to stand alone and know no kin, she describes him as having countrymen and kin. To her, one's city and family necessarily define one's identity. Just as she cannot imagine herself apart from Rome, she cannot imagine anyone apart from city and family. Rendered silent by Coriolanus's silence, Volumnia concludes by vowing that her silence will be short-lived: "I am husht until our city be afire, / And then I'll speak a little" (5.3.181–82). If she disowns her son now, she will curse him later.

Still silent, Coriolanus takes his mother's hand. He "[h]olds her by the hand silent" (s.d. 5.3.182). In *Coriolanus*, hands are often syncedoches for the grip of force or necessity, especially in matters of death.[34] At other times, however, they are the external signs of the bonds between people.[35] Hands go together with the blood of life and with the blood of death—with Coriolanus's origin and end, with the conditions for his virtue and the virtue that tries to free itself from those conditions. They involve the touching that harms or bonds. Here, Coriolanus's holding his mother's hand—the outward and literal sign of his reaffirming the lineal bond—at once reunites him with his family and announces that he will not attack Rome. A silent, symbolic gesture, it tacitly disavows his proud scorn for the body. Not the belly, as Menenius thought or hoped, but the womb, as Volumnia stressed, has forced him to forfeit his imitation of the gods and to realize that he is not Mars, but Martius.[36]

"O mother, mother! / What have you done?" Coriolanus finally exclaims. "Behold, the heavens do ope, / The gods look down, and this unnatural scene / They laugh at" (5.3.182–85). Coriolanus sees himself as acting a part before the gods. He is a stage actor; the gods are his audience. What is tragedy for him, however, is comedy for them. The gods, Coriolanus suggests, inspire men to scale heaven, but then laugh when men, attempting to "imitate the graces of the gods" and become more than human, are brought down by their own humanity (see 1.1.255). If man affirms his nature by trying to surpass his nature, his nature finally causes him to fail. What spurs him on, trips him up. Coriolanus describes the scene as "unnatural." By "unnatural," he seems to refer not to a Roman warring against Rome or a mother pleading with her son for mercy, but a heroic warrior melting to such pleas (cf. 1.1.171–73).[37] In order not to be "[f]alse to my nature" (3.2.16)—to be "the man I am" (4.5.47)—Coriolanus has had to oppose his nature. He has had to denature his nature in order to be true to his nature. What is "unnatural" to him is for him to submit to his common human "nature" or "instinct" (5.3.25, 33, 35).

It is to recognize that he is not author of himself and to yield to the natural bonds of birth.

Volumnia does not answer Coriolanus. In fact, she does not say another word. Just as she left without acknowledging his reluctant decision to flatter the Roman people (3.2.137), she never even begins to say what she thinks of his agreeing not to attack Rome. Their reunification is also their final break.

Although imagining that he is on stage before the gods, Coriolanus seems to forget that he is on public stage before the Volscians (cf. 5.3.92–93). Instead of attempting to portray his yielding as a victory for both the Volscians and the Romans, as Volumnia had belatedly suggested (5.3.121–22, 132–40), he characterizes it as a complete victory for the Romans: "O my mother, mother! O! / You have won a happy victory to Rome" (5.3.185–86). Virtually confessing his betrayal of the Volscians, he presents his acceding to his mother as both his and the Volscians' defeat. "But for your son, believe it, O, believe it," he sorrowfully insists, "Most dangerously you have with him prevail'd, / If not most mortal to him" (5.3.187–89). Never able to disguise victory, Coriolanus is unable to disguise defeat. He recognizes, however, that his submission is dangerous and might be fatal to him—that his yielding to his "mortal" bonds might prove "mortal" to him. Yet, he seems stoically to accept his fate: "But let it come" (5.3.189). His spirited defiance now seems gone. At the same time, Coriolanus, who never sees himself as betraying anyone, appears to place himself above his twin betrayals. While silent about his having betrayed the Romans, he makes light of his betraying the Volscians. Although unable to keep his promise to the Volscians (". . . though I cannot make true wars . . ." [5.3.190]), he says, he will nevertheless frame a suitable ("convenient" [5.3.191]) peace. But despite his apparently thinking that a peace short of full victory could satisfy the expectant victors, Coriolanus finds it necessary to justify his submitting to the suitors' pleas. Addressing him as "Aufidius," including "good Aufidius," thrice in four lines and, in particular, framing his explanation with Aufidius's respectful name (cf. 1.8.7; 4.5.55), he justifies his yielding to his family ties by appealing specifically as his mother's son: "Now, good Aufidius, / Were you in my stead, would you have heard / A mother less? or granted less, Aufidius?" (5.3.191–93). Coriolanus's rhetorical question points up the critical difficulty: only someone "in [his] stead"—only the suitor's son—would have yielded to her pleas. Oddly, Coriolanus seems to expect Aufidius to understand and forgive him. He appears to have forgotten why the Volscians thought they needed to make him swear not to relent (5.3.80–82). "I was mov'd withal," Aufidius answers, with ominous reserve.[38] Coriolanus's spiritedness, in surrender, takes the form of self-justification and a curious kind of boasting. "I dare be sworn you were," he replies, adding, "And, sir, it is no little thing to make / Mine eyes to sweat compassion" (5.3.194–96). Instead of "sweat[ing] with wrath" at his enemies (1.4.27), he has sweated tears of compassion for his mother. The warrior who has brought tears to the eyes of many Volscian widows and mothers (2.1.175–78) cries when his mother pleads (cf. 4.1.25–27). Aufidius will not forget his words or his tears.

Although he recognizes that his submission to his mother may be danger-ous to him, Coriolanus announces, without explanation, that he will not re-turn to Rome but will go, instead, with Aufidius to Antium, and he asks for Aufidius's support in the matter: "I'll not to Rome, I'll back with you; and pray you, / Stand to me in this cause" (5.3.198–99). Then, he no sooner ex-pects Aufidius to treat him as a loyal ally and defend his decision than he cries out, "O mother! wife!" (5.3.199). As though having forgotten the "world['s] . . . slippery turns" (4.4.12), he trusts the political loyalty of a man whose country he has betrayed and whose political interests he threatens. Aufidius, in an aside, welcomes Coriolanus's yielding. He is delighted that Coriolanus has set his "mercy" and his "honour" at odds (5.3.200), and he will take advantage of his surrender to "work / [Him]self a former fortune" (5.3.201–2). Nevertheless, despite Coriolanus's capitulation, Aufidius evi-dently thinks that he must still work underhandedly to restore his position to what it was before giving Coriolanus joint command. However much he may have disappointed the Volscians, Coriolanus, the great warrior, might still have a bright future in Antium.

After offering the suitors a traditional gesture of peace ("[W]e will drink together" [5.3.203]), Coriolanus masculinizes the women, not only assigning them a Roman duty—to carry the official treaty of peace back to Rome—but suggesting that they deserve a high public honor for having achieved what no army of men could have achieved for Rome. "Ladies, you deserve / To have a temple built you," he says. "All the swords / In Italy and her confed-erate arms / Could not have made this peace" (5.3.206–9). Plutarch tells that the Roman Senate built a "temple of Fortune of the women" (Plutarch, Cori-olanus, 37.2; North, 2:186). Shakespeare puts the proposal for such a temple in Coriolanus's mouth. Coriolanus, confessing or even boasting that he gave away, from private duty and love, what no army could ever have won from him with swords, proposes a sacred memorial to his own submission to his mother and hence to his own mortal nature. In his final words to Romans, he obscures the distinctions between male and female, and public and pri-vate, and narrows the distinctions between virtue and fortune, war and peace. Indeed, his final word to a Roman is "peace"—a word he spoke in Rome only in bitter scorn of the people.[39] If in seeking to sever virtue from birth he undermined the patricians' central claim to political power, Coriolanus, forced to repudiate the possibility of separating them, comes to deny everything that he has always stood for. He will be a very different man from what he was, when we see him, next, in Antium.

Act Five, Scene Four

1.
Menenius had not wanted to go to Coriolanus, fearing that he would be rebuffed like Cominius. However, the tribunes, whom he had blamed for Rome's plight, persuaded him to go, assuring him that he could not fail. Menenius soon came to believe their assurance (4.6.89ff.; 5.1.1–62). Now, much as he originally feared that he would fail because Cominius had, Menenius is certain the women have failed because he did. Displaying a spirited form of hopelessness in the face of expected doom, he defends his own failure, while at the same time implicitly renews his blame of the tribunes for Rome's plight by insisting that the women's task is impossible. "If it be possible for you to displace [the cornerstone of the Capitol] with your little finger," he says, "there is some hope the ladies of Rome, especially his mother, may prevail with him." (5.4.4–6). The impossibility of Menenius's condition implies his conclusion: "But I say there is no hope in't, our throats are sentenced and stay upon execution" (5.4.4–8).

Sicinius looks for some reason for hope and thinks he finds it in Coriolanus's attachment to his mother. "Is't possible," he asks with disbelief, "that so short a time can alter the condition of a man?" (5.4.9–10). Menenius, intending to correct him, emphasizes Coriolanus's great change. "There is differency between a grub and a butterfly," he explains, "yet your butterfly was a grub. This Martius is grown from man to dragon: he has wings; he's more than a creeping thing" (5.4.11–14). Throughout his exchange with Sicinius, Menenius speaks in likenesses—in analogies, comparisons, synecdoches, metaphors, and similes. Likeness lends itself to hyperbole and exaggeration.[40] Thus, Menenius, seeking both justification of himself and blame of the tribunes, describes Coriolanus's pitilessness and Rome's peril in likenesses in virtually every sentence. Coriolanus has, of course, previously been likened to a dragon. When leaving Rome, he described himself as "[l]ike to a lonely dragon" (4.1.30), and Aufidius told of his fighting "dragon-like" for the Volscians (4.7.23). Dragons are both solitary and menacing, hence like Coriolanus in battle. Menenius, however, stresses what Coriolanus has "grown from" and what he has "[grown] to." He speaks as Coriolanus had wished— to rise above his human origins and become something more than human.

Ironically, unbeknown to Menenius, Coriolanus's natural origins have proved to limit what he could become. What he has grown from has confined what he was able to grow to. On the other hand, no less ironically, Sicinius, desperate for hope, is correct in spite of himself.

In contrast to Menenius, Sicinius, seeking hope rather than self-justification and censure, speaks literally and briefly. "He loved his mother dearly," he replies, slipping into the past tense. Menenius counters, "So did he me" (5.4.15–16). Menenius makes no distinction between being a parent and being "call'd" (5.1.3) a parent. In defending his own failure, he disregards what was essential to Volumnia's success. Menenius then continues to describe Coriolanus by means of embellished likenesses. He first compares him to a horse: "[H]e no more remembers his mother now than an eight-year-old horse" (5.4.16–17). Coriolanus can remember only his wrongs and his wished-for revenge. Menenius then offers a series of likenesses, alternating similes with metaphors, which may or may not be meant to be taken entirely figuratively:

> The tartness of his face sours ripe grapes. When he walks, he moves like an engine and the ground shrinks before his treading. He is able to pierce a corslet with his eye, talks like a knell, and his hum is a battery. He sits in his state as a thing made for Alexander.
>
> (5.4.17–22)

Coriolanus's look, walk, sight, and sound produce effects that are beyond what is natural or even possible for humans. Fittingly, Menenius compares Coriolanus not to Alexander the Great, but to his statue. Coriolanus sits on his chair of state as though he were a statue of Alexander. Pointing beyond Alexander himself, he resembles an idealized resemblance of the conqueror (cf. 2.1.263–64). And as Menenius unites image and reality, so, too, he unites speech and its effect: "What he bids be done is finished with his bidding" (5.4.23). The separation between speech and deed vanishes. Not surprisingly, Menenius, having begun with the bestial, concludes by explicitly comparing Coriolanus to a god: "He wants nothing of a god but eternity, and a heaven to throne in" (5.4.24–25). The more Coriolanus is remote from, or above, man, the more Menenius is freed from blame for his failure to assuage him, and the more the tribunes are to blame for his rage and Rome's imminent destruction.

Sicinius replies ambiguously, "Yes, mercy, if you report him truly" (5.4.26). "[M]ercy," here, may be a noun or an exclamation. Sicinius may mean that if Menenius's report is accurate, Coriolanus lacks another attribute of a god, namely, mercy, as Volumnia had suggested (5.3.149–53). Or he may be exclaiming his fear. Or he may mean both. Each would seem to imply the other. Menenius, answering Sicinius's hopeful doubt (". . . if you report him truly"), declares that he "paint[s]" Coriolanus "in the character" (5.4.27). His portrait is true to life. Once again exonerating himself while excoriating Sicinius, Menenius affirms, "There is no more mercy in him than there is milk in a male tiger; that shall our poor city find; and all this is long of you" (5.4.28–30).

Sicinius calls upon the gods to show the mercy: "The gods be good unto us" (5.4.31). But Menenius warns of the gods' stern justice. The gods support a moral order in which respect for virtue also shows respect for them: "No, in such a case the gods will not be good unto us. When we banished [Coriolanus], we respected not them; and, he returning to break our necks, they respect not us" (5.4.32–35). Wishing to punish Sicinius by forcing him to rue Coriolanus's banishment, Menenius, paradoxically, retracts his blame that the tribunes alone were responsible for all the trouble ("all this is long of you"). Just as when he first heard that Coriolanus was leading Aufidius's army against Rome, Menenius, seeking to remove any hope whatsoever of his mercy, concludes that it was "we" who did not respect the gods when "we" banished Coriolanus, and it will be "our necks" that he will break, because the gods respect not "us" (cf. 4.6.122–24, 138–39 and 4.6.89, 96–99, 101, 118–19, 130–37, 147–48). He spreads the blame, so he can make the destruction complete. Menenius cannot punish Sicinius thoroughly enough without also punishing himself.

2.

Menenius's warning is followed immediately by a messenger's. The Messenger warns Sicinius to flee for his life, saying that the plebeians have captured Brutus and will give him a painful, protracted death unless the women return with good news. If Menenius shared responsibility for Coriolanus's banishment in order to punish Sicinius, the people deny their own responsibility in order to punish his fellow tribune.

A second messenger arrives with the astonishing news that the ladies have, indeed, prevailed, the Volscians have withdrawn and Coriolanus is gone. In the Messenger's opinion, Rome has never had a happier day, not even when the Tarquins were expelled. When an incredulous and stunned Sicinius presses him to confirm that the news is certain, the ecstatic Messenger, thinking no one could doubt it, declares that he is "[a]s certain as I know the sun is fire" (5.4.46). Then, poeticizing the effect of the news on the sun, while calling upon Sicinius to listen for himself ("Why, hark you!" [5.4.49]), he says that the music and shouts of the "recomforted" (5.4.49) Romans flooding through the city's gates "[m]ake the sun dance" (5.4.50–52). Reversing the cries of death accompanying Coriolanus's sword as music following a dancer (2.2.109–10), the sun itself dances to the music of the celebratory Romans. If anger has poetic exaggeration, so do relief and joy.

With the joyful sounds in the air, Menenius, weighing her worth against that of the rest of Rome, at once praises Volumnia and disparages the tribunes. While "[t]his Volumnia" is worth "[a] city full" of consuls, senators, and patricians, she is worth "[a] land and sea full" of tribunes such as Sicinius (5.4.53, 55, 56). Menenius's mention of "[t]his Volumnia" is the only time her name is spoken in the play. Her name, like her son's, marks her Roman triumph. Despite his disparagement of the tribunes, however, Menenius no longer blames them for anything. His anger and despair giving way to his sudden and surprising relief, Menenius even seems to forget what he said just a moment ago about the gods not listening to the Romans' prayers. "You have pray'd well today," he compliments Sicinius (5.4.56). Unexpected relief not only makes him more gracious, but reverses his view of the gods' justice, which, he warned, prevented their answering the Romans' prayers (5.4.32–35). Sicinius, too, becomes more gracious. He asks the messenger, whom he says the gods bless for his tidings, to "[a]ccept [his] thankfulness," as well (5.4.60). Never before has either tribune offered thanks to anyone for anything, not even when flattering the people. Where Sicinius wanted to whip the slave who reported bad news (4.6.60–62), he heartily thanks the messenger who delivers good news.

Hearing that the women are about to enter Rome, Sicinius concludes the scene by saying, "We'll meet them, / And help the joy" (5.4.62–63). Despite their usual mutual antipathy, Sicinius and Menenius are given the same final word. While Menenius speaks of the sound of the crowd's joy ("Hark, how they joy!" [5.4.58]), Sicinius, echoing him, ends by saying, "And help the joy." They end in united joy. We can be sure, though, that the harmony will not last long. While foreign wars bring Romans together, domestic strife begins when those wars are over. Freed from fighting for their lives, the Romans quarrel through ambition. Nevertheless, however briefly, nothing ameliorates class enmity in Rome so much, it seems, as the narrow escape from certain death and destruction.

Act Five, Scene Five

Volumnia's return to Rome mirrors Coriolanus's Roman triumph (2.1.161ff.). Like her son, Volumnia has saved Rome from the Volscians. Where he was seen by the Romans as the god of war (2.1.216–19), she is seen by the Romans as the "patroness" (5.5.1) or protectress of the city. The one brought death to Rome's enemies, the other brings life to Rome. Volumnia not only brings life, however, but is "the life of Rome" (5.5.1). She saves Rome by embodying the claims of life or birth. Where Coriolanus's untempered virtue ultimately denies maternal claims, Volumnia saves Rome by asserting those claims and pulling her son back from public and private matricide.

Volumnia saves her country, but loses her son. Much earlier, she said that had Coriolanus died in battle, his fame would have been her son (1.3.20–21). But just as she failed to recognize the tension between his unconditioned virtue and his loyalty to his kin, she similarly failed to see the tension between his virtue and his service to Rome. Ironically, it is she, not he, whom Rome finally honors. Rather than his fame being her issue, her honor is his redemption. "Unshout the noise that banish'd Martius; / Repeal him with the welcome of his mother" (5.5.4–5). Rome's welcome of Volumnia nullifies its banishment of Coriolanus. The honor of the mother cancels the shame and punishment of the son.

Coriolanus's repeal—stated twice, once as a double negative—is a double reversal. Besides revoking his banishment, it implicitly reverses what Rome honors. While Rome publicly honors manliness, it is saved by what it scorns (2.2.83–85, 95–97). Indeed, in addition to being saved by women and the bonds of birth rather than by the manly scorn of death, Rome is saved by the private rather than the public—by Coriolanus's regard for his own that is indifferent to his city. As is signified by Coriolanus's own final words to Romans, the city is saved by the denial of its first principles.

Act Five, Scene Six

1.
Aufidius sends a letter to "the lords o'th'city" with accusations against Coriolanus, the truth of which, he says, he will make good to "theirs and . . . the commoners' ears," in "th'market-place" (5.6.1–4). Meanwhile, he says, Coriolanus "[i]ntends t'appear before the people, hoping / To purge himself with words" (5.6.7–8). Coriolanus will do in Antium what he would not lower himself to do in Rome. He not only will plead his case to the people, but counts on them for support. Commentators often suggest that Coriolanus undergoes no change during the play, that "the Coriolanus of the first scene is the same Coriolanus at the end of the play."[41] But, right away, we see that Coriolanus has changed very greatly since capitulating to his mother. Realizing that his virtue cannot be unconditioned, he has abandoned the aristocratic principle and now openly courts the Volscian commoners.

An aggrieved Aufidius, bitterly resenting that he has been destroyed by his own generosity, meets several members of his faction with whom he has previously begun plotting against Coriolanus. While common Volscian soldiers consider Coriolanus "our general" (5.2.5, 48, 50–53, 108), one of these officers greets Aufidius with that title (5.6.10). A second conspirator assures Aufidius that they can free him from his "great danger" (5.6.15) if he still wants their help. But Aufidius is hesitant. He thinks he must take his cue from the people. "We must proceed as we do find the people" (5.6.16). As in Rome, the people hold the balance. The Third Conspirator, however, the fiercest of the group, dismisses the concern. The people can be safely disregarded, he argues. So long as Aufidius and Coriolanus disagree, the people will remain uncertain. "[B]ut the fall of either / Makes the survivor heir of all" (5.6.18–19). Aufidius can disregard the people, not because they are unimportant, but because they will go with the winner. Action, not words, will determine their support.

Aufidius, agreeing ("I know it" [5.6.19]), begins to rehearse his "pretext" (5.6.20) for striking at Coriolanus, which he says can be given an honorable ("good" [5.6.21]) interpretation. Aufidius complains that he raised Coriolanus to a position of power and pledged his honor for his loyalty ("I rais'd him, and I pawn'd / Mine honour for his truth" [5.6.21–22]), but, having been raised to a position of power, Coriolanus flattered Aufidius's supporters to win their favor: "being so heighten'd, / He water'd his new plants with dews of flattery, / Seducing so my friends" (5.6.22–24). Besides ignoring his own intention to betray Coriolanus (1.10.12–29; 4.7.6–8, 17–26, 56–57), Aufidius ignores Coriolanus's successes in leading the Volscian army up to the walls of Rome (4.6.76–80, 91–96, 103–6; 5.3.1–2). He speaks as though nothing accounted for Coriolanus's high stature except his own favor and Coriolanus's flattery. While Aufidius had expected Coriolanus's "nature," which, he said, is "no changeling" (4.7.10, 11), to produce his downfall in Antium as in Rome, now, he says, that nature has changed. In flattering Aufidius's friends, Coriolanus has "bow'd his nature, never known before / But to be rough, unswayable and free" (5.6.25–26). Instead of always being harsh, inflexible, and free-spoken, he is now pitying, pliant and politic. Whereas his "stoutness" and "lack of stooping," as the Third Conspirator describes it (5.6.27, 29), cost him the consulate in Rome, in Antium he will stoop to conquer.

Aufidius tells how he received the banished Coriolanus, gave him joint command, allowed him his way in everything, let him pick his best troops as his own, personally served his undertakings, helped him harvest all the fame, and even took some pride in doing himself this wrong, until, finally, he "seem'd his follower, not partner," and Coriolanus "wag'd [him] with his countenance, as if / [Aufidius] had been mercenary" (5.6.39–41; cf. 4.6.125–27). Coriolanus not only was ungrateful, but shamed his benefactor by assuming authority and then paying him with patronage as though he were his hired soldier. He patronized him, in two senses of the word (cf. 4.5.101–2). The First Conspirator, agreeing and prompting Aufidius, introduces the aborted attack on Rome: "[A]nd in the last, / When he had carried Rome, and that we look'd / For no less spoil than glory" (5.6.42–44). The Conspirator expands Aufidius's private complaint. Not Aufidius alone, but everyone, expected to gain from Coriolanus's victory. Their expectations having been raised to a presumed certainty, the Volscian people could be turned against Coriolanus for their perceived loss. Tellingly, the Conspirator speaks of what Coriolanus was expected to win as though he had already actually won it ("When he had carried Rome"). The subjunctive slips into the past indicative.[42] The absolute confidence that Coriolanus inspires in his troops can be used against him. Anything short of the expected spoil and glory can be made to seem a loss.

The Conspirator's prompt provides Aufidius with what he needs. "There was it," he replies, "For which my sinews shall be stretch'd upon him" (5.6.44–45). The people can satisfy Aufidius's personal resentment by punishing Coriolanus for their disappointment. For a few cheap women's tears, Aufidius continues, summing up his proposed accusation, Coriolanus "sold the blood and labour / Of our great action. Therefore shall he die, / And I'll renew me in his fall" (5.6.47–49). Coriolanus's death will be Aufidius's rebirth.

Aufidius no sooner states his plan than events bear out the gravamen of his bitter private complaint. While Aufidius entered "[his] native town" (5.6.50) like a mere messenger "[a]nd had no welcomes home" (5.6.51), Coriolanus now "returns / Splitting the air with noise" (5.6.51–52). Aufidius returned to his native city amid silence; Coriolanus returns to his adopted city amid loud festive fanfare and great welcoming shouts: *Drums and trumpets sound, with great shouts of the people* (s.d. 5.6.49). The Second Conspirator is indignant at Coriolanus's reception. "And patient fools," he says of the people, "Whose children he hath slain, their base throats tear / With giving him glory" (5.6.52–54). The people are so foolish, feckless, and fickle that they will tear their own throats in shouting glory upon their children's killer (cf. 4.4.1–6).

The Third Conspirator, making more explicit what he previously suggested, urges Aufidius to kill Coriolanus before he has a chance to speak: "Therefore, at your vantage, / Ere he express himself or move the people /

With what he would say, let him feel your sword, / Which we will second"
(5.6.54–57). The people have already forgiven Coriolanus the deaths of their
children. They might forgive him anything. Rather than allow Coriolanus to
explain himself, Aufidius, with the conspirators' assistance, should kill him
and then give his own account of Coriolanus's actions: "When he lies along,
/ After your way his tale pronounc'd shall bury / His reasons with his body"
(5.6.57–59). By killing him before he can speak, Aufidius will, in effect, give
Coriolanus a double burial. His version of Coriolanus's actions will bury Coriolanus's version along with his body.

2.

Certain Volscian lords enter. These are the ones to whom Aufidius sent his
letter and whose support he seeks. When he initially talked of bringing
charges, Aufidius mentioned some unspecified actions which Coriolanus had
left undone and which, he said, "shall break his neck or hazard mine /
Whene'er we come to our account" (4.7.25–26). The First Lord, however,
makes light of those charges: "What faults he made before the last, I think /
Might have found easy fines" (5.6.64–65). Aufidius seems to have exaggerated the seriousness of the omissions, at least in the eyes of the Volscian nobles. The new charges, however, are quite different. "[B]ut there to end /
Where he was to begin," the Lord continues,

> and give away
> The benefit of our levies, answering us
> With our own charge, making a treaty where
> There was a yielding: this admits no excuse.

> (5.6.65–69)

The Lord, "griev[ing] to hear" (5.6.63) the new charges, says that Coriolanus
committed three unpardonable faults in stopping the action when it should
have begun. He gave away the advantage the Volscians had gained by raising
an army, repaid them by returning merely their expenses and came to terms
with an enemy after it had yielded. Although he will deny the charges, we
must wonder whether Coriolanus made a critical error in not having con-
sulted with the Volscians who had put their trust in him as well as in con-
ducting his exchange with the suitors in public.[43] Aufidius, despite having
evidently advised Coriolanus on the terms of the treaty after Rome's yielding
(5.3.196–97), will soon seize upon both mistakes. Now, however, contrary to
the Third Conspirator's advice, he lets Coriolanus speak: "He approaches:
you shall hear him" (5.6.70).

3.

"*Enter Coriolanus marching with drum and colours, the Commoners being with him*" (s.d. 5.6.70). Coriolanus, who, unwilling to bend, finally broke, becomes in Antium the opportunist he refused to be in Rome. He becomes the very thing he loathed—a flattering demagogue who uses the people for his own political ends. Aufidius may be driven to kill him by nothing but resentment and envy, but Coriolanus's turning to the people for support presents a genuine threat to the Volscian nobles, just as his refusal to do so in Rome helped to keep the city free.

Coriolanus never explains why he chooses to go to Antium rather than return to Rome. There seems little doubt that the Romans, relieved, full of joy and thanks, and ready to "unshout" his banishment (5.4.41–63; 5.5.1–6), would have allowed, even gladly welcomed, his return. But pride or shame would likely have prevented Coriolanus from doing in Rome what he is now willing to do in Antium. Although he has forsaken the aristocratic principle, he is not without shame. And his having forsaken the principle exposes him to shame, for it seems to show that he flattered himself when he claimed the principle, flatters the people now when he abandons it, or both. And while flattery is shameful, shame is deeper before intimates than before strangers: the closer the intimacy, the deeper the shame.[44] Coriolanus can thus do in Antium what he cannot do in Rome. He can stoop without mortifying himself in Antium, but not in Rome.

Coriolanus immediately reassures the nobles that nothing has changed. "Hail lords, I am return'd your soldier," he brightly greets them;

> No more infected with my country's love
> Than when I parted hence, but still subsisting
> Under your great command.
>
> (5.6.71–74)

Coriolanus then proceeds to talk only of the results, and not of the causes, of what happened. "You are to know," he reports,

> That prosperously I have attempted, and
> With bloody passage led your wars even to
> The gates of Rome.
>
> (5.6.74–77)

Contradicting Aufidius's complaints in his letter, Coriolanus, claiming success, states that the Volscians' spoils exceed their expenses by one-third and that they made peace "[w]ith no less honour to the Antiates / Than shame to th'Romans" (5.6.80–81). He does what his mother first suggested, prudently presenting disappointments as successes (cf. 5.3.132–40). It seems that, had he heard her plea in private, peace could have been struck between the two cities, and, despite his having yielded to her for purely personal reasons, the terms of peace could have been publicly presented to the Volscians as a victory. Now, however, the public circumstances of her pleading and his yielding prevent that. Owing to the publicity, Coriolanus's private motives are public knowledge. In the name of integrity and full transparency (5.3.2–4), Coriolanus has made it impossible to keep Aufidius from discussing—or rather taunting him for—his motives. In his attempt to deny himself everything personal, he has allowed what is personal to himself to become the crucial issue.

When Coriolanus hands the lords the treaty reached with Rome, Aufidius, not wanting it read (at least partly because it evidently contradicts his accusations and partly because he advised on its terms), bids the nobles not to read it but instead to tell "the traitor in the highest degree" (5.6.85) that he has abused their powers. Coriolanus, once again not seeing himself as a traitor to anyone, answers as he did in Rome: "Traitor? How now!" (5.6.87; cf. 3.3.67). And when Aufidius, provoking him as the tribunes did in Rome, reaffirms the charge ("Ay, traitor, Martius" [5.6.87]), Coriolanus becomes furious at being stripped of his honorific name (cf. 5.1.11–13). "Martius!" he exclaims (5.6.87). Aufidius, inciting both him and the Volscians, then indignantly responds,

> Ay, Martius, Caius Martius! Dost thou think
> I'll grace thee with that robbery, thy stol'n name
> Coriolanus, in Corioles?
>
> (5.6.88–90)

The name Coriolanus is the unmistakable sign that Coriolanus is the Volscians' hateful enemy, as Coriolanus himself had acknowledged and even boasted to Aufidius—"a good memorial, / And witness of the malice and displeasure / Which thou should'st bear me" (4.5.72–74). Aufidius, however, suggests that victory does not entitle Coriolanus to the name that he won in Corioles. His name is a "stol'n name," a "robbery." Yet, even as he denies that his achieved victory entitles Coriolanus to his surname, Aufidius claims in his next breath that the Volscians' anticipated victory entitles them to Rome. "You lords and heads o'th'state," he says, addressing the nobles and turning from the Volscians' past defeat to their recent disappointment,

> perfidiously
> He has betray'd your business, and given up,
> For certain drops of salt, your city Rome,
> I say "your city," to his wife and mother.

(5.6.91–94)

Echoing the First Conspirator (5.6.43), Aufidius argues that Rome became the Volscians's city by right of presumed conquest. For Coriolanus not to have conquered what he was confidently expected to win is for him to have surrendered perfidiously what belonged to the Volscians. Anything less than triumph was treachery. Having accused him of stealing his name from the Volscians and giving away what was theirs, Aufidius charges Coriolanus with breaking his oath not to yield to Roman pleas and with failing to consult a war council on whether to make the peace. The former accuses Coriolanus of betraying the Volscians by breaking his word of honor; the latter, by acting alone. Aufidius then, finally, describes Coriolanus's yielding to his mother's pleas, weeping at her weeping:

> [A]t his nurse's tears
> He whin'd and roar'd away your victory,
> That pages blush'd at him, and men of heart
> Look'd wond'ring each at others.

(5.6.97–100)

Coriolanus not only betrayed the Volscians, but did so in the most unmanly of ways. While men of courage were astonished, even lackey pages blushed at his shame. The manly and the unmanly alike viewed him with deep contempt.

Whether from moderation or wrath, Coriolanus remains largely restrained. Instead of answering Aufidius directly, he appeals incredulously to Mars: "Hear'st thou, Mars?" (5.6.100). The god of war, he seems to say, would vouch for his virtue. But Coriolanus's invocation of Mars only plays into Aufidius's hand: "Name not the god, thou boy of tears!" (5.6.101). Only manly men may invoke Mars. And when Coriolanus indignantly exclaims ("Ha!" [5.6.101]), Aufidius compounds the insult and provocation with a play on words, at once denying that he is more than a boy and commanding his silence in the face of the outrage: "No more" (5.6.102). Perhaps finding the half-truth more unbearable than an outright lie,[45] Coriolanus, defending his manhood, exaggerates the falsity of Aufidius's taunt, suggesting that it is a boundless lie: "Measureless liar, thou hast made my heart / Too great for what contains it. 'Boy'! O slave!" (5.6.103–4). Yet, despite claiming that Aufidius's lie has made his heart swell so much with rage that it threatens to burst, Coriolanus, still trying to maintain his restraint, apologizes to the nobles for his anger: "Pardon me, lords; 'tis the first time that ever / I was forc'd to scold" (5.6.105–6). Ironically, this is the first time that he has ever asked pardon for his anger.[46]

Coriolanus is, nevertheless, unable to resist refuting the purely personal affront. Appealing to their own judgments, he entreats the lords to " give this cur the lie"—a term of contempt he used for the plebeians when they banished him (3.3.120; also 5.6.112)—and then declares that Aufidius's awareness of his own wounds will belie the affront:

> [A]nd his own notion,
> Who wears my stripes impress'd upon him, that
> Must bear my beating to his grave, shall join
> To thrust the lie unto him.
>
> (5.6.107–10)

The scars that Coriolanus has inflicted on Aufidius and Aufidius will carry to his grave shall make him answer for his lie. The scars are proof of Coriolanus's prowess.

Although the First Lord, asking to be heard, calls for peace, Coriolanus can no longer contain himself. After offering to let the Volscians kill him to refute the taunt ("Cut me to pieces, Volsces, men and lads, / Stain all your edges on me" [5.6.111–12; cf. 4.5.96–97]), he triumphantly tells of having harmed not only Aufidius but "your Volscians." "'Boy!' False hound!" he cries out;

> If you have writ your annals true, 'tis there,
> That like an eagle in a dove-cote, I
> Flutter'd your Volscians in Corioles.
>
> (5.6.112–15)

With an ill-timed boast of the harm he has caused those whom he has asked to judge him, Coriolanus asserts that he was an eagle to the Volscian doves, a noble bird of prey to frightened birds of peace. Moreover, "Alone I did it. Boy!" (5.6.116), he brags, echoing his earlier taunt of Aufidius on the battlefield (1.8.8). All tact gone, Coriolanus defends his manhood by boasting of having single-handedly fluttered the Volscians in Corioles. Far from being a mere "boy" (5.6.104, 112, 116), he carved his surname out of Volscian hearts and wrote his deeds in their blood.

Aufidius, turning to the lords, provokes them and compounds his insult by attributing Coriolanus's victory to mere fortune. "Why, noble lords," he asks, by way of shaming them,

> Will you be put in mind of his blind fortune,
> Which was your shame, by this unholy braggart,
> 'Fore your own eyes and ears?
>
> (5.6.116–19)

The Volscians' shame is twofold. Coriolanus not only shamed them on the battlefield by winning by chance rather than by virtue, but he has shamed them again, right now, by insulting them to their faces by reminding them of their shame. He has increased the insult by obliging the insulted to witness it. Dishonor, as we have seen, is all the greater when delivered directly to one's face. Aufidius, of course, does not mention that that is exactly what he has been doing, right now, to Coriolanus.

Incited by the conspirators' cry ("Let him die for't" [5.6.119]), the people turn against Coriolanus, demanding his immediate death for killing their family members: "Tear him to pieces! Do it presently! He killed my son! My daughter! He killed my cousin Marcus! He killed my father!" (5.6.120–22). The people want to kill Coriolanus not for halting his attack on Rome, but for pursuing his attack on Corioles—not to revenge their disappointed greed, but to revenge their familial losses. The Second Lord, wanting to avoid an "outrage" to a man who is "noble" and whose "fame" encompasses the world (5.6.123, 124), pleads for the rule of law and peace. Ignoring the Volscians' deaths and defeat, and focusing wholly on the aborted attack on Rome, he states that Coriolanus's "last offences to us / Shall have judicious hearing" (5.6.125–26). In his view, if Aufidius would stop his provocation, the peace could still be preserved: "Stand, Aufidius, / And trouble not the peace" (5.6.126–27). But Coriolanus, enraged, can think of nothing but revenge. Echoing his mother's curse on Sicinius (4.2.26–28), he wishes, "O that I had him, / With six Aufidiuses, or more, his tribe, / To use my lawful sword" (5.6.127–29). The man to whom the claims of generation prevailed over the demands of revenge now wants his revenge against not only Aufidius but his entire line of descendants. No longer seeking the glory of defeating only Aufidius in a duel ("I'd . . . make / Only my wars with him. He is a lion / That I am proud to hunt" [1.1.233–35]), he would take revenge on his full progeny. If the ambition for unconditioned virtue seeks to separate oneself from one's parental origins, the desire for the most complete revenge seeks to destroy one's enemy's entire bloodline, along with the man himself. Not surprisingly, just as Coriolanus's final thought is of revenge for a personal insult, his final word is "sword"—his "lawful sword" because his complete revenge against Aufidius, he indignantly believes, would be thoroughly justified.

When Aufidius cries, "Insolent villian!" (5.6.129), the conspirators shout to kill Coriolanus: "Kill, kill, kill, kill, kill him!" (5.6.130). The plan was for Aufidius to strike Coriolanus and then for the conspirators to second him ("[L]et him feel your sword, / Which we will second" [5.6.56–57]). But Aufidius evidently has no hand in the actual killing. "*The Conspirators draw, and kill Martius, who falls*" (s.d. 5.6.130).[47] Aufidius depends entirely on their assistance.

In the play's opening scene, the people of Rome wanted to kill Coriolanus. In the closing scene, several conspiratorial nobles of Antium kill him, with the people's approval, while other nobles look helplessly on. The political difference between the two cities seems to lie in the fact that no noble in Rome seriously threatens the other nobles by courting the people, as Coriolanus does in Antium (and Caesar will in Rome), and that there are tribunes in Rome to put a brake on popular violence, reach compromises with the nobles, and mask political violence under the guise of law, as the Second Lord may have sought to do, here. The tribunate helps to prevent in Rome what conspiracy and murder produce in Antium. While Rome has a mixed regime in which the plebeians lay claim to an equal share in the government and possess a political office, in Antium, although the people have the power of sheer numbers, the city is governed by an aristocracy,[48] one which Coriolanus, having become a demagogue, seeks to subvert. Ironically, the difference between their regimes is crystallized by the contrast between the presence in Rome of what Coriolanus had opposed there in the beginning and the absence in Rome of what he seeks to bring about in Antium in the end.

Aufidius stands upon Coriolanus's corpse (s.d. 5.6.130). Volumnia had said that Coriolanus would "beat Aufidius below his knee, / And tread upon his neck" (1.3.46–47). Instead, Aufidius kills Coriolanus and treads upon his body. He kills the man and debases his corpse. What he could not do to the man alive, he does to his dead body. An example of spirit animating the inanimate in order to punish it, Aufidius treats Coriolanus's corpse as though it were the living man himself.

The moderate lords are appalled by Aufidius's actions. The First Lord exclaims Aufidius's personal name in dismay, "O Tullus!" (5.6.131). The Second Lord accuses Aufidius of cowardice: "Thou hast done a deed whereat valour will weep" (5.6.131–32). And the Third Lord, asking for all to be quiet, admonishes Aufidius, "Tread not upon him" (5.6.133). Aufidius, defending his action, claims to have acted "in . . . rage / Provoked by [Coriolanus]" (5.6.135–36) and with prudence for the nobles' interests. His act was both honorable and advantageous, he claims. Promising to explain to the senate at a later time "the great danger" (5.6.136) which Coriolanus posed for the nobles or else face their heaviest censure, he says that the nobles will "rejoice / That he is thus cut off" (5.6.138). Aufidius will presumably argue, as the tribunes did in Rome, that Coriolanus sought "one sole throne, / Without assistance" (4.6.32–33), though, here, with the support rather than the opposition of the commoners. An important sign of the danger, in addition to we have already seen, is that when he entered Antium surrounded by the people, Coriolanus not only emphasized the plunder that he brought back to the city (cf. 1.1.248–49; 1.5.4–8),[49] but quickly slipped twice into the royal "we"—"Our spoils we have brought home . . ."—which he repeated three times in the next seven lines (5.6.77[twice], 79, 80, 84). The embodiment of the aristocratic regime becomes the prototype of the Caesarian regime.

The nobles nevertheless appear divided. The First Lord seems unimpressed by Aufidius's defense. Calling upon the Volscians to mourn for him, he says that Coriolanus should be buried with dignity and "regarded / As the most noble corse that ever herald / Did follow to his urn" (5.6.142–44). Coriolanus, to him, is the noblest hero who ever lived. On the other hand, the Second Lord, who accused Aufidius of cowardice, now splits the blame. "His own impatience," he says, referring to Coriolanus's rage, "[t]akes from Aufidius a great part of blame" (5.6.145). The spirited quality of the soul that elevates Coriolanus in the First Lord's eyes at least partly convicts him in the Second's.

Aufidius, now that his "rage is gone," is—or says he is—"struck with sorrow" (5.6.146, 147). His envy and resentment, finally satisfied, disappear and give way to magnanimity. Calling for a solemn ceremony to honor Coriolanus, Aufidius orders "three o'th'chiefest soldiers," whom he will join, to be pallbearers (5.6.148), a drum to be beat so that "it speak mournfully" (5.6.149), and steel pikes trailed along the ground, a military gesture of respect.[50] Although he dishonored Coriolanus's corpse, Aufidius will honor his memory with a memorial and posthumous fame:

> Though in this city he
> Hath widow'd and unchilded many a one,
> Which to this hour bewail the injury,
> Yet he shall have a noble memory.
>
> (5.6.150–53)[51]

In Rome, Coriolanus was dishonored by those whom he benefitted. In Antium, he is honored by those who still grieve his grievous injuries.

Coriolanus is honored for what he did before submitting to his mother, before yielding to the natural bonds of birth. While Aufidius, whose concluding word, fittingly, is "[a]ssist" (5.6.154), could not defeat him without assistance, Coriolanus is honored for the virtue that allowed him to act "alone." *Coriolanus* seems to end twice—once when Coriolanus submits, and again when he is killed. The first marks his destruction as a hero; the second, his death as a human. The two episodes have an obvious connection. Coriolanus's submission to his mother gives Aufidius what he needs to orchestrate his death. They are connected more deeply as well, however, by the fact that Coriolanus's submission rests on his recognition of his mortal nature. His submission to his mother is his submission to his birth and hence to his mortal nature. His recognition of what is "most mortal to him" proves "most mortal to him." The play's two endings, one pointing to birth, the other to death, indicate the natural conditions from which Coriolanus sought to sever his virtue and himself. It seems ironic that although we hear of slaughter throughout the play, Coriolanus's death is the only one we see. The man who kills countless others is the only character to die. Coriolanus's tragedy lies, however, not in the circumstances of his death, but in the tension within his soul between virtue and life. To be human, man must seek to surpass himself. Owing to his dual nature, man must go beyond himself in order to be true to himself. But owing to man's dual nature, the soul cannot succeed in doing that without ultimately destroying itself. In spiritedly defying death, it ultimately denies life. Thus, just as Coriolanus's unconditioned virtue would destroy Rome, so, too, it would destroy his soul. As we see in *Coriolanus*, the soul's spirited fulfillment is also the soul's tragic death. Turning back against itself, the perfection of the soul proves, tragically, to be the destruction of the soul.

Notes

1. Plutarch, *Coriolanus*, 31.4; North, 2:179; also Dionysius of Halicarnassus, 8.36.4.

2. *OED*, s.v. Passable, 2 and 3.

3. See, e.g., 1.1.242; 1.10.13–16; 2.1.136–41; 4.1.21; 4.5.115–16; 5.3.47–48.

4. Abbott, §294.

5. Aristotle, *Rhetoric*, 1379b3–4; *Politics*, 1328a1–5.

6. Parker, 332.

7. Coriolanus, as previously noted, has often used a question not to get an answer but to make a reproach. Here, he uses the same rhetorical figure in self-reproach, as he will soon repeat (5.3.27–28, 56–57).

8. Bliss, 253.

9. E.g., 1.1.73; 2.1.170; 3.2.75; 4.6.22–23; 5.1.5–6, 65.

10. Most modern editors, following Alexander Pope (1723), change the Folio's "hope" to "holp," i.e., "helped," making Volumnia's words retrospective rather than prospective.

11. C. Porter, in Furness, 536.

12. For Roman piety as devotion to both kin and country, see, e.g., Cicero, *De inventione*, 2.66, 161; *Republic*, 6.16.1; Livy, 27.9.11.

13. Quintilian, 6.1.33.

14. Anonymous, 2.50; Cicero, *De inventione*, 1.106–9.

15. Anonymous, 4.38.

16. Anonymous, 4.51; Quintilian, 8.3.67–69.

17. Anonymous, 4.66.

18. Anonymous, 4.21.

19. Coriolanus speaks in rhyming couplets only here and in his soliloquy at 2.3.112–23.

20. Quintilian, 3.8.12–13.

21. See act 3, n8, above.

22. Quintilian, 3.8.34.

23. Aristotle, *Rhetoric*, 1392a6–7; Cicero, *De oratore*, 2.336, 3.205; *Orator*, 56; Quintilian, 4.1.49; 9.2.17.

24. Aristotle, *Rhetoric to Alexander*, 1438b34, 39a4.

25. Aristotle, *Rhetoric to Alexander*, 1438a19–23, 34–36; Cicero, *Partitiones oratoriae*, 97; Quintilian, 3.8.62.

26. Cicero, *De oratore*, 2.335; Quintilian, 3.8.34.

27. Cicero, *De oratore*, 2.104–13.

28. Anonymous, 2.5; Cicero, *De inventione*, 2.32.

29. Anonymous, 2.19.

30. Anonymous, 2.28–29, 46.

31. Anonymous, 2.38.

32. Brockbank, 295.

33. E.g., Anonymous, 4.21, 36; Cicero, *De oratore*, 2.343–49; *De inventione*, 1.36; *De orator*, 39.135; *Topica*, 18.68–71; Peacham, s.v. Cataplexis; Apocarteresis.

34. E.g., ". . . his mail'd hand . . . wiping" (1.3.35); "Wash my fierce hand in's heart" (1.10.27); "Lay hands upon him" (3.1.220, 225; also 3.1.176); "He shall be thrown down the Tarpeian rock / With rigorous hands" (3.1.264); "The noble tribunes are the people's mouths / And we their hands" (3.1.269–70); "Within his eyes sat twenty thousand deaths, / In thy hands clutch'd as many millions . . ." (3.3.70–71); "His good sword in his hand" (4.2.25); ". . . fisting each other's throat" (4.5.126). See also 1.1.54; 4.5.150; 4.6.118.

35. E.g., when Coriolanus returned to Rome ("Your hand, and yours!" [2.1.192]) and when banished ("Give me thy hand" [4.1.57]), he held his mother's and his wife's hands; when Volumnia arrived to beseech him, she had "in her hand / The grandchild to her blood" (5.3.23–24). See, also, 4.5.133, 148.

36. Bliss, 59.

37. E. K. Chambers, in Furness, 550.

38. Wilson, 239.

39. 1.1.168; 3.2.13; 3.3.36. Following his initial exclamation demanding the suitors' silence ("I beseech you, peace!" [5.3.78]), Coriolanus mentions peace four times, always with approval (5.3.191, 197, 209; 5.6.79).

40. Aristotle, *Rhetoric*, 1413a18–35; Cicero, *Topica*, 45; Anonymous, 4.62; Quintilian, 8.6.67–76.

41. Rosen, 187; also Arthur Rossiter, *Angel with Horns* (New York: Theater Arts Books, 1961), 250.

42. Abbott, § 361.

43. Plutarch, *Comparison of Alcibiades and Coriolanus*, 4.3.

44. Aristotle, *Rhetoric*, 1384b25–29.

45. E. A. J. Honigmann, *Shakespeare: Seven Tragedies Revisited* (Hampshire: Palgrave, 2002), 184.

46. But see 5.3.43.

47. The Folio's stage direction ("*Draw both the Conspirators, and kill Martius, who falls*"), while confusing the number of conspirators by reducing them to two, underscores Aufidius's inaction.

48. Dionysius of Halicarnassus, 6.62.4.

49. Cf., e.g., *Julius Caesar*, 3.2.90–92.

50. Fortescue, 1:116.

51. For Aufidius's only previous rhymes, see 4.7.54–57.

Index

~

About the Author

Jan H. Blits is professor, University Honors Faculty, at the University of Delaware. He received his B.A. from St. John's College, Annapolis, Maryland, and his Ph.D. from the New School for Social Research in New York City. He has served as secretary of the Navy Distinguished Fellow at the U.S. Naval Academy and has won the University of Delaware's Excellence in Teaching Award. He is the author of *The End of the Ancient Republic: Shakespeare's "Julius Caesar,"* and *The Insufficiency of Virtue: "Macbeth" and the Natural Order,* both published by Rowman & Littlefield. His books *Deadly Thought: "Hamlet" and the Human Soul* and *The Soul of Athens: Shakespeare's "A Midsummer Night's Dream"* were published by Lexington Books, an imprint of the Rowman & Littlefield Publishing Group. His articles have appeared in *Political Theory, The Journal of Politics, Interpretation, Educational Theory, The Southern Journal of Philosophy, Apeiron,* and other journals.